Strategy and Management

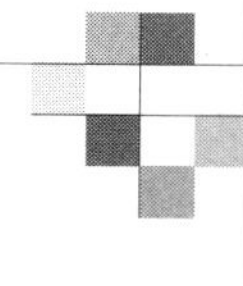

A New Zealand Casebook

Bryan Poulin
Bob Mills
Dorothy Spiller

Addison Wesley Longman New Zealand Limited
46 Hillside Road, Auckland 10
New Zealand

Associated companies throughout the world

First published 1998

ISBN 0 582 73954 3

Typeset in Palatino 10.5/12

Produced by Addison Wesley Longman New Zealand Limited
Printed in Malaysia through Longman Malaysia

Contents

Preface

Strategy and Management: A New Zealand Casebook contains case studies of 12 interesting and important New Zealand organisations. Some of these organisations are small, entrepreneurial and regional in outlook. Others are larger and international in outlook. The cases are representative of a range of New Zealand organisations. Many are very good, even excellent organisations. But none claims to be perfect. And they all face strategic challenges about their possible futures. This makes them both informative to read about and challenging to analyse.

The book offers a selected sample of case studies of organisations which, together, illustrate the many strategic challenges facing leaders and managers in New Zealand today. The cases also suggest the kinds of challenges that New Zealand leaders and managers have faced and will continue to face in the future. The leaders and managers of these organisations must continue to wrestle with long-term strategy while managing the current issues of day-to-day 'business'. Lessons to be learned from the cases should be transferable to both New Zealand and international students of strategy and strategic management. Partly, this transferability is due to the more deregulated environment both in New Zealand and worldwide. And partly it is because New Zealanders and New Zealand leaders and managers, like many other peoples, are resourceful and creative. For these reasons, a serious study of these cases will lead to meaningful learning about strategy – today and tomorrow.

We know you will share our gratitude for the generous co-operation shown by the leaders, managers and other people in these 12 organisations. But please, do not directly contact people in these organisations. These people are very busy and we would not want to 'wear out' our welcome. Instead, we invite you to contact one of us with your questions, suggestions and comments. We really would appreciate hearing from you.

Dedication

In September 1987, Associate Professor Harold Chambers proudly introduced a 'new business policy lecturer' to the School of Management Studies at the University of Waikato. Chambers had credibility. He was a graduate of the Harvard Business School Advanced Management Programme. As well, he had been a senior manager with a large New Zealand international firm. He had foreseen problems with the strategic direction of the firm, but others prevailed. Harold Chambers stepped aside and joined the School of Management Studies at the University of Waikato. Here he was responsible for business policy, the most integrative course in the School. He was firm in his view that the Harvard case study method is the most effective way of exposing students to the challenges of real strategy situations. Associate Professor Chambers did not just talk. He demonstrated his view by taking the new lecturer on a tour of a company he was writing up as a case study for one of his classes in 'policy'.

The way that Chambers fondly dwelt on the name 'Harvard' was testimony to the confidence that he placed in the Harvard case method. His legacy to the School includes his tenacious defence of the case study method, his pioneering work in writing New Zealand strategy cases for the School of Management Studies, and his oversight of the development of the 'Management Lodge', a purpose-built combined residential and seminar facility used for continuing education by middle and senior level managers. But the most memorable part of his legacy was his dream. He dreamed of the day when the School of Management Studies at Waikato would be regarded as the 'Harvard' of the Asia-Pacific region.

Harold Chambers was not only a man with an important message, he was also a fine man. Tragically, Associate Professor Harold Chambers died in 1990. His own excellent cases are now dated and they could not be included in this book. But Chambers and the example he set influenced many people. His dream lives on through these people. One example is the 'new business policy lecturer' who 'graduated' to become one author of this book. This book is dedicated to the memory of Associate Professor Harold Chambers.

Acknowledgments

Many people have helped us with the preparation of this book of strategy cases and, unfortunately, it is not possible to formally thank all. But we must now formally mention a few people without whom the book would not have been at all possible. First, our publisher, Max Loveridge of Addison Wesley Longman, has always offered us steady encouragement, timely suggestions and sound advice. But even more importantly, he soon became part of the collaborative effort that resulted in this book of cases. Other sources of inspiration came in the persons of Dr Chris Kirk, founding Director of the Technology Management Innovation Unit at the University of Waikato and Mr Dermot McNerney of TRADENZ, an early supporter in five of the case studies. We thank Jared Paisley for his latest version of the Black Water Rafting case. Students in both New Zealand and Canada have been enthusiastic over an earlier version and we expect a similarly enthusiastic response to his latest version. We also thank our students who have 'trialed' the cases by attempting to 'solve' them.

We are especially grateful to the people of the University of Waikato – specifically those of the Department of Strategic Management and Leadership of the School of Management Studies, the Department of Technology of the School of Science and Technology, and the Teaching and Learning Development Unit of the University of Waikato – for their generous loan, use and provision of resources and, always when required, for their unique expertise. Special mention goes to Lotta Bryant and Diane Curry of the Management Research Centre for their help in reformatting the 'bits and pieces' of the cases to a consistently high standard.

Appreciation is due both to David Quinlan, third-year student in graphic design at the Waikato Polytechnic, for his creative input into the cover design brief, and to Marie Low, designer for Addison Wesley Longman, for the final artwork and cover design.

Finally, and certainly not in the least, we are indebted to the leaders, managers and other talented people of the 12 organisations that were studied. These busy people generously gave of their time and their wisdom. Then they patiently corrected our misconceptions and filled in the missing pieces. Finally they gave us permission to publish the case study of their organisation. We credit the fine people in these 12 organisations for the accuracy of the information that has been provided. We accept responsibility for the errors or omissions that remain.

Introduction

Everything has actually been practiced in a good many companies, if only in bits and pieces.

(from *Management, Tasks, Responsibilities, Practices*, Peter F. Drucker 1974, p. 300)

A Story About Learning

Once there was a teacher who had the finest reputation in the land. But one day this teacher began to teach using methods unfamiliar to other teachers and students in the school. The teacher would ask a question and wait, sometimes for a long while, until some venturesome student would answer the question. At other times the teacher would ask the students to ask their own questions about a particular topic. In the beginning, the silence was deafening. Yet, most students began to think. A few became inspired, enthusiastically seeking their own questions and finding answers from many sources. These students flourished, achieving hitherto undreamed-of possibilities. In short, the teacher behaved as if teachers were not the sole source of knowledge. All was well, or so it seemed.

However, a few students were offended at having to learn in ways so different from other courses in the school. These students started complaining to the teacher and to other students. The teacher would patiently suggest to them, 'Come back when you have read something on the subject, and then we will discuss your complaints.' But they took no mind of the teacher's suggestions. One angry student even began to spread a rumour about the teacher, saying, 'The teacher is not a teacher at all.' The rumour was unfounded, yet it grew. It 'tingled the ears' of some students and many teachers at the school. Meetings were called. Some time later, the teacher left the school.

Years went by. A student came to regret the rumour. This one student decided to 'put things right' and seek out the teacher. When finally the teacher was found, the student anxiously asked, 'Do you remember me?' To which the teacher replied, 'I remember you well.' The student continued, 'I'm so sorry about the rumour I spread so many years ago. Please, tell me what must I do to put things right?' Replied the teacher, 'Take a feather pillow and scatter the feathers to the wind.' The student did not understand. But it seemed a simple enough thing to do. So the student did it. When the student returned, the teacher said, 'Now I want you to collect all the feathers and put them back in the pillow.' Surprised, the student asked, 'But isn't that impossible?' Then the lesson sunk in, and the student was very sad. For one moral of the story is this: it is easier to gather up feathers scattered to the wind than it is to take back a rumour (adapted from a Hasidic tale as reported in Telushkin 1991).

The Teaching and Learning Context

A second point to the story of learning above is that often the most valuable lessons are difficult to grasp. This point applies especially to strategy. A third point which might be teased from the fable follows from these themes. The former student can see the impossibility of perfectly reconstructing the pillow from the scattered feathers, but is the question purely rhetorical? Gathering up feathers offers a constructive learning opportunity, as well as an unattainable goal. A perfect theory may not grow out of the welter of events, actions and decisions which take place in an organisation. However, common themes and principles will emerge from the particular to the general, from the one case study to another, and be seen in action. Frameworks for the gathering and organising of experience can be constructed, and serve as a springboard for further questions. Organising the 'bits and pieces', found scattered everywhere, will foster better understanding of management practice. The unending process of enquiry, at first arduous, becomes ingrained as a habit of mind.

The story also reflects a number of key themes that recur in the contemporary literature on teaching and learning. One of these themes is the marked trend away from teaching as the delivery of information by 'expert' teachers.

By contrast, newer models of teaching and learning emphasise providing students with opportunities for engaging with their own ideas and their own interpretations of ideas, in challenging and practical ways. Most important, since it dictates everything else, is the idea of independent or self-directed learning. (See, for example, Poulin and Spiller 1996; Gibbs 1995; Baume 1994; Race 1993; and Ramsden 1992 and Bonham 1989.)

Students do need teachers to guide their learning. But students also need to take increasing responsibility for their own intellectual and personal growth, especially at tertiary levels. The incentive for greater responsibility is that students can acquire greater control and direction over their learning. Students, not just teachers, can learn to make informed choices about questions of study, project design, topics of discussion and other means of study that may turn out to confirm, or challenge, prevailing orthodoxies.

However, the learning context needs to be redesigned in order to facilitate this potential for more independent and self-directed learning. A participatory learning approach is required where teacher and student value each other in a context where teacher and student both become learners. Of course the teacher begins as the senior 'partner' in such a learning process. But this kind of teaching and learning aims to close the gap in learning ability between teacher and student. Then, as the student 'graduates' to the status of self-directed learner, the teacher and student will be able to approach the learning collaboratively, that is, interdependently.

Close interdependence is particularly relevant in a field of study such as strategy since the subject's major aim is to prepare students for future senior management or senior academic careers. Such collaboration is not only desirable, it is essential.

Close interdependence between teacher and student is evident in the preparation of these case studies. Some have been written by the teacher and practising managers; some have been written by the teacher and student together; and others have been written by senior students with guidance by the teacher. We, as teachers, are not seen as the sole dispensers of knowledge. We inform and guide students as necessary. Students are invited to inform us as teachers in a process of reciprocal learning. In turn, the academic institution is influenced by this interaction between teacher, students and practising managers. Together we search for and find meaningful 'realities' that can even inform the marketplace.

Teachers and students of strategy and management will find these cases particularly suitable for independent and interdependent learning. In this sense, the cases reflect the two important contemporary teaching and learning themes, 'learning by doing' (Race 1993; Gibbs 1988; and Kolb 1984) and 'doing the right things right'. (See Bennis 1989; Weick 1985; and especially Drucker 1974.)

Selection and Use of Case Studies to Teach Strategy

The book is principally about how things are in each of the organisations, not about how they might be or, perhaps, should be. The last is the 'job' of the student who is, hopefully, a 'budding strategist'. In this respect, the case studies in this book simulate the dynamics of real organisations.

The Harvard Socratic Case method of encouraging questions will provide students with a sound approach for absorbing the blend of historical, current and projected situations reported in the cases. Students will be prompted to ask questions such as:

- 'What is going on?'
- 'Why is it happening?'
- 'How can the future best be approached?'

This initial inquiry will then provide information which can be integrated into the information already with each student. Then the student needs to place the information into suitable strategic frameworks to develop a simplified, but not simplistic, model of the organisation. After these steps, detailed and deep analysis of the case is possible.

Such a whole or holistic approach to the case studies will provide students with opportunities to:

1 vicariously 'experience' an organisation (the case)
2 reflect on that experience (the issues of the case)
3 form abstract concepts (theory that applies to the case)
4 test ideas in detail (solutions to the case).

This idea of a four-stage process of learning is associated with David Kolb (1984) who was inspired by Kurt Lewin. Kolb's 'Lewinian' model of experiential learning is presented as Figure A (see next page).

Gibbs (1988) makes an important observation that is consistent with Kolb's experiential learning model. He observes that the learning is more effective when teacher and student perceive the case to represent, as closely as possible, a situation in real time. But the Kolb model also indicates that the experience needs to be 'concrete'. In other words, the experience needs to be as realistic as possible. That means that students and teachers need to relate to each case realistically, and personally, just as real managers must realistically and personally relate to the organisation and the people involved with the organisation.

However, most students and some teachers may want to take a singularly dispassionate, analytical approach – the 'consulting' role. While a consulting role is preferable for the analytical (reflection) and theoretical (formation) processes,

Figure A: Kolb's Experiential Learning Model

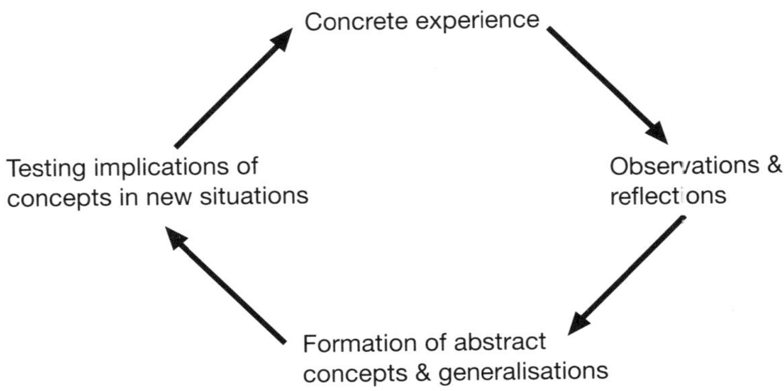

Source: Kolb (1984, p. 21)

it is not suitable for the experiential (experience) and implementational (testing) processes. The use of a short role-play on a key analytical issue of the case can bridge the gap between the two types of processes, analytical and implementational, both of which must be present for involved, meaningful learning.

An implementation issue can also be challenging and fun to enact. But, as Bourgeois and Brodwin (1984) point out, implementation is complex. Students can be challenged in many ways. Some examples include prompts like these:

- In implementing the new technology, who is to use the technology?
- Who is advantaged?
- Who is threatened? Let's hear from the people affected!
- What can be done to overcome the challenges?
- How can 'real' conflicts be resolved!

Use the roles suggested by the case: the CEO, the marketing manager, the production manager, the financial manager, the employee representative, the 'old-timer', and so on. Learn something 'real', realistically. Have some fun! These cases can really be made to 'come alive'!

To help guide users on the selection and use of the 12 New Zealand strategy cases that are contained in this book, the cases are first arranged into three groups by relative size of organisation, and then classified by type. The three groups are:

1 smaller, for example, Black Water Rafting (adventure tourism operator)
2 mid-size, for example Healtheries (health food and vitamin supplement manufacturer)
3 larger, for example Tower (financial services provider).

Each of the cases has been classified in this manner and they are presented in Figure B.

Figure B: Classification of Cases

Size	Name of Case	Description
Smaller	Black Water Rafting Champion Flourmills Auckland Credit Union Waikato Mills Reef Winery Subway Hamilton Central	Adventure tourism Food manufacturer Financial services Wine producer Fast food services
Mid-size	The Gallagher Group Healtheries New Zealand PEC (New Zealand) Tidco International	Electronic fencing Food manufacturer Electronic products Heavy equipment
Larger	Fisher & Paykel (Electronics) The Tower Group of Companies Wattie Frozen Foods	Whiteware products Financial services Food manufacturer

The particular need for New Zealand students of strategy and management is that they should be able to carry the insights the field provides into the small to medium-sized enterprises who will be their likely employers, as well as into the national and multinational organisations where this field of study was initially developed.

In New Zealand the manager is not far from the shop floor. Technical innovation and strategy, analysis and strategy development, and implementation, may all be intertwined in the hands of an individual or small group. To add value in such organisations and teams the strategist must be equipped to think holistically, and on the right scale.

These cases capture a representative cross-section of New Zealand organisations at work, dealing with a mix of local, regional, national and multinational environments, and they emphasise the role of strategy at all levels.

Suggestions for Analysing the Cases

Perhaps surprisingly, we have found that many students do not know how to go about reading a case properly. Reading a case analytically is a skill that has to be developed.

We recommend that students read each case as if they were (strategic) detectives, asking questions about what is written, and 'reading between the lines'. For example, a student should be continually asking questions such as:

- 'What is being said here?'
- 'What does this mean in terms of my opinions, strategy principles from the text book, or theory introduced by the teacher?'

The student should also imagine what it might take for the organisation to improve, asking questions such as:

- 'How might the company offer more exceptional value to others – customers, employees, community, nation?'

In this process of asking questions, students might note their observations in the margins or spaces provided.

Perhaps few strategists or organisations can reach the exalted heights where people at all levels, inside and outside the organisation, sense something lasting and special is being created. But such a possibility poses intriguing strategic challenges. Each of the cases described in the next few pages has this potential.

The idea is for students to identify and then strategically resolve the complex challenges and problems in each case. We have found that a variation of the usual approach to strategy cases is useful. This approach considers how 12 forces (three groups of four forces) interact so as to influence the organisation, both competitively and cooperatively, in its industry and in society.

Two of the three groups of forces – societal and industrial – are external to the organisation. The third group of forces is internal to the organisation. From the most general to the most specific level, these three groups of forces are:

1 **Societal** – the four societal forces that affect all industries. These societal level forces are known by the well-accepted acronym STEP (Social, Technological, Economic and Political-legal forces).
2 **Industry** – the four forces that affect all competitors in an industry, identified by Porter (1980). These industry level forces can be recalled by the acronym 'BEST' (Buyers, Entrants, Suppliers and Technologies). Porter identifies competition, or rivalry, between organisations in the same industry as the fifth force but competition, and co-operation may also be considered an outcome of all forces.
3 **Organisation** – the four forces of organisation, identified by Poulin (1996). These internal forces at the organisational level can be recalled by the acronym BITS (Beliefs, Identity, Technology, and Structure).

One easy way for students to remember all 12 forces or pieces to the competitive 'puzzle' (4 bits x 3 levels) is to think of a competitive dance step and simply repeat the following acronymous word-sentence:

STEP to the BEST BITS of Competition!

In summary, the STEP forces affect the competitiveness of all industries in a society, the BEST forces affect competition within an industry, and the BITS forces affect the competitive capability of each organisation. This view is an extension of standard strategic representations of external and internal 'environmental' forces. These are contained in most standard reference texts in strategy, for example, *Strategic Management* (Hunger and Whellen 1996).

The whole or holistic framework shown as Figure C indicates how these strategy forces relate to each other and across the three groups or levels. Figure C indicates a 'balanced' view of strategy by representing:

1 the external view – an adaptive response to environmental conditions (Hofer and Schendel 1978)
2 the internal view – a creative intention to influence society, industry and organisational conditions (Weimer and Vining 1989, Poulin 1996).

Technology is the common element at each level: society, industry and organisation. Technological activities range from building castles from play blocks to creating scenarios of the future based on expert opinion. The fact that technology is inextricably connected to change has been recognised by New Zealand educationalists who have integrated technology into the secondary and tertiary curriculum.

Figure C: Holistic Force Model of Organisation In Its Context

* Michael Porter (1980) has identified five forces of industry competition: buyers, new entrants, suppliers, substitutes and rivalry among competing firms.

The direction of the forces indicated by the arrows in Figure C indicates that strategy is both a responsive and a creative process. The direction of the arrows from outside inwards indicates strategy in its adaptive mode. Inside outwards indicates strategy in its creative mode. Both modes are required for strategic balance, and this holistic or integrated model implies how a simplifying, but not simplistic, model of strategy can be usefully applied. The 'building blocks' are the people who are responsible for the design and renewal of the basic dimensions which make up organisation, industry and society.

However, most important is what is not seen in this simplifying model. These are the forces inside each organisation. This observation is centred on what Deming (1984) called the philosophy of organisation, or that set of beliefs and values from which trust, and trustworthiness and lasting integrity, can be built. Deming is emphatic in stating that 'philosophy' is the most important factor behind the longest-lasting strategies and their manifestations, that is, 'whole' organisational cultures (Weick 1987). But are coherent beliefs and values really necessary? The most recent ideas on strategy, that is the competences(ies) and resource ideas (Hamel and Prahalad 1994 and Barney 1991) might suggest these are sufficient. But how do specific competencies develop in the first place? And, more importantly, why? Figure D and Figure E represent a model of the organisation that helps to answer such important questions.

Figure D: Top View of Poulin's (1996) Framework of Organisational BITS in Industrial Context

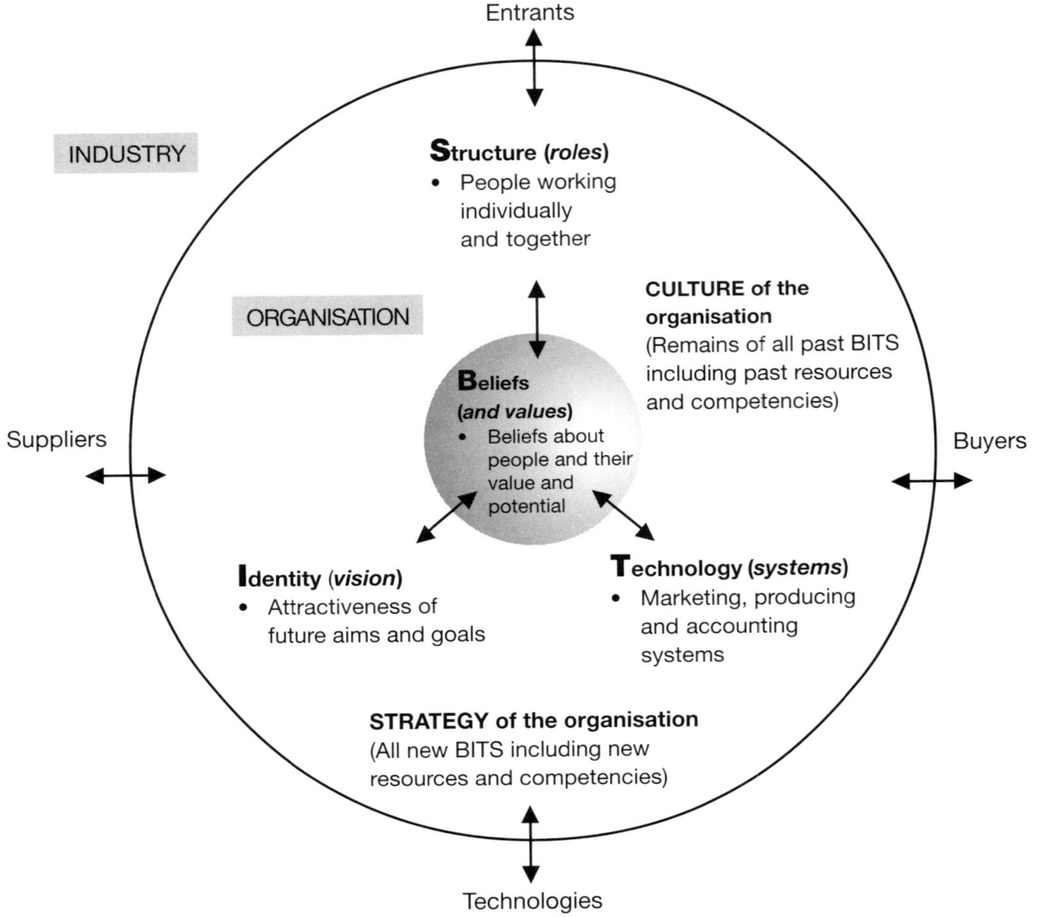

Entrants
INDUSTRY
Structure (roles)
• People working individually and together
ORGANISATION
CULTURE of the organisation
(Remains of all past BITS including past resources and competencies)
Beliefs (and values)
• Beliefs about people and their value and potential
Suppliers
Buyers
Identity (vision)
• Attractiveness of future aims and goals
Technology (systems)
• Marketing, producing and accounting systems
STRATEGY of the organisation
(All new BITS including new resources and competencies)
Technologies

Source: Poulin (1996)

Figure E: Side View of Poulin's (1996) BITS Framework in Industrial and Societal Context

Beliefs
Identity
Technology
Structure
Buyers
Entrants
Suppliers
Technologies
Social
Technological
Economic
Political
Competitors
Organisation (BITS)
Industry (BEST)
Society (STEP)

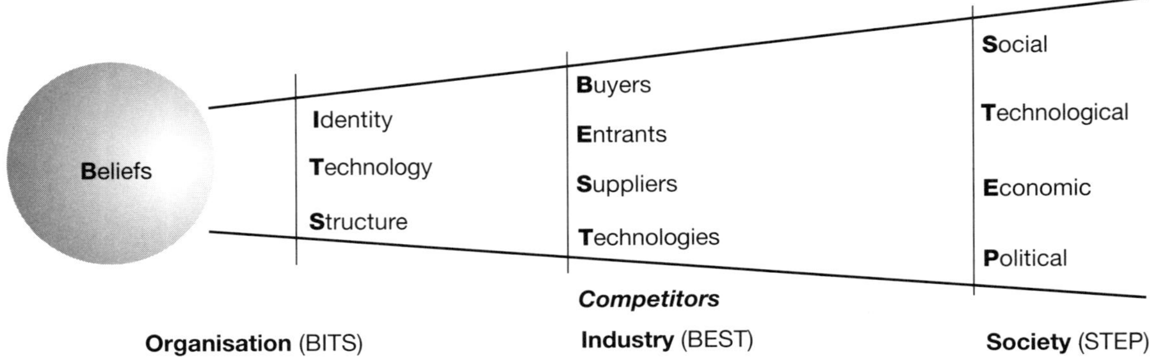

Source: Danny Ngatai, a senior management student at the University of Waikato, likes to view beliefs as the source light that projects outward, like the bright light behind the film of a movie projector: beliefs first enlighten the organisation 'screen' (identity, technology and structure), the remaining light shines through onto the industry screen, and, eventually, the residual light shines through onto society. Let your light shine!

A study of Figure D and Figure E also implies that organisational beliefs and the values attached to these beliefs provide the basis for understanding an organisation, as Deming (1984) and Weick (1985), among others, suggest. And, in a review article, Dennison (1990) contends that organisational effectiveness depends on the culture of the organisation. But the centre of culture is beliefs and values (Kroeber and Kluckholm 1952). Could this be so?

Consider the timeless classics of economic and social thought. For example, consider how Mosaic law (1700 BC) and Aristotle's ideas on ethics (384 BC) might be combined to explain the efficacy of businesses operating 'freely', subject to a moral standard. The result might be what Adam Smith (1776) foresaw when he imagined the 'invisible hand' of the market advancing the public or social interest. And the market, when it is subject to a high standard of laws that are properly administered in a democratic society, has performed remarkably well. And so Smith's ideas have endured.

In short, the framework of Figure D and Figure E is constructed upon the idea that strategy, and culture, are most essentially expressions of beliefs and values (Deal and Kennedy 1982; Deming 1984; Weick 1987). The definitions of strategy and culture are interesting because, as Weick (1985) first noted, the term 'strategy' can be substituted for 'culture', and vice versa. For if strategy is about planning for and moving towards a vision of a desired future, culture is the embodiment of past strategies. The point is that strategy and culture can and do influence people in the organisation, for better or worse. Poulin (1996) advances this definition of organisational culture:

> A holistic culture is that manifestation of coherent philosophy, or coherent set of beliefs and values. The philosophy provides meaning to the leaders' vision, inspiring commitment by followers in all dimensions of human existence: mental, physical and spiritual. Culture begins with strategic leaders and ends with strategic managers who leave a legacy of corporate history, heroes, structures, systems and rituals.
>
> A holistic culture requires continuous development and periodic renewal by managers and leaders, without which the culture will flounder in a morass of dead tradition, inflexible structures (and technology), antiquated control systems and rituals. This last condition is the antithesis of a holistic culture. (p. 182)

It is interesting to see how the ideas of other pioneers can be incorporated within this organisational framework. For example, Deming's 14 points of 'total quality management' (TQM) can be superimposed onto the three-dimensional framework shown as Figure E. An interesting exercise is to ask students to place each of the 14 main issues contained in Deming's 14 points of TQM – the heart of which Deming said was 'philosophy' (or beliefs). In this way, students come up with different 'solutions' to how Deming's notions might represent an ideal organisational strategy and culture. We have found general consistency in the themes of identity, technology and structure but we have also found great diversity in the way that the students choose to place the 14 points or issues of total quality management (TQM).

Such superimposition is meant to represent a holistic and dynamic view of organisational life, where gaps between what now exists and what may exist are highlighted by comparing how far each case meets (or falls short of) the ideal. Since strategy is about designing improved, technology-driven systems and delegating structures to accomplish the vision, everything that needs change is strategic in nature. Conversely, since culture is the established way of doing things, practices that are perceived as not needing change are cultural in nature.

Figure F: Exercise in placing Deming's 14 Points of TQM onto Poulin's (1996) Holistic Framework (with indication of placement)

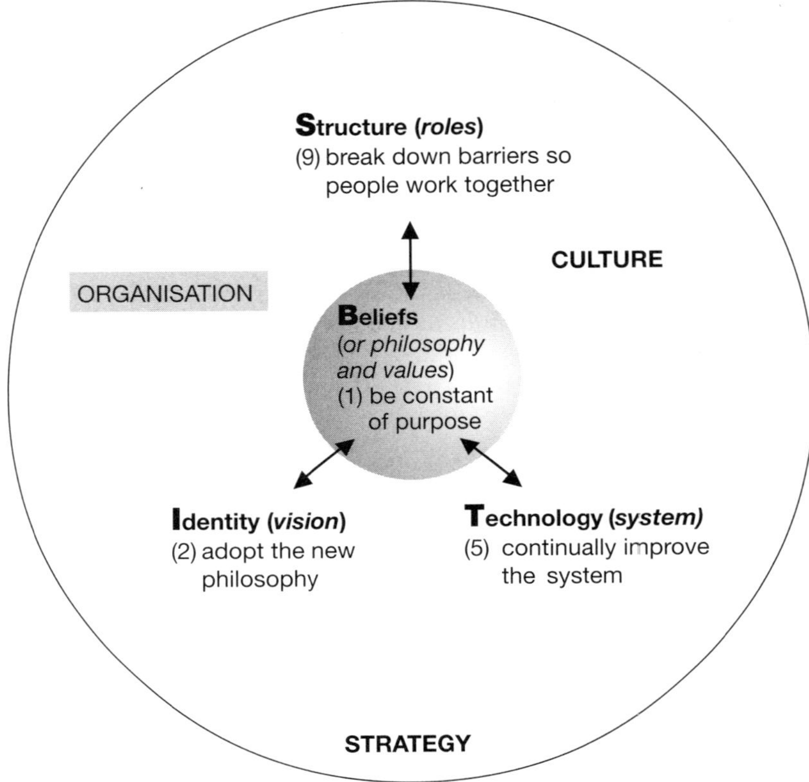

Summary of Deming's (1984) 14 points of Total Quality Management (TQM)

(1) Be constant of purpose.
(2) Adopt the new philosophy.
(3) Build in quality in the first place.
(4) Have one trusted supplier.
(5) Continually improve the system.
(6) Train on the job.
(7) Help people and gadgets do a better job.
(8) Drive out fear so people work effectively.
(9) Break down barriers so people work together.
(10) Substitute leadership for slogans.
(11) Eliminate management by numbers.
(12) Eliminate barriers to workmanship.
(13) Institute education.
(14) Engage everyone in the transformation.

However, perceptions can be deceptive, and there are strategic priorities to consider. Strategic leadership is required to find the priorities. Strategic leadership is also required to balance the simultaneous need for strategic change and some sense of cultural stability. The essential BITS of the firm can be thought of as a projection onto the industry and societal environments. An interesting exercise for students is having them project the BITS in this manner. The result might look like a telescope with the BITS at the narrow end, and the STEP environment at the broad end. One student thought that the intensity of the projection increased in scope and decreased in effect from the narrow to broad end of the telescope. (Compare this analogy with the film projector analogy of Figure E.)

Three key observations can be made in looking at Poulin's idealised framework and the placement of the 14 points of Deming's TQM. They are these:

1 All aspects of the organisation need to be related to the underlying philosophy, or basic beliefs and values. The culture is the outcome of the social interaction of people who are drawn together, or otherwise, by the identity imparted by the attractiveness of the future or vision of the organisation.
2 People are assisted, or otherwise, in pursuing the vision by both the technology-driven systems and the structural roles that influence the motivational, physical and conceptual practices within the organisation.
3 Organisations and enterprises exist because the larger social environment accepts, or changes to accommodate, what it represents. However, the organisation, industry and society need continual renewal to continue to do well. The organisation must create opportunities and not just respond to threats from industry competitors or social governance.

In addition, there is the important observation that the difference between the strategy and culture constructs is not so much in their make-up but in their emphasis and timing, with strategy preceding the cultural changes wrought by the strategy, and culture in turn influencing the new strategy. Some of the most effective examples of business and their organisations suggest that their cultures are dynamic and subject to a process of continual renewal of vision. Visionary renewal is the process of fashioning and nurturing a culture that will engender commitment and release individual potential, thereby creating lasting corporate identity and corporate effectiveness. In short, effective organisations raise and do not just meddle with the human condition.

The vision itself, and every derivative of the vision, must be tested by the underlying philosophy and truth contained, or denied, by that philosophy. In the spirit of truth-seeking, moral means must be found to accomplish attractive ends (Wilson 1993).

Success in accomplishment is then a matter of involving more and more people in all aspects of the organisation, including finding ways to improve existing practices and creating altogether new ideas that add richness and depth to the process of renewal.

Potentially, this transformation will lead to more enlightened systems, higher-order roles of delegated authority and responsibility, and increasing competence by everyone. Eventually, extraordinary results might be considered astounding only by the fact that the people appear so 'ordinary' (Peters and Waterman 1982). The framework shown in Figure D is advanced to capture such a process of creative renewal in organisations. Here students are encouraged to continually test the appropriateness of the three dimensions of identity, technology, and structure, and even to question the organisation's fundamental beliefs and values.

Hopefully, the guiding framework should make clearer the major elements of, and the unique combinations and processes in, each organisation. The implication for this case study book is that an integrated view needs to be taken for each of the cases. We hope this introduction will help students overcome what Schein (1985) and Drucker (1974) say is the human tendency for simplistic and uni-dimensional answers.

A glossary of some of the terms used in this introduction follows a brief summary on each of the 12 cases contained in this book, listed in alphabetical order.

We hope you will find these cases relevant and interesting. We are indebted to the many people who have helped us in the development of these ideas and the preparation of this book.

Bryan, Bob and Dorothy

Summaries of the Cases on Strategy and Management

Black Water Rafting

New Zealand is renowned for its friendly people, for its unique flora and fauna and for its varied and unique scenery. In short, New Zealand is an 'outdoors' country that is attracting more and more tourists, people who seek a thrilling experience of the natural wonder of the land. Black Water Rafting is about the invention of a unique form of adventure tourism – the underground experience of 'black' water rafting in caves located in the upper central part of the North Island. But what began as a simple tourism business becomes complicated. 'Success' of the venture brings with it competitors who increase the 'bidding' for what is a limited use for the land and the caves. This land use issue is complicated by the different views of land use and status of land ownership by Maori in New Zealand. The owner-operators respond to these challenges by expanding their present business and adding a new restaurant business. But to what extent are these businesses compatible? And how might the owner-operators contain their risks while planning for future opportunities?

Champion Flourmills Auckland

Marketing had almost ground to a halt at Champion Flourmills Auckland when Ron Bates was appointed manager in 1988. Focus had been on a small line of products for a few big customers and so variety and interest in production was not a regular stimulus. By 1994 sales volume had increased by 50 per cent and overheads reduced by 27 per cent. The mill was humming and the product range had increased dramatically. Bates had decided to work on the only resource that had not been refined by the passage of time – his staff. This case retraces the process of first changing people and encouraging their growth. He believes that, through people, the practices of the workplace can be changed. But his concern is that such change may be a veneer displayed by the incumbents and will not be 'hereditary'. Has enough been done so that the change may be retained even when Bates moves on?

Credit Union Waikato

Credit Union Waikato is faced with a dilemma. It is large enough to attract those smaller credit unions that cannot survive in the competitive environment of the financial services industry. But at this stage Credit Union Waikato is too small to offer the expanded range of services needed by its own owner-members. So does Credit Union Waikato pre-empt the market and put into place the new services, hoping that they can eventually be paid for by an expanded customer base, or acquire other smaller credit unions, or both? Or does Credit Union Waikato accept the overtures of a suitable merger partner? The governing body of Credit Union Waikato, the Board of Directors, are of two minds. On one hand, there is the conservative view that Credit Union Waikato exists to serve members by offering prices lower than the cost of some services. On the other hand, there is the view that credit unions should become a competitive alternative to the banks, and charge 'customers' competitive prices for all services. What should Credit Union Waikato do?

Fisher & Paykel Electronics

Henry van der Heijden is general manager of the electronics company that has made a clothes washing machine directly driven by an electric motor made substantially from plastic when General Electric said it could not be done. Fisher & Paykel call themselves 'The Innovators' and during their 55-year history have turned their technology importing enterprise into a $670 million export business. This case looks at the contribution of strategic alliances, blended with a home-grown product and process innovation philosophies, in the development of the business. How should van der Heijden move the company into the future? Should the best blend of 'opportunities that arise' govern the direction of the company or should the strategy of 'world-class innovators' prevail? And what will be the position of their allies and competitors in the future?

The Gallagher Group

By the end of the 1980s John and Bill Gallagher recognised that the 50-year-old company started by their father was in danger of losing its way. They then made a change from largely mechanical agricultural equipment to animal containment and security systems based on solid state electronics. The international distribution system was improved. But still the business was getting tired. This case looks at the impact of two new managers, John Walley and Neil Richardson, as they worked with John and Bill to change the culture of a company already led by technological innovation. New operations and management systems were introduced and attention to the progress of the many new products was intensified. Perhaps the biggest change was how management saw their role – as coaches on the sideline. But what now? Where is the way ahead? What more can be done?

Healtheries New Zealand

Healtheries New Zealand Ltd is one of the icons of New Zealand business, having virtually pioneered health foods and vitamin supplements in this country during the 1960s. However, in the early 1980s, Healtheries was headed for serious trouble. Only in 1991 did the company emerge from a very stressful turnaround situation that saw the number of its managers and employees halved. The turnaround was engineered by a new managing director, Mark Mathews, a relatively recent graduate of a New Zealand business school. As managing director, Mathews first diligently 'followed the book', and then added his own challenge to turn around the company. And the people in the company responded to the challenge. Within three years, the reputation of Healtheries was restored and, today, Mathews is held in high esteem by shareholders, managers and employees alike. But now the company is faced with looking beyond the turnaround. How is Healtheries to proceed from here?

Mills Reef Winery

Mills Reef Winery is one of a number of excellent wine makers in New Zealand. Mills Reef has its own unique way of doing things. Partly this uniqueness is a reflection of the Prestons, a family who chooses to own a winery business and a restaurant business. This special set-up may be due to the location of Tauranga, a seaside tourist area that is not ideal for growing grapes. In fact, the Prestons started out making wine from kiwifruit and they consistently continue to win top medals for kiwifruit wine. Mills Reef also wins awards for their grape wines, made using grapes from another region of New Zealand. The challenges for the Prestons are not in the making of good wine but in the marketing, selling and distribution of wine. Does Mills Reef operate their restaurant only to expose their wines to the public? What other options are there?

PEC (New Zealand)

PEC is about using breakthrough innovations to supply a global market from 'small town' New Zealand. The story is seen through the eyes of managing director John R. Williams, who was made the senior executive of a rural mechanical engineering company specialising in fuel pump equipment in 1965. He was then 28 years old and given free rein by his father. In 1977 PEC introduced the world's first microprocessor-based fuel pumps. By the 1980s major companies including the London Underground were buying PEC electronic security systems. By the early 1990s sales were doubling each year. John Williams has retained the sense of 'family' and has strong views about family values but needs to face issues of the growing 'family' and its future welfare. Which markets should be tackled and when? What should his successor emulate?

Subway Hamilton Central

Subway, a fast-food restaurant in the central district of Hamilton (hence Subway Hamilton Central) will capture the imagination of those interested in the rapidly expanding market of fast food and franchise businesses in New Zealand. The story of how Subway was started by a student and his scientist-mentor illustrates how unconventional business and marketing strategy can be. From a dismal start, Subway has become amazingly successful in the US and internationally. And students will be surprised to find that the Subway sandwich chain has recently overtaken KFC and Pizza Hut to become the second largest franchisor of fast-food outlets after McDonald's. Subway Hamilton Central has survived its first year of operation in Hamilton's competitive fast-food market. Now what?

Tidco International

Tidco International, in the tiny Waikato town of Matamata, is home to the 'Barmac', the most innovative rock-crushing machinery in the world. The company experienced a wrenching period due to impending financial losses that totalled almost $6 million on total sales of less than $14 million, during an 18-month period in 1991 and 1992. That the company could turn around a year later and record profits of $1 million was testimony to the managerial skill of the new managing director, his team, and the confidence of everyone, including the new owners. And much also had to do with the potential of the construction equipment invented by the Matamata-based company. However, there is no guarantee that Tidco can hold its technological leadership forever, and competitors could develop a variation of the Barmac's unique designs. How can the company retain its technological leadership?

The Tower Group of Companies

The Tower Group of companies is another one of the remarkably recent New Zealand success stories. From a poor performance in the 1970s and 1980s, Tower has overseen a process of change to out-perform its larger rivals in the highly competitive financial services industry. This success is a story about sound management. The fact that all Tower's considerable improvements are done with such uncommon good sense as valuing its people, yet challenging them, sets the stage for introducing effective strategic principles. In many ways, Tower sets a standard for students to match or beat in their analysis of other cases. But this is not to say that Tower does not face its own challenges. How does this financial services company compete in the long term with the international giants of the industry? Can management maintain its goal of 'fairness' in the face of such fierce competition?

Wattie Frozen Foods

Wattie Frozen Foods, formed in 1986, faced the prospect of a $10 million loss in its first year of operation and something had to be done. Gerard La Rooy was one of the executive management team facing the problem and in this case he describes the solution, a radical move to the creation of a work centre management system. The idea was to restructure operations by creating 'businesses' for each stage in the transformation of fresh food to frozen or dehydrated groceries. Meaningful business performance measures had to be created and reported to each business on a daily basis. Now, as part of the international food giant H.J. Heinz, there is a need to face the prospect of a new culture and, possibly, a new direction for the processing plants as the company adopts a work centre approach. What home-grown philosophies should be preserved? How can their essence be characterised as a contribution to the new international 'family'?

Glossary of Key Terms

External factors are both societal forces which affect every industry, that is, the 'STEP' factors and changes (social, technological, economic, political/legal factors and changes); and the forces identified by Porter (1980) which affect competition, namely Buyers, (new) Entrants, Suppliers, and Technological substitutes, or 'BEST' forces of industry competition.

Internal factors are those Beliefs (and values); Identity (vision); Technology (system) and Structure (roles) or 'BITS' central to the strategy and culture of the organisation (Poulin 1996).

Competencies are groups of skills that have value in themselves, and beyond, in the creation of unique products and services (Hamel and Prahalad 1994).

Resources are Valuable, Inimitable, Rare and Organisationally unique (VIRO) assets and capabilities that, together, achieve sustainable competitive advantage (Barney 1991).

Beliefs are those opinions that are so closely held that they determine the very character of the people involved with the organisation, both inside (employees and owners) and outside the organisational boundaries (customers and suppliers).

Identity is that projection into the future of the driving ideas of the organisation. It includes the competing vision that enables leader(s) of the organisation to attract followers and to apply and harness timeless truths about the potential of human nature.

Technology represents the physical system that assists people and process in their functions, for example marketing system, production system, management accounting system. System also involves reward or censure. Effective use of technology is dependent on the vision that is, in turn, grounded in beliefs about people.

Structure is the means of resolving the tension between directing people in their roles and delegating authority and responsibility that goes beyond formal roles. The most effective structures may be based on leading by example and driving out fear so that people can work effectively, individually and together.

Strategy is about what change is needed to improve the organisation, its products and services, and how change is to be accomplished. Strategy begins with beliefs and identity or vision and ends with technology and structure, for better or worse. Renewal of the organisational culture is the first and final challenge of strategy.

Culture is the result of the enactment of all past strategies, including the heritage of past visions, technology and structure. Culture needs continual development and vigilant redirection, in spite of its general resistance to change.

References

Barney, J. (1991) 'Firm Resources and Sustained Competitive Advantage', *Journal of Management*, Vol. 17, pp. 99–120.

Baume, D. (1994) 'Developing Learner Autonomy', SEDA Publications, Birmingham.

Bennis, W. (1989) *Why Leaders Can't Lead*, Jossey-Bass, San Francisco.

Bonham, L. A. (1989) 'Self-directed Orientation Toward Learning: A Learning Style', Oklahoma Research Center for Continuing Profession and Higher Education, University of Oklahoma.

Bourgeois, L. J. and Brodwin D. R. (1984) 'Strategic Implementation: Five Approaches to an Elusive Phenomenon', *Strategic Management Journal,* Vol. 5, pp. 246–264.

Deal, T. A. and Kennedy, A. A. (1982) *Corporate Culture,* Addison-Wesley, Reading, Massachusetts.

Deming, W. E. (1984) *Out of the Crisis,* M.I.T. Press, Cambridge, Massachusetts.

Dennison, D. R. (1990) *Corporate Culture and Organizational Effectiveness,* Wiley, Los Angeles.

Drucker, P. E. (1974) *Management Tasks, Responsibilities, Practices,* Harper and Row, New York.

Gibbs, G. (1988) 'An Extract from Learning by Doing; A Guide to Teaching and Learning Methods', FEU Publications, Oxford.

Gibbs, G. (1995) 'Learning in Teams', The Oxford Centre for Staff Development, Oxford.

Hamel, G. and Prahalad, C. K. (1994) *Competing for the Future,* Harvard Business School Press, Boston, Massachusetts.

Hofer, C. and Schendel, D. (1978) *Strategy Formulation: Analytical Concepts,* West Publishing Company, St. Paul, Minnesota.

Hunger, D. J. and Whellen, T. L. (1996) *Strategic Management,* Fifth Edition, Addison-Wesley, Reading, Massachusetts.

Kolb, D. A. (1984) *Experiential Learning: Experience as the Source of Learning and Development,* Prentice-Hall, Englewood Cliffs, New Jersey.

Kroeber, A. L. and Kluckholm, C. (1952) *Culture: A Critical Review of Concepts and Definitions,* Vintage Books, a division of Random House, New York.

Peters, T. and Waterman, R. (1982) *In Search of Excellence: Lessons from America's Best-run Companies,* Harper and Row, New York.

Porter, M. E. (1980) *Competitive Strategy: Techniques for Analyzing Industries and Competitors,* Free Press, New York.

Poulin, B. J. (1996) 'Strategy, Culture and Enterprise Effectiveness', unpublished doctoral thesis, University of Waikato, Hamilton, New Zealand.

Poulin, B. J. and Spiller, D. (1996) 'Universities in Transition: Towards Credibility and Integrity in Teaching and Learning', proceedings, International Council for Higher Education, Vancouver.

Race, P. (1993) 'Never Mind the Teaching, Feel the Learning', SEDA Publication, Birmingham.

Ramsden, P. (1992) *Learning to Teach in Higher Education,* Routledge, London.

Schein, E. H. (1985) *Organizational Culture and Leadership,* Jossey-Bass, San Francisco.

Smith, A. (originally published in 1776) *The Wealth of Nations,* Modern Library, New York.

Telushkin J. (1991) *Jewish Literacy,* William Morrow and Company, New York.

Weick, K. E. (1985) 'The Significance of Corporate Culture', in P. J. Frost et al. (eds), *Organizational Culture,* Sage, Beverly Hills, California, pp. 381–389.

Weick, K. E. (1987) 'Organizational Culture as a Source of High Reliability', *California Management Review*, Vol. 29, pp. 51–64.

Weimer, D. L. and Vining, A. R. (1989) *Policy Analysis: Concepts and Practice,* Prentice Hall, Englewood Cliffs, New Jersey.

Wilson, J. Q. (1993) *The Moral Sense,* The Free Press, New York.

1 Black Water Rafting

In a way, we find ourselves in the same position as the Waitomo District Council. Business is good right now, and there are a number of potential developments on the horizon.

(Peter Chandler, Co-owner, Black Water Rafting, 1996)

Introduction

'I guess this means we've got ourselves a legitimate business now,' remarked John Ash (49) about the buzz of a chainsaw and the pounding of builders' hammers. He and Peter Chandler (34), co-owners of Black Water Rafting, were seated at a picnic table adjacent to their newly acquired Black Water Cafe, currently undergoing extensive renovations.

Business had been good. Since the introduction of their unusual float-through cave tours in 1987, customer numbers had grown steadily from under 2000 in the first year (1987–88), to about 20,000 per year by 1991–92, and almost 24,000 in 1995–96. However, in April 1996 the two managers found themselves pondering how their business might be affected by increased local competition, and by proposed changes to the management of Ruakuri Cave.

Amid the steady rumble of tour buses on their way to the Glow Worm Cave, John and Peter reflected on the current situation. They had originally gone into business with five basic goals in mind:

1 for self employment
2 to provide the best in underground experiences
3 to foster an enterprise that will benefit the wider community
4 to encourage the responsible use, management and monitoring of caves, and
5 to have fun!

Now their business was in the midst of a large capital expansion, yet the future of their traditional 'float-through' cave tour was somewhat uncertain. They had recently purchased a 10 per cent share of another property approximately 30 minutes' drive from the cafe, which included two caves and 60 hectares of pine forest. The owners of that property (including John and Peter) were in the process of deciding how it might best be used. Initial plans included a possible mix of forestry and cave tour operations.

Acknowledgments This case was prepared by Jared W. Paisley as a basis for classroom discussion rather than to illustrate either effective or ineffective handling of an administrative situation. The cooperation of John Ash, Peter Chandler and the Department of Strategic Management and Leadership, University of Waikato, is gratefully acknowledged.

The Early Years

Situated at the village of Waitomo Caves, in the central North Island, Black Water Rafting was started by Peter Chandler, an Earth Sciences graduate from Hamilton's University of Waikato. He had participated in many trips through nearby Ruakuri Cave, which featured an underground stream, and one night came up with the idea of offering a float-through cave excursion to the non-caving public.

After discussing the idea with his friend and fellow spelunker John Ash, a former University of Auckland Geology graduate, the two scrounged up some wetsuits, old tyre tubes and caving helmets. Peter's old car and John's van were used for transport and, in October 1987, Black Water Rafting was launched with a total of 22 customers in the first month.

Arrangements were made with the Waitomo Museum of Caves to act as their booking agent. Across the street, the local Rugby Club provided shower and changeroom facilities, and formal arrangements were made with the cave's owners to allow access.

A typical trip took about three hours. Customers were outfitted with wetsuits at the Rugby Club, then transported in a van to a 'jump off point' near the cave. Some initial training exercises preceded a 15-minute walk across farm paddocks to the well-hidden cave entrance. After about an hour of walking and floating through the cave, the group of 12 customers and two guides emerged at the cave's stream exit sporting big smiles. Then it was back to the Rugby Club, to change and have some soup and toast before heading home to tell their friends.

The New Zealand Tourism Industry

During the early 1990s the New Zealand tourism industry sector was booming. Over a period of five years, the annual number of holiday visitors increased by about 66 per cent (see Figure 1.1), with a significant increase in visitors from Asia (see Figure 1.2). This was particularly good news for the New Zealand economy, considering the general spending habits of Asian tourists (see Figure 1.3), and the fact that the tourism industry provided, directly, about 10 per cent of all jobs in New Zealand.

Figure 1.1 New Zealand Holiday Visitor Arrivals by Year

Year	No. of Visitors	% Change
1990	464 545	
		+5.8%
1991	491 591	
		+5.6%
1992	519 274	
		+14.3%
1993	593 415	
		+18.3%
1994	702 945	
		+10%
1995	773 379	

Figure 1.2 Visitor Arrivals in New Zealand: Percentage Distribution

Area of Origin	1991	1992	1993	1994
Australia	40	38	37	33
USA	16	15	14	14
Japan	12	14	13	13
Asia (excl Japan)[1]	7	9	11	15
United Kingdom	10	10	10	10
Europe (excl UK)	8	8	9	9
Canada	4	3	3	3
Other Areas[2]	3	3	3	3
Total (%)	**100**	**100**	**100**	**100**

[1] Including: Taiwan, Hong Kong, Singapore, S. Korea, Thailand, Malaysia
[2] Including: Indonesia, Fiji, New Caledonia, Tahiti
Source: Statistics New Zealand, *New Zealand Yearbook 1995*.

Figure 1.3 Expenditure by Tourists From Selected Countries 1993

Country of Residence	Mean Expenditure per Day (NZ$)
Japan	237
Singapore	192
Taiwan	174
Hong Kong	163
USA	135
Germany	105
Australia	96
Canada	73
United Kingdom	70

Source: Statistics New Zealand, *New Zealand Yearbook 1995*.

The Waitomo Caves area is famous for its variety of cave resources, particularly the world-renowned Glow Worm Cave, which is home to many thousands of small luminescent grubs.

Waitomo's central North Island location is within a three-hour drive of more than half the country's population, and on a busy day it is not uncommon to record over 2000 visitors to the Glow Worm Cave. The village of Waitomo Caves (pop. 300) had very little in the way of infrastructure or buildings (see Figure 1.4), but had become the centre of one of the country's premier tour areas. In total, more than 400,000 visits were recorded at the Waitomo area attractions during 1995.

Early in 1996 there were eight different tourist operators in the Waitomo area, all of whom had an interest in promoting the region as a tourist destination. A Hamilton-based organisation known as Tourism Waikato annually provided about $20,000 in promotional assistance to the Waitomo District Council, and an Internet site had recently been set up by the Council to help advertise local tourist attractions. In nearby Hamilton, plans were being developed for a NZ$40 million tourist hotel complex, which had the potential to make the Waitomo Caves area a very important day-trip destination for visitors from overseas.

Figure 1.4 The Waitomo Caves Area

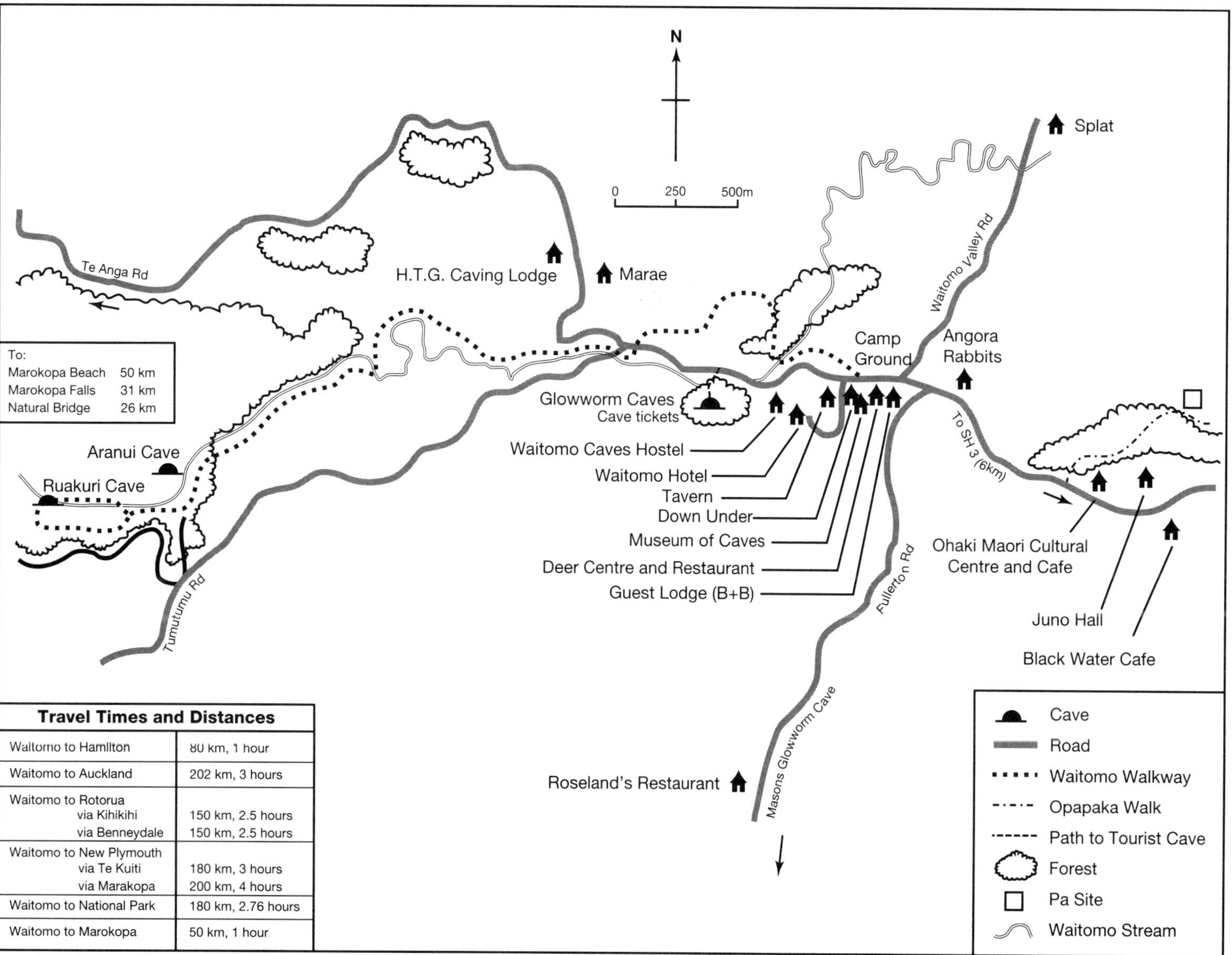

Travel Times and Distances

Waitomo to Hamilton	80 km, 1 hour
Waitomo to Auckland	202 km, 3 hours
Waitomo to Rotorua via Kihikihi	150 km, 2.5 hours
via Benneydale	150 km, 2.5 hours
Waitomo to New Plymouth via Te Kuiti	180 km, 3 hours
via Marakopa	200 km, 4 hours
Waitomo to National Park	180 km, 2.76 hours
Waitomo to Marokopa	50 km, 1 hour

Despite the steadily increasing number of tourists, the Waitomo District Council, according to John and Peter, had not yet developed a formal long-range plan to protect and manage the village and its surrounding resources. However, the District and Regional Councils did coordinate environment and management plans, and there was control and licensing of some tourism operators in the area.

The Early 1990s

From its humble beginnings, Black Water Rafting grew to the point where it was accommodating over 3000 customers per month during the busy summer season (see Figure 1.5).

Figure 1.5 Black Water Rafting Customer Numbers

	1993–94	1994–95		1995–96	
	BWRI	BWRI	BWRII	BWRI	BWRII
April	1 782	1 972	255	1 931	247
May	1 122	1 126	127	1 136	145
June	795	984	161	707	120
July	914	931	190	883	66
August	912	855	142	786	111
September	958	1 070	145	1 041	98
October	1 562	1 565	168	1 520	134
November	2 005	2 295	223	2 037	311
December	2 828	2 885	315	2 956	349
January	3 562	3 182	388	3 390	432
February	2 861	2 672	305	2 794	90
March	2 555	2 660	276	2 411	299
Total	**21 856**	**22 197**	**2 695**	**21 592**	**2 402**

In 1994, a new tour called 'BWRII' was added to give customers a more advanced caving experience. This tour, which included a 30-metre abseil (rope slide) down a tomo (vertical shaft), started in a 'dry' section of Ruakuri Cave and linked up with their traditional underground stream route. The 'experience' is constantly reappraised and changes are made which can affect customer numbers. For example, in November 1995, the BWRII trip was shortened from six hours to four hours with less emphasis on abseil training. And, in February 1996, the BWRII trip was cancelled for three weeks to allow maintenance of the abseil shaft. Black Water Rafting's offerings are indicated by the 1996 brochure shown as Figure 1.6.

John and Peter felt their operation had outgrown the Rugby Club's facilities, and in April 1995 they attended an auction and bought a tearoom from a local couple who had not achieved much success running it as a restaurant. The building was ideally located on the outskirts of town, on the left side of the main road into Waitomo Village. Just across the road was a recently constructed youth hostel.

In late 1995, without interrupting their normal business operations, Peter and John set about organising improvements to their restaurant and its five-acre (2.02-ha) site. The building included a large dining area, a licensed lounge complete with bar, piano and fireplace, and a large deck overlooking the surrounding countryside. The kitchen was upgraded, and an office and souvenir shop were constructed. Outside, a septic system was installed to accommodate the new shower and changeroom facilities. The company's latest expansion had been recently featured in the local media (see Figure 1.7).

Figure 1.6 Black Water Rafting 1996 Brochure

LET NATURE GRAB YOU!!

Black Water 'Rafting'

Invented cave tubing ("rafting") – the sport of navigating along subterranean rivers aided by constellations of glowworms. Our trips strip you of your worldly belongings, squish you into a wet suit, provide you with the necessary safety equipment and then lure you into a delicate underground environment full of adventure, mystery, awe and even fun.

BWR I – allow 3 hours
The original award-winning cave "rafting" tour.
Dynamic, natural, fabulously mysterious fun in Ruakuri Cave.
Age limit 12 and over 40kg.

BWR II – allow 6 hours
Abseil/rappel into the blackness of the Ruakuri Cave river for a more advanced and exhilarating adventure. Age limit 16 and over.
No prior experience necessary.

ALL TOURS INCLUDE:
- FREE entry to the excellent WAITOMO MUSEUM OF CAVES.
- Transport from Museum.
- Showers – soup, toast, tea, coffee.

YOU NEED:
- Swimsuit or something to wear under a wetsuit (thermal underwear helps in winter).
- Towel for a shower (soap/shampoo).
- Maybe a camera.
- Know that in the interests of safety, we reserve the right to cancel tours and assess clients prior to departure.

BOOKINGS:
- Phone: (64) 0-7-878 6219
- Fax: (64) 0-7-878 6184
- Write: Box 13 Waitomo Caves
  NEW ZEALAND

"Sensationelle!"
"Great fun. Simply brilliant!!"
A "MUST DO" for any NZ visitor!!

Figure 1.7 Newspaper feature on Black Water Rafting

Caves visitors cool off with rafting company

By TONY WALL

Thousands of people from around the world have found a perfect way to cool off from the scorching King Country sun while exploring ancient underground caves.

The Waitomo Caves-based Black Water Rafting company is enjoying booming business as up to 160 people a day take the hour-long journey on inner tubes through some of New Zealand's most spectacular but hidden scenery.

The firm is one of several in Waitomo expanding to meet a growing demand overseas and nationally for the unique adventure activities the area has to offer.

It has built a new $300,000 base facility at a site next to the Black Water Cafe, which is now also part of the operation.

It has employed more staff over summer to cope with demand and currently has 20 guides. The business was previously based at the Waitomo Caves Domain and used rugby clubrooms as changing facilities.

Just after Christmas a crane was called in to move shipping containers used to house rafting equipment to the site, which has new changing rooms, showers and toilets.

Staff worked into the night to set up the new base and to ensure the business did not have to shut down during the peak season.

Black Water Rafting operations manager Van Watson says overseas tourists tend to take the firm's guided tours through the cave system at Ruakuri during winter, while New Zealanders turn out in their hordes in summer when the water is far warmer.

"They've got more sense, they like to frolic rather than flinch."

Two guides take tours of 12 people through the cave system, which features glow-worms and waterfalls.

English tourist Chris Storey said he had never seen anything like it. "It's very peaceful. Looking at the glow-worms is like staring at hundreds of little stars."

Source: *Waikato Times*, 8 January 1996, p. 3.

The property includes a large parking area with convenient access off the main road. A big black 'tyre tube' with the words 'Black Water Cafe' painted on it, served as a distinctive marker to the carpark entrance. Peter commented on their new facilities:

> This new facility provides opportunities for additional added value activities, but anything we do can't just be for our own benefit – it has to serve the customers' needs, otherwise they'll stop coming here. Our main objective is not necessarily to diversify into the restaurant business, but to provide really good facilities for people after their trip, so they can have more than just soup and toast.

On the advice of their accountant, John and Peter formed a limited company which owned the building and property, which in turn leased them back to Black Water Rafting to operate the tours and cafe. By the time it was all finished, the total project (including renovations) cost close to $800,000. Financing was arranged through their own cash reserves, and by a mortgage against the property. A summary of Black Water Rafting's financial statements is presented in Appendix 1 and Appendix 2.

By early 1996, the business employed 10–15 full and part-time guides and 10 cafe/office staff. There were plans to install a computerised trip booking system at the cafe and this would be linked to the central trip reservation system at the Waitomo Museum of Caves.

Employee Concerns

A number of Black Water Rafting staff had been with the company from the beginning. After eight years, these loyal employees felt they were a part of the company, and the company was a part of them. However, some were questioning their future role in the growing business. John commented:

> Some of our most capable and loyal staff are thinking about going off and doing their own thing, which would probably be creating more competition for us. They've put a lot of effort and energy into Black Water Rafting, and want to know where the business is going and what's in it for them.
>
> Guide professionalism is the cornerstone of our business; without it we would become like many other tourist operations. Our guides need to feel that they are respected for their knowledge, expertise and experience. They need to be given the opportunity to develop all of these within the business framework. They've invested time and creativity in this business and we've invested in their training.
>
> Some of our guides are the best in the business and they are very versatile. We have people who can jump in the water to lead a caving trip, then go and cook meals in the cafe. They realise that Black Water Rafting isn't just John and Peter and Ruakuri Cave – it's them too.

Peter and John were considering other ways to organise their business, which would allow more autonomy to employees wanting to 'do their own thing'. One idea discussed was to create semi-autonomous business units, each with its own coordinator and staff. Peter commented on this proposal:

> Having separate business units with their own managers is a great idea, as long as those managers can be partially rewarded for their successes and be partially responsible for their failures or non-successes.

These units would report on a regular basis to the 'parent company', and liaise among themselves for shared resources.

The business units might include:

- Black Water Rafting (cave tour) operations
- Cafe
- Corporate Groups and Tours
- Merchandising
- Education and School Groups
- New Developments (e.g. spa pools).

Marketing and Competition

'I happen to be reading a great little book at the moment,' said John Ash, 'called *The Small Business Handbook*. It has about eight lines on marketing with respect to competition. According to the book there are basically three ways to compete: (1) you match the competition with your product, (2) you try to reduce your prices, possibly risking a price war, or (3) you concentrate on what you want to do and what they don't do.'

John continued:

> We don't have a monopoly any longer. There are now four cave rafting businesses in New Zealand: two here in Waitomo and two in the South Island. Apart from the usual annual fluctuations, our customer numbers seem to have plateaued in the past year or so. I think we are doing pretty well. Although there are more tourists, the market is getting more competitive and there are more tourist operators offering a very wide variety of activities.

In 1992, a Maori-owned business, trading under the name Waitomo Down Under, started offering underground rafting trips in a different cave, in direct competition to Black Water Rafting. The Maori business opened their own booking office right next door to the Waitomo Museum of Caves, and offered trips of a similar nature and price (see Figure 1.8). John stated:

> We haven't taken an attitude of competing with Waitomo Down Under; they offer a different tour. When they first started, their price was $40 and ours was $50 because we wanted to make a statement that we are in a different business. They have recently put their price up to the same as ours.
>
> We believe, from listening to people, that there is more customer distinction among the trips than there was two years ago, and our customer numbers really haven't dropped.
>
> We've created a trip to fit into a cave system, but by flooding part of their (privately owned) cave, Waitomo Down Under has created a cave system to fit a trip.

To add even more confusion to the marketplace, John and Peter recently learned that one of their South Island competitors had printed brochures using the name 'Black Water Rafting', yet their trip was completely different. John and Peter were in the process of preparing an application to the Commerce Commission, in a effort to stop the other operator from using their business name.

Figure 1.8 Waitomo Down Under 1996 Brochure

WAITOMO

DOWN UNDER

A UNIQUE NEW ZEALAND EXPERIENCE

Box 24 • Waitomo Caves • New Zealand

Come and try one of our exciting adventure packages

Adventure One

Cave Tubing

Explore the subterranean world of Glowworms and Spleotherms on a rubber tube.
Try the jumps and waterslide.
Learn about the history and folklore of the Maori people.
Time: Allow 3 hours
Require: Towel and swimwear
Maximum: 12 people
Cost: $55.00*

Adventure Two

Cave Tubing • Abseiling

A 150 foot drop!
Perform acrobatics upside down, or even no hands at all!!
Once you reach the bottom then it's off to Cave Tubing.
Time: 4.5-5 hours
Require: Sturdy clothes & Togs
Maximum: 6 people
Cost: $110.00*

Meet us at Taware House next to the Museum

Hot showers and light meal provided
Free entry to Museum of Caves
Tours depart every day

Special Group, Student, YHA, Business and School Discounts available

**Please Note: All costs subject to change without notification October 1995*

FOR FURTHUR INFORMATION OR BOOKINGS

TELEPHONE (07)8786577 FACSIMILE (07)8786565

If that initiative proved successful, they planned to formally apply to the Trademark Office for registration. Peter commented:

> We invented the 'Black Water Rafting' and have put a lot of effort into developing our business. Our name isn't generic like 'White Water Rafting', but once a name is generally adopted as a generic term there's not much you can do about it, even if you have a registered trademark.

By way of illustration, the names of famous branded products such as Windsurfer, Kleenex, Roller blade, and Frisbee had all become 'generic'. From the original producers' point of view, this is not considered an ideal situation.

Land Ownership Disputes

Black Water Rafting's tours were conducted in a small part of a large cave system known as Ruakuri Cave, located about 5 km from their new headquarters at the

Black Water Cafe. Up until 1988, Ruakuri Cave had been the site of a very popular 'dry' cave tour which was operated by the Government's Tourist Hotel Corporation (THC). However, in that year a dispute arose between the THC and the cave's major owner, resulting in a 'No Trespassing' sign being erected in a privately owned section of the cave, forcing its closure to tourists. According to New Zealand law, property owners own any caves underneath their land.

In 1994, a new survey was conducted and it was discovered that there were in fact *three* owners of the part of the cave in which Black Water Rafting operated: the original private landowner, the Waitomo District Council (which owned the part of the cave underlying the 20-metre road allowance), and the Department of Conservation (DOC) which owned the cave's tourist entrance located on a public scenic reserve. See Figure 1.9 for a detailed cave map.

To further complicate matters, the scenic reserve (containing the cave's tourist entrance) was being claimed back from the government by the local iwi, under terms of the 1840 Treaty of Waitangi. In summary, there were effectively *four* parties with ownership claims on the northern end of the cave: the private landowner, the Waitomo District Council, the Department of Conservation, and the local iwi.

The Helicopter Line Proposal

In late 1995, a Dunedin-based company was negotiating with the various owners of Ruakuri Cave for the rights to re-open the tourist portion of the cave. The Helicopter Line was a large concern which owned and operated a fleet of campervans, rental cars, buses, and a range of tourist activities such as helicopter and jet boat rides, rafting, heliskiing, and Kelly Tarlton's unique aquarium in Auckland.

A tentative agreement was reached to re-open the cave's tourist route sometime later in 1996. However, before a final agreement could be signed, some members of a local hapū (sub-tribe) who hadn't attended the earlier meetings, pointed out that the area in and around the tourist entrance had long ago been a sacred Maori site or wāhi tapu. They felt it was inappropriate to re-open that part of the cave to tourists, especially since it was the subject of a land claim. Furthermore, the Maoris went on to say that the boundaries of the wāhi tapu should include not only the cave's tourist entrance, but should extend back as far as daylight would normally reach. This had the effect of extending the 'off limits' area at least one-third of the way down the main cavern.

John elaborated on this situation:

> I think it's important that people should understand where Maori people are coming from, and I think that's very difficult. I've been fortunate because I've sat down for lots of cups of tea with many Maori families, and believe I have acquired a sense of what some of them are thinking.
>
> A hundred years ago the Maori people were experienced business operators in New Zealand. When the Europeans first came, the Maoris took over and operated 80 per cent of the shipping trade, as well as flax mills, flour mills and other businesses. Eventually that was taken over by the Europeans, so the Maori people have had a huge gap in their history where they've had little opportunity to develop their business acumen.

Figure 1.9 Ruakuri Cave: Tourist Section

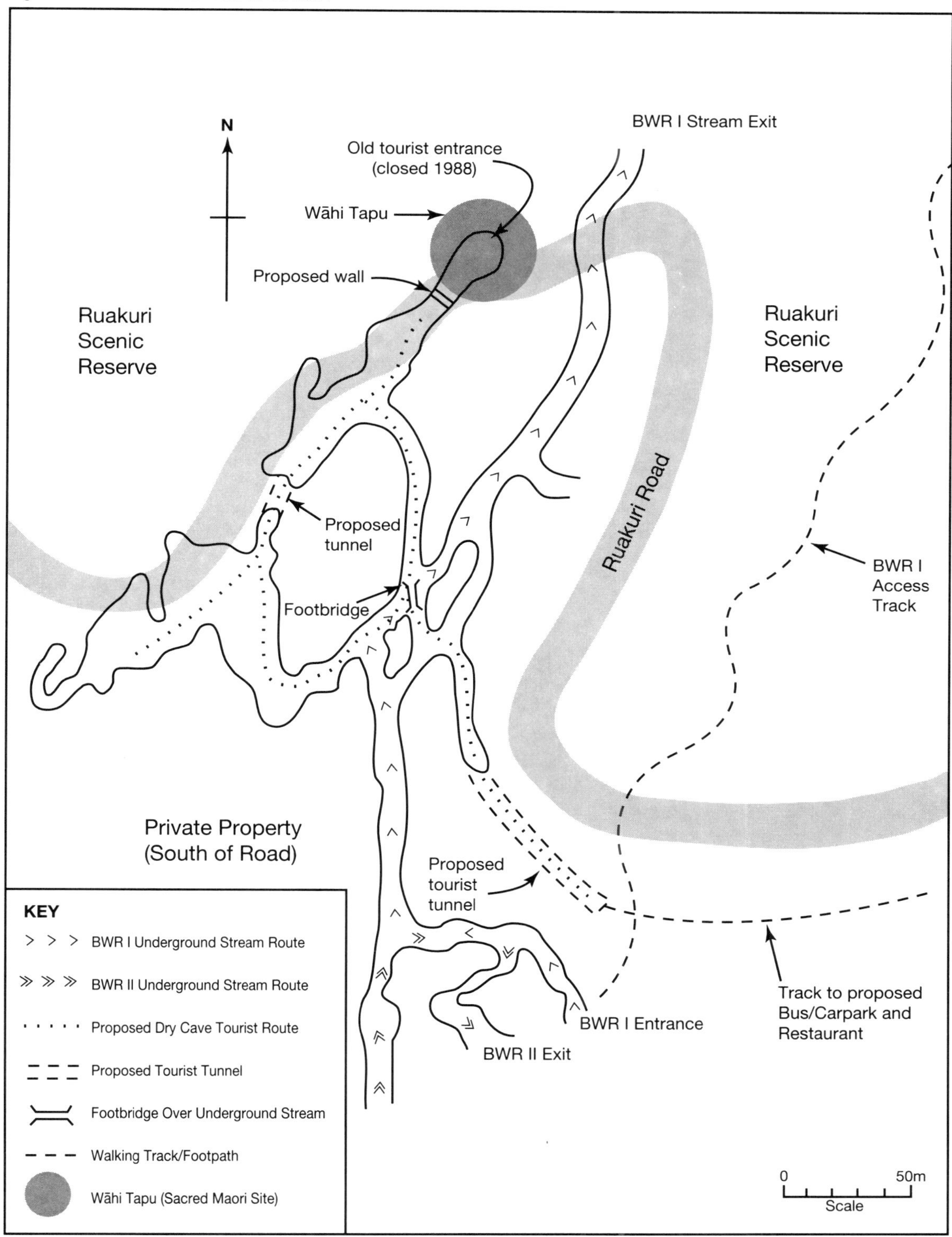

> Now, with the handing back of land and resources, they've been forced to form groups and trusts and inter-family relationships which they never had before, and that places an incredible amount of stress on their people. One group will say one thing and another group will say something entirely different, and who actually has control is important.
>
> We had a local example here just recently, where an old historic marae was being rebuilt. They young people decided they were tired of seeing no action, so they went up there with a whole lot of materials and started rebuilding. Then the older people said, 'You can't do this, it's in the wrong place.' So they had to stop and shift everything to another location.
>
> Sometimes the Europeans miss out. We tend to assume the Maori people can't agree among themselves, but that's not entirely true. It's a complex series of interrelationships that is very difficult for us to understand.

Not to be deterred by the hapū's concerns, the developers put a much bigger proposal on the table for discussion.

The Revised Ruakuri Cave Proposal

A new proposal, costing an estimated NZ$8 million, called for construction of a steep 90-metre long tunnel, to be drilled into a hillside on the private landowner's property, linking into the existing Ruakuri Cave system (see Figure 1.9). Inside this tunnel, a motorised walkway was planned, and the entrance would feature an artificial waterfall, behind which tourists would walk to gain entrance to the tunnel.

Other proposed improvements included a large restaurant and gift shop near the cave's new entrance, along with a huge carpark capable of accommodating 30 tour buses. Inside the cave, the plan included drilling another shorter tunnel to allow a circular tours route, and putting up an artificial wall at the extent of the wāhi tapu, perhaps featuring a video interpretation area.

By working in cooperation with the highly popular Glow Worm Cave – perhaps by offering package deals to high volumes of tourists – initial profits (after operating expenses) of $0.25 million per month were forecast for the new cave tour.

From Black Water Rafting's point of view, this new development plan could have a significant impact on their future operations. The proposed 'new entrance' was directly in the path Black Water Rafting took to get to their traditional cave entrance and would almost certainly have a negative impact on the aesthetics of that part of the trip. Inside the cave, the proposed tourist route bridged directly over the underground stream used by Black Water Rafting. Nobody could say for sure what effect thousands of tourists walking through the cave might have on the general underground environment.

The private landowners were in the process of negotiating a lease agreement with The Helicopter Line, and part of that agreement was contingent on The Helicopter Line coming to an acceptable sub-lease arrangement with Black Water Rafting. According to John Ash, there had also been some talk of The Helicopter Line possibly being interested in buying a 50 per cent share of Black Water Rafting.

Peter offered a final comment: 'What we really need is a long-term strategy to help guide our business into the future.'

Appendix 1: Black Water Rafting Consolidated Income Statement for Year Ending 31 March 1996

Income	
Sales:	
BWRI	1 036 600
BWRII	230 929
Cafe	202 665
Souvenirs	23 395
Other Trips	59 687
Total Sales	**1 553 276**
Interest Income	1 695
Total Income	**$1 554 971**
Expenses	
Cost of Sales:	
BWRI	448 611
BWRII	147 704
Cafe	241 007
Souvenirs	12 557
Other Trips	41 450
Total Cost of Sales	**891 329**
General and Overhead Expenses:	
Advertising and Sponsorship	19 360
Depreciation Expense	12 377
Food (inc. Staff Lunches)	22 678
General Operating & Administrative Expenses	22 067
GST	97 122
Insurance	21 848
Interest & Bank Charges	10 621
Legal Expenses	4 840
Printing & Stationery	12 013
Rent	12 649
Staff Training	1 442
Staff Bonuses	20 753
Staff Wages	125 829
Telephone	11 316
Vehicle Expenses	17 546
Total General & Overhead Expenses	412 461
Total Expenses	**$1 303 790**
Gross Profit	**$251 181**
less Income Tax @ 33%	82 890
Net Profit	**$168 291**

Source: Unaudited Company Records.

Appendix 2: Black Water Rafting Consolidated Balance Sheet as at 31 March 1996

Current Assets	
Bank Deposits	27 498
Inventory	14 756
Accounts Receivable	41 141
Other	2 050
Total Current Assets	85 445
Fixed Assets	
Land, Buildings & Equipment (at cost less depreciation)	674 614
Improvements to Buildings & Site	236 907
Total Fixed Assets	911 521
Total Assets	**$996 966**
Current Liabilities	
Accounts Payable	51 269
Bank Overdraft	42 855
GST Payable	26 660
Income Tax Payable	16 587
Accrued Holiday Pay	13 823
Trip Deposits	292
Total Current Liabilities	151 486
Long Term Liabilities	
Bank Loan	393 142
Loans from J. Ash & P. Chandler	308 080
Other Loans (from family and friends)	90 000
Total Long Term Liabilities	791 222
Total Liabilities	**$942 708**
Partners' Capital	54 258
Total Liabilities & Equity	**$996 966**

Source: Unaudited Company Records.

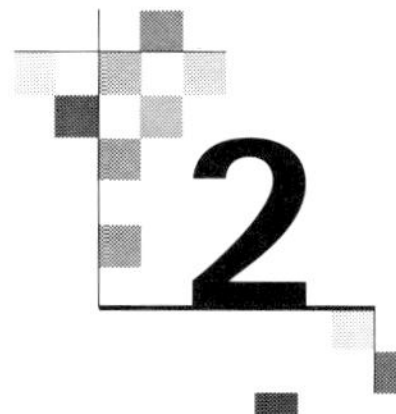

2 Champion Flourmills Auckland

Our annual training costs worked out at $43 per person. We don't have any training 'costs' at all now, instead we make investments in our staff.

(Ron Bates, Champion Flourmills Auckland, 1994)

Introduction

This case is about company growth through a commitment to the development of people.

Champion Flourmills Auckland increased its sales volume by 50 per cent between 1988 and 1994. The utilisation of grain improved by 5 per cent and overheads were reduced by 27 per cent during that time. Although staff numbers were reduced from 81 to 61, staff morale improved. These figures represent a remarkable achievement in such a mature industry. How was it done?

A variety of models were used to enhance understanding of behaviour and implement appropriate changes. The Team Management Index, Yung's behavioural models, and Matataki techniques, processes, methods and experiential learning, were all explored and used. Porter's Value Chain and Value System concepts helped identify how staff in each part of the process could add value to company products. This resulted in a 'total value improvement process'.

The importance of both the internal and external customer became evident to all employees. Staff agreed that product conformance was the major issue for customers and set about writing quality system documentation in a language they could understand. Translation to ISO 9000 series quality standards was an afterthought, not a driving force.

The thrust of Champion's winning strategy is for all staff to consider themselves as part of the sales team, rather than only the seven sales specialists. All company performance results are shared and all staff benefit from the commitment to development.

Acknowledgments This case study was developed for teaching by Bob Mills and is based on interviews with Ron Bates, North Island Manager for the Goodman Fielder Ltd subsidiary Champion Flourmills and invaluable contributions from Garth Gillam, Mike Enesa and Ken Peat. The case was originally commissioned by TRADENZ for an Innovation Leadership Programme for CEOs in the Food and Beverage Industry held at Hotel du Vin, 6/7 March 1995. The authors would like to thank Champion Flourmills Auckland for their time and their willingness to share their experiences and philosophies. The case is to be used for classroom discussion and not to illustrate effective or ineffective handling of a strategic or administrative situation.

The Company and its History

The Fort Street site in Auckland was purchased for a flour mill in 1875. In 1888 the Auckland Roller Mills Co Ltd was incorporated with the mill and was amalgamated a year later with Firth's First Eight Hour Roller Mills, which had been established at Quay Street. In 1899 the company's name was changed to Northern Roller Milling Company (NRM). On 1 July 1992, the name was changed again to Champion Flourmills Auckland (CFA).

A variety of oatmeal products as well as wheat flour was produced until 1954. NRM's merger with Fleming and Co Ltd of Gore saw the oatmeal plant dismantled and transferred south. A physical remodelling to increase capacity occurred in 1961 when the old NRM flour mill in Quay Street finally closed.

Further extensive remodelling of the mill took place in 1982/83, including the installation of new milling machinery. The new machinery is expected to maintain full efficiency until well into the twenty-first century and meet consumer needs for the foreseeable future. Champion Flourmills is a 100 per cent owned operating unit of Goodman Fielder Mills (NZ) Ltd. The old building and restrictive site make logistics planning very much a 'just-in-time' operation. A production flow of 24,000 tonnes must pass through the 400 square metre warehouse each year.

In 1985 the Fort Street mill employed 140 people. By 1988 staff numbers had been reduced to 81 and today only 61 are employed in spite of a 50 per cent increase in production in six years. Seventeen nationalities are represented, made up of 62 per cent New Zealanders, 19 per cent Pacific Islanders, 7 per cent Asians, 6 per cent from Britain and another 6 per cent from the rest of Europe. Staff are employed in the seven functional areas of production, packing, dispatch, engineering, administration, sales and customer services.

The Industry and Environment

Prior to 1987, flour milling was the most regulated industry in New Zealand. The New Zealand Wheat Board, established in 1933, sold all the wheat supplied to New Zealand mills and purchased back all the flour. Profit was fixed at 12.5 per cent of written assets in the company accounts, and had no relation to the amount a flour mill produced or how cost effective its operation was. Mills could, however, increase trade in the relatively static market by purchasing quota. Mill numbers have been reduced from 35 in 1933 to 14 today.

Mill ownership has changed from grower cooperatives and small family businesses to the situation today where three Australasian parent companies, Allied Foods, Defiance Milling and Goodman Fielder, have 91 per cent of the trade. In 1989 Goodman Fielder Wattie closed the mill at Mount Maunganui and transferred the trade to Champion Flourmills in downtown Auckland, now the largest in the country. This transfer provided up to 30 per cent of the increase in sales volume in the five years prior to 1994.

New Zealand uses about 220,000 tonnes of flour each year. In 1992, 25,000 tonnes were packed into retail bags (in up to 10-kilogram bags), 55,000 tonnes were packed for industry (in up to 60-kilogram bags) and the rest was sent out in bulk to large bakeries. Deregulation in 1987 meant finding a new way of doing business. A strategy was required to meet competition, survive and grow. All this was to be done within the constraints of an established and stable market and a relatively new plant run by a 'league of nations' in old, inadequate premises.

The Change Agent

Ron Bates qualified as a miller in 1975 and has worked in flour mills all his working life. After spending a year as a Head Miller (Production Manager) in the South Island he worked in a bakery for two years to learn more about flour. He moved to Auckland as business unit manager for Goodman Fielder in the regulated environment for four years and, in the following three years, he readied four mills for deregulation as a general manager for Goodman Fielder Mills. Bates focused on establishing a five-year development plan for all staff. After the merger with Wattie in February 1988, Bates found himself in charge of the Fort Street mill and faced a significant challenge.

The Fort Street Mill in 1988

Up to this point, management style at Fort Street had been autocratic and gave priority to cost reduction rather than to being cost competitive. The company had little market focus and few marketing skills. As a result, production was oriented to large customers and the product range was small. Staff were highly competent but not enpowered to make decisions. Very little time and effort was spent on staff training. In fact the annual budget averaged $43 per person.

There had been an expectation that the site would be sold, so little money had been spent on maintenance in the previous four years. A high-speed packing machine had been purchased but not installed for the same reason. The share and property market crash of 1987 put paid to any chance of an early shift from the site. The decision was made to stay on the site for at least eight years, but this meant there was pressure, not only to reduce costs, but also to spend an extra $500,000 on repairs and maintenance in the next year. Another pressure arose because Goodman Fielder Wattie (GFW) had a number of mills in Australia that could supply all of New Zealand's needs and closure of the Auckland mill could increase returns to shareholders.

What Had to be Done

Ron Bates and his senior managers put together the following 'to do' list:

- Strive for quality
- Get staff committed to internal and external customers
- Reduce overheads to 55 per cent of existing level
- Differentiate the product in order to:
  - lift the image of flour from being a mere commodity
  - increase margins
  - retain market leadership
- Reduce fear. Staff were scared to step outside their safety zone, as many others had lost their jobs
- Change staff attitudes:
  - from production to marketing
  - from merely attending the job for payment to enjoyment of the work
- Provide a consistent product
- Bring the factory up to good working repair

- Install new technology – high speed packer and automatic palletisation
- Upgrade management information systems.

Some way had to be found to get staff working together to design and implement the changes. All the senior staff team were very capable and keen to develop and accept more responsibility and accountability. But how could this be implemented?

The Change Process

In June 1988 GFW arranged an Advanced Management Programme at Matataki Lodge, Pauanui. Matataki are specialists in people and company development. There, Bates met instructors with a mindset that matched his management style and way of thinking. The strength of their approach was considered to be the ability to facilitate thinking, vision and learning. It was at this Programme that Ron was also introduced to the Team Management Index (TMI), a tool for measuring the differences in people's role strengths. The technique explains how people can work together harmoniously as a team once their role is understood.

In October 1988 the senior management team at Champion, including supervisors, attended a two-day workshop on the TMI model. The technique explores the relationships between the roles of advisers, innovators, promoters, developers, organisers, producers, inspectors, maintainers and linkers. Teams are said to be more effective if they include all of these attributes. The Champion staff began to appreciate the strengths and weaknesses of others. They also saw the benefit of collecting contributions from all team members before decision making. During the next 12 months senior staff met weekly to discuss production and planning changes. Two additional sessions at Matataki were held for senior staff, one for developing a five-year strategic plan and the other for preparing an action plan for the following year.

In order to measure team progress another tool called a Management Practices Audit (MPA) was used. The mechanics of the system is that each individual answers 40 questions about his or her own practices, and five other staff members also score that individual. The leadership practices that are measured include experimenting and taking risks, asking 'what can we learn', looking for ways to improve and innovate, inspiring a shared vision, modelling the way, enabling and encouraging others. The results provide a soft and anonymous way of comparing individuals' self-perceptions and the observations others make about their progress. MPA has continued to be used each year since then. By the end of 1989 it was considered that TMI was useful for the senior team but not for a company-wide programme to extend thinking, learning and innovation.

Company-wide Change

The change that Ron Bates sought was now focused on three areas:

1 Management style such that:
   - All staff are able to have their say
   - Team participation is expected and encouraged
   - Loyalty is earned
   - Respect and trust are developed

- Job satisfaction is understood and developed
- Job satisfaction is gained and returned
- People and resources are better used.

2 Quality improvement such that everyone is responsible for quality and the following sequence occurs from recognising quality people to becoming a quality company:
   - Quality people
   - Quality training
   - Quality product
   - Happy customers
   - Quality environment
   - Quality company

3 Staff training such that each person:
   - Understands his or her function
   - Is capable of carrying out the function, doing more than one task and of being promoted
   - Works well and is happy in his or her contribution.

It was very important, as Bates saw it, that the Senior Team accept the vision of total company involvement as it was their positions and their status that would change the most. Matataki Lodge was asked to arrange a one-day outdoor environment seminar during a weekend in February 1990 and all Champion staff were invited. Seventy-five per cent came. Learning experiences included canoe trips, snorkelling, rock walks and a launch ride. During this programme Ron shared his company-wide vision. Everyone had to understand how the company worked, how each department operated and how to satisfy their suppliers and customers. The major model used to accomplish this understanding was the Porter Value Chain. As well, Yung's behavioural and conflict models, de Bono's thinking hats and Ishikawa fish bone diagrams were devices used during the process.

The Value Chain sequence at Champion was developed and found to be different to that expected by traditional thinking. For Champion the Value Chain was:

- Customer
- Customer Services
- Dispatch
- Packaging
- Production
- Purchasing
- Sales and Marketing
- Accounts
- Technical Support
- Administration.

The Value Improvement Process became part of the fabric of life at Champion. Staff developed a mission statement: 'To do what our customers want, I will professionally own my part of the company'. It was seen as less remote than the company's mission statement. Quality attributes were given the following priority ranking:

1 Conformance
2 Serviceability
3 Reliability
4 Performance
5 Features
6 Aesthetics
7 Durability
8 Perception.

The values that the company decided to pursue were set in 1990 as:

- Professionalism
- Responsiveness
- Flexibility
- Personal Service
- Supportiveness
- Continuous Learning.

In 1992, 'Creativity' was added to the list of values, as Champion adopted the Drucker statement, 'We do different things and we do things differently', as a theme for the year.

Continuous Improvement Process

The Senior Team has been transformed into Value Champions. They meet for 45 minutes every three weeks under a rotating chairpersonship. Ideas, plans and knowledge are exchanged and developed. Themes are selected for the company for the period; for example, waste management, power savings, quality improvement, cost saving. Value Champions' meetings are followed by departmental meetings where the themes and information are considered and actioned.

Ron Bates believes that thinking time must be provided if innovation is to occur (after de Bono), and brainstorming sessions are encouraged. Staff are trained to present new ideas in a simple but effective form for presentation to Value Champions. Unless capital costs need verification, the Value Champions can give ideas the 'go ahead'. Rewards to individuals are various and have included shopping vouchers, time off, a company jacket or jersey, and dinner out with partner. However, departmental teams get the greatest enjoyment from advertising their success.

Capital installations have now been completed. Upgraded labourers take full responsibility for the new machines rather than hiring a technology expert. This has resulted in reduced costs, upskilled staff and staff members becoming more interested in their job. Even the service contract on some machines may not be renewed next year. Company results are shared with staff at a 'State of the Nation' talk twice a year. Staff are entrusted to keep confidences, do their task and support one another.

The Results

- A 2.93 per cent increase in yield of flour from wheat grain and a 1.76 per cent decrease in grain use. These figures amount to operational savings exceeding $1 million per year
- Overheads have been reduced by 27 per cent
- There are now no costs, only investments
- Staff numbers have been reduced from 81 in 1988 to 61 in 1995
- ISO 9002 Accreditation was achieved in October 1992 and the parallel Value Improvement programme has been able to be wound down
- Product range has increased from fewer than 20 to over 80 lines
- A family atmosphere has been created, everyone talks to each other and is helpful
- Greater staff skills, creativity and understanding of the business make staff more marketable
- The company is more responsive to its customers.

The Future

Champion Flourmills Auckland has been transformed. While Bates and his senior staff are running the mill the change process and its benefits will be ingrained in the way things are done. The relentless grinding down of inefficient operations will see continued pressure on companies in the milling industry to perform and excel. A further concern for management is whether the experiences of existing workers can be vicariously absorbed and owned by new staff. Should the company set in place a plan to renew shared experiences on a regular basis or is it time to look for new stimuli? How should change be managed for the future?

3 Credit Union Waikato

I can't go to the community and say we are great until we truly are great.

(Janet Hodgson, Manager, Credit Union Waikato, 1996)

Introduction

Since 1991 Credit Union Waikato has undergone significant changes in the way it does business. In response to its changing environment, changes in the credit union's strategic direction are redefining the policies which have distinguished the union since its founding in 1967. For example, recent promotional moves to increase membership are threatening the very characteristics which historically differentiated credit unions from the banks. But how else can Credit Union Waikato compete with the banks who are becoming more aggressive every year?

What is a Credit Union?

A credit union is a not-for-profit financial cooperative, owned and operated by its members. A credit union has three functions: to encourage members to save with the union; to lend the resulting funds to other members; and to provide its members with additional financial services that they may require. Members save by lodging deposits with the credit union like a bank. However, unlike banks, for every $1 deposited the member receives one share in the credit union's Members' Funds Capital Account.

Credit unions are regulated under the Friendly Societies & Credit Union Act of 1982. To register with the Act a credit union must submit a 'trust deed', an important element of which is the instrument called a 'common bond'. This instrument refers to the particular connection (such as employment at the same organisation) between all members of a credit union. By definition it becomes the main criterion for membership. Each credit union has its own common bond which is approved by the Registrar of the Friendly Society and Credit Union Act 1982.

Acknowledgments This case was prepared by Roger Honore-Morris, Heath Kerr and Robert Kelman under the supervision of Bryan Poulin of the School of Management Studies, University of Waikato. Special thanks go to Janet Hodgson, Manager, Credit Union Waikato, for her cooperation and valuable contribution. The case is to be used for classroom discussion and not to illustrate effective or ineffective handling of a strategic or administrative situation.

History

In 1967 the employees of Waikato Hospital decided to form their own credit union. They named their new organisation Waikato Hospital Employees Credit Union. Part of the philosophy of this credit union was the financial education of members. The common bond was that the person had to be an employee of the Waikato Hospital, the main criterion to be eligible for membership. The employee restriction had two advantages. First, it provided for controlled growth. Second, bad debts were almost non-existent because borrowers were aware that they were effectively borrowing money from their working colleagues.

Over the next 20 years, changes in the national health system saw the Waikato Hospital expand its area of responsibility to include the regional Taupo, Te Awamutu, Morrinsville, Tokoroa, Te Aroha and Huntly hospitals. To allow these other hospital employees to become members of the credit union, the common bond was amended to include all 'employees of the Waikato Area Health Board'.

The name of the credit union was changed to Waikato Area Health Board Credit Union to reflect these changes, including the changes to the health system. Mostly, these changes meant expansion of Credit Union Waikato. Expansion did not really change the functioning of the union. The organisation was just bigger. But there have been exceptions to a general expansion such as when employees of Rotorua Hospital first belonged to this Credit Union (Waikato) and then formed their own when they were 'big enough'.

In 1991 a further change was made to the national health system with a few large Regional Health Authorities (RHAs) replacing Area Health Boards. The net result was considerable employee redundancies as the RHAs 'rationalised' (made leaner) their operations within the hospital system and small hospitals were closed. These changes had a dramatic effect on hospital-based credit unions. This was because past employees lost their eligibility for membership. Membership dropped considerably.

The Board of Directors decided to seek approval from the Registrar to broaden the common bond in 1993. The application was successful and in 1993 the common bond became simply 'residency' in the Waikato, Rotorua, Coromandel, Taupo and King Country districts. The name Credit Union Waikato was chosen to reflect the shift to a wider community base from its traditional employee base. The Board's new Statement of Purpose for the credit union simply stated:

> This Credit Union is a member-owned cooperative that aims to provide services enabling each member to achieve personal financial understanding and stability.

The move from the health industry base to a wider community base was significant for two reasons. First, credit unions were historically formed by people who shared homogeneous characteristics, and this commonality became more fragmented. Secondly, the financial advantages offered by the hospitals to the credit union were dramatically reduced. For example, no longer did the hospital provide rent-free office space, and no longer did it provide a free telephone and free postal service.

Also in 1993, a new manager was appointed with a title change from manager to chief executive officer (CEO). The directive for the new CEO was to create growth for the purposes of gaining a higher profile as a financial service supplier and to become a real alternative to the banks. Specifically the new CEO was to increase memberships, increase loans, increase profit, and enhance the not-for-profit philosophy of 'people before numbers'.

Following the appointment of the new CEO, the infrastructure of Credit Union Waikato was modified to allow more direct action by the CEO rather than the reactive style of management experienced in previous years under the Board of Directors. The appointment of the CEO also helped the Board move from being a Board of 'managers' to a Board that would oversee progress. This new role was to 'set policies, philosophies and overall guidance' for the board of management. From 1993 to 1994, loan demand, new memberships and new funds all increased, and initial developments were made in the area of improving technology and management information systems. However, late in 1994 the CEO resigned to pursue other interests.

In early 1995, Janet Hodgson was appointed as the new manager and the more corporatist title of CEO was not maintained. Janet Hodgson brought from Trust Bank to Credit Union Waikato over 20 years' experience in retail banking, an area which she left because she 'felt it was losing its traditional "people" and "community" focus.'

Currently, Credit Union Waikato operates three offices: the Waikato Hospital (original office), Ngaruawahia, and the Central City office (headquarters). In 1996 a Hamilton East branch was closed because it was only being used by members for deposits and withdrawals. Members wanting loans or ancillary service such as insurance tended to visit the other branches, particularly the city branch. The premises of the Hamilton East branch are on the market to be sub-leased. The Hospital branch remains profitable mainly because of the large number of members who still work at the hospital. The Ngaruawahia branch is profitable because it has extremely low overheads and is the only credit union in a town which has limited banking options.

Industry Information

As mentioned previously, credit unions are controlled by the Friendly Societies and Credit Union Act 1982. But credit unions are also regulated by the Security Regulations 1978, the Financial Reporting Act 1993 and the Income Tax Act 1976. This multiplicity of regulation is restrictive for credit unions in that it places an unfair burden on credit unions compared with other financial service organisations competing in the deregulated finance market. In 1994 the government announced that there would be no change to the current credit union regime because the 'appropriate government resources were busy with higher priorities'. The government did, however, indicate that eventually there would have to be amendments. From the government's point of view, the present tax exemption status is a primary issue. The New Zealand Association of Credit Unions continues to wait (now for five years) for a discussion paper promised by Treasury on these issues.

A major project of the New Zealand Association of Credit Unions is for the credit union movement to be allowed greater self-regulation, but under the umbrella of the New Zealand Association of Credit Unions. Presently, a credit union can be formed and promote a credit union status without being a member of the New Zealand Association of Credit Unions (NZACU). The NZACU argues it is too easy to form a credit union, and monitoring of quality, performance and security of non-association members is poor. It is concerned that the failure of a credit union, even one outside its organisation, will have serious negative repercussions for the credit union movement as a whole. In effect, the association wishes to encourage higher levels of responsibility by increasing the barriers to entry.

Another major issue for credit unions is a decision on whether to charge fees on 'on-call' (withdrawals can be made immediately and at any time) savings accounts. Recently credit unions have been attracting many customers whose only source of income is a social welfare benefit, and this is also true for Credit Union Waikato. A significant reason for this inflow is that many credit unions, including Credit Union Waikato, do not charge fees on on-call savings accounts whereas all the major banks do. The major banks introduced fees for withdrawing from savings accounts for two reasons. First, the idea is to move closer towards a user-pays system where account holders pay for the cost of each account banks operate and each transaction banks handle for customers. Secondly, income from interest has fallen and account charges provide a form of non-interest income.

Credit unions are now learning how expensive it is to serve an account for a person who does not save and cannot borrow. These accounts are costly because some customers, including beneficiaries, tend to maintain a very low level of funds. These customers are not contributing to funds which can be lent to others and earn interest revenue for the credit union. So, with the other members effectively subsidising a non-profitable account, Credit Union Waikato must decide how it maintains its 'people before profit' philosophy without compromising the credit union philosophy of 'members helping members'.

It is also becoming more evident that if credit unions are to compete effectively with other suppliers of financial services, managers and directors of credit unions will require higher qualifications and expertise in the management of organisational resources. Staff training is currently restricted because of the limited financial resources, but if the credit unions are to offer more ancillary services in order to become a person's 'total bank', then it is inevitable that training will become a more important issue.

Structure at Credit Union Waikato

Credit Union Waikato is governed by a Board of Directors consisting of a chairperson, a treasurer, a secretary and eight other directors. Seven of these other directors are voting members. One is non-voting, and the manager sits in on board meetings in ex-officio (non-formal) capacity and does not vote. Certain board members are delegated specified authority under legislation and under the credit union's rules. Four directors are also trustees of the assets held by the credit union.

Directors and trustees are voted onto the board at each annual general meeting for a two-year period, after which they must resign, but may immediately stand again for re-election. The Board of Directors appoints the manager (and staff) to carry out the daily operational needs of the credit union. The manager reports directly to the chairperson and/or treasurer, depending on specific matters. The formal structure is indicated by Figure 3.1.

Figure 3.1 Credit Union Waikato: Organisational Structure

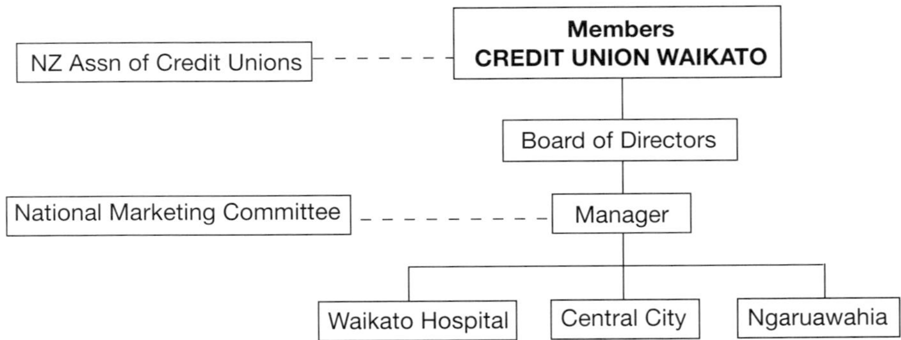

The Board of Directors

Historically, the board has been comprised of hospital employees with little or no formal business experience or commercial acumen. Persuading the board to move on 'the best business decision' was difficult at times. However, the current board composition is improving with a mix of people from a variety of occupations who represent a greater range of interests. Ann Livingston, one such director, is a trustee on the board who has given long-standing service to Credit Union Waikato and the community at large. She suggests that the board may still make too many decisions without understanding or appreciating the members' long-term interests. For instance, over 1992–93 the board decided that members would not want Automatic Teller Machine (ATM) access to their funds.

Electing capable directors who have the time available is also a future problem. The New Zealand Association of Credit Unions has attempted to rectify this problem through correspondence courses which train directors in their role. But the limited resources of most credit unions prevent them from employing the assistance of consultants if it is required.

Every opportunity is taken when appointing staff to develop a personnel team with a mix of skills to cover all bases, and informal in-house training is undertaken when possible.

Competition and Performance

The deregulation of the financial markets in the 1980s and 1990s has created a fiercely competitive banking industry. Net-interest margins are continuously being 'squeezed'. Mergers and acquisitions have been one strategy adopted by financial firms to reduce costs to combat the tighter net-interest margins.

Consolidations have reduced the number of players in a market which has often been labelled by analysts as over-banked. In the last five years major consolidations include: ANZ Bank acquiring Post Bank; the National Bank purchasing the Rural Bank; and Westpac Banking Corporation buying Trust Bank. The sale of Trust Bank to Westpac now means that none of the major banks operating in New Zealand is New Zealand-owned or controlled.

The Credit Union movement has also experienced consolidation in the last four years. Specifically, consolidation has arisen because compliancy costs are becoming too great a burden for small credit unions. For example, in 1993, Credit

Union Waikato acquired Ngaruawahia and Hamilton East Community Credit Unions. Early in 1996 Credit Union Waikato accepted a Term of Engagement from Thistle Credit Union (Anchor Company's employee credit union), and is currently undertaking to accept a Term of Engagement from Trigon's employee credit union.

Smaller credit unions are approaching Credit Union Waikato requesting to be taken over because they can no longer break even on their own. While small organisations with approximate asset value of $100,000 make little contribution to a $7 million credit union, Credit Union Waikato looks to the possibility of absorbing larger credit unions whose asset base is closer to $1 million. Such contributions may enable serious competition with the banks. (See Appendix 1, 2 and 4 at the end of the case for financial positioning of Credit Union Waikato.)

Frequently named advantages of credit unions over banks are the not-for-profit orientation, the low service charges, the sense of customer ownership, and the friendly staff. Disadvantages, however, are the location of branches, the low security of funds and lack of access to funds via ATM cards. Janet Hodgson explains the opportunities for credit unions:

> Banks still think of us as very tiny and the 'poor man's' bank. They don't really see us as a threat at all as we [credit unions] have less than 1 per cent of the market share. But in Australia, credit unions are about the size of Trust Bank, and that's where I see credit unions going.
>
> Because banks don't see us as a threat, there is an opportunity to sneak in the back door, and before they know it, we will be competing. The advantage credit unions have over banks at the moment is that as a cooperative we are not here just to be profit driven for the benefit of a few shareholders. We are here to make a profit to pay back to the members.

However, credit unions are aware that the large banks could easily make it difficult for credit unions to operate because they rely on banks for access to a cheque clearing house. Banks also provide daily 'cash' requirements which enable the credit union to meet the withdrawal demands of their customers.

Credit Union Waikato has been fortunate in that Trust Bank Waikato has not charged it for providing the 'cash' service. However, now that Trust Bank Waikato is controlled by Westpac, this free service is under threat. The present market rate for offering this service is approximately $28,000 per annum.

As at 30 June 1995, Credit Union Waikato was the ninth largest in terms of assets with the New Zealand Association of Credit Unions, and the largest association member with a 'dominant base of employees from the same occupation on a payroll system'. (See Appendix 3 for a general comparison of credit unions over time and see Appendix 4 for the relative position of Credit Union Waikato, in comparison with other credit unions in New Zealand.)

Currently, the top performing credit unions in New Zealand are Baywide (Hawke's Bay) Credit Union and Mount Maunganui Credit Union. One reason for these organisations' recent financial success is that they have both increased their revenue base by charging account fees. Nonetheless, the present board and management of Credit Union Waikato still oppose charging account fees for ordinary savings accounts.

Other major credit unions in Hamilton are the Clerical & Industrial Credit Union and Credit Union Hamilton. Credit Union Hamilton is the third largest credit union registered with the NZACU with total assets two and a half times the size of Credit Union Waikato. Credit Union Hamilton has a common bond which is almost identical to that of Credit Union Waikato, but as Janet Hodgson states:

> We don't see them (other local credit unions) as competition because we're both too small to fight against each other. We may as well join forces in our marketing to fight against the banks. If I believe in the 'people' philosophy of credit unions, then I should be happy if they [Credit Union Hamilton] get a customer away from a bank.

Marketing and Range of Services

Janet Hodgson is soon to be elected onto the national credit union Marketing Committee. The Marketing Committee was collectively formed by a group of credit unions around the country to enhance public awareness of the credit union movement as a whole, rather than each credit union attempting to market themselves individually.

Most of the committee members are also managers of the larger credit unions, but all credit unions affiliated with the Marketing Committee are required to implement the strategies which are approved by the Marketing Committee. Each individual credit union continues to operate and profit independently in all other areas of business.

The Marketing Committee's focus is to continue promoting public awareness of credit unions and what they represent. One of the major achievements of the Marketing Committee has been the creation of a brand logo as an umbrella logo for all affiliated credit unions. This logo now appears on the stationery and advertising for 24 credit unions in New Zealand. The branding logo is shown as Figure 3.2.

Figure 3.2 Credit Union Logo

In addition to the Marketing Committee, Credit Union Waikato has its own marketing strategies. The union acknowledges that it is much cheaper to retain and increase the business of existing customers than to attract new ones. By improving and extending the services offered to existing members, Credit Union Waikato aims to take the banking business the members may be doing with banks.

Before being appointed manager, Janet Hodgson was only familiar with the savings and Christmas account services offered by Credit Union Waikato. But, as manager, she soon discovered the importance of marketing the lesser known services to existing customers. She states:

> Credit unions in general need to promote themselves more, because I was a potential target for more business. I had been a member for a

> couple of years before I became manager and yet Credit Union Waikato had not become my total bank. So straight away I knew that current members were not really being targeted to increase their business with the union. I believe we can be a person's total financial institution.

A large share of Credit Union Waikato's customer base consists of low to medium income earners with a hospital employment history. Examples include nurses, typists, receptionists, cleaners, general administration staff and auxiliary service staff (for example, transport workers). There are also retirees and the beneficiaries mentioned earlier.

The Credit Union Waikato Board of Directors is concerned that too many beneficiary type accounts may disrupt the credit union's core values. Subsidising beneficiary accounts does not fit in with the philosophy of members working together for mutual benefits. Long-time board members would prefer Credit Union Waikato to grow by capitalising on its 'good base' of original members, by increasing each member's financial transactions and targeting family members, friends and work colleagues. These people are likely to share similar socio-economic backgrounds, personal characteristics and core values. Consequently, the members are more likely to share similar interests in the financial services they require from the credit union. A credit union which has like-minded members requiring similar services in facilities, loans and investment is in better stead to cope with the stringent regulatory requirements and make a profit. However, Janet Hodgson believes that a lot of beneficiaries do not want to be beneficiaries so, in keeping with its people before profit philosophy, Credit Union Waikato should service them.

Management have estimated that, of the current 6500 members, less than half are 'productive' members, that is, members generating revenue for the credit union. There may be a large potential for increasing the level of business provided by the current membership if all contributed something.

Credit Union Waikato now offers most core retail financial products and services including:

- mortgages
- personal loans
- on-call deposit and savings accounts
- Christmas Club savings accounts
- bill payment facilities
- personal loan protection insurance
- personal house and contents and car insurance
- free friendly financial assistance.

Technology

Before Janet Hodgson can promote Credit Union Waikato as a comprehensive retail financial institution, it must first introduce an EFTPOS (Electronic Funds Transfer at Point of Sale) card to provide members with convenient access to their money through Automatic Teller Machines. At the moment members have to go to the branches to withdraw or deposit funds, but an ATM/EFTPOS card is planned to be available by the end of 1996.

The introduction of an ATM/EFTPOS card, however, will result in Credit Union Waikato having to change their 'no fees' policy. Janet Hodgson has labelled the fee a 'cost recovery charge' to recognise that the credit union cannot afford to subsidise the cost of operating an ATM/EFTPOS system. Only members who choose to have a ATM/EFTPOS card will be charged.

Credit Union Waikato does not offer cheque accounts, and has no plans to do so in the future. Cheque accounts are costly to administer and monitor, and research shows that consumers are moving towards electronic banking mediums like ATM/EFTPOS as cash alternatives to cheques.

In 1986 the credit union installed a data processing system, which when first installed was considered to be a very progressive banking software package. The system has aged with minimal upgrades over the last 10 years, but the system still has direct dialling facilities and ATM/EFTPOS facilities to manage ATM and EFTPOS.

The bill payment system is one further service which Credit Union Waikato sees a demand for and pushes heavily. While many banks charge for this service, Credit Union Waikato offers the bill payment service free of charge. Quite simply, members authorise the credit union to pay bills on their behalf. Due to payment timing logistics, the credit union benefits from having the use of the aggregated funds for a few days interest free.

Although in other countries credit unions have been successful as an individual's total financial institution, credit unions in New Zealand will find it difficult because there are too many individual credit unions who alone could not finance the systems required to offer the necessary services. Janet Hodgson and Ann Livingston, a member of the board, agree that before Credit Union Waikato can pro-actively implement marketing strategies, it must be able to offer more services such as ATM access to members' funds.

Merger Options

Credit Union Waikato and Credit Union Hamilton

A merger between Credit Union Waikato and Credit Union Hamilton would realise quite significant cost savings. But historical, cultural and emotional issues have yet to be satisfactorily resolved. For instance, Credit Union Hamilton was originally the St Mary's Catholic Church Credit Union, whereas Credit Union Waikato has historical ties to the old Anglican Credit Union. If a successful merger is one day achieved, the combined credit union would be the largest listed with the New Zealand Association of Credit Unions.

Credit Union Waikato and Clerical & Industrial Credit Union

The management of Credit Union Waikato approached the Clerical & Industrial Credit Union in 1993 to discuss a merger. The board of Clerical & Industrial felt a merger would effectively give Credit Union Waikato control over their credit union and would not be in the best interests of their members. While Clerical & Industrial declined the invitation on this occasion the door may not be permanently closed. Clerical & Industrial only have assets of $1.3 million, so may find it difficult to operate if the compliancy regulations are further increased.

The Future

Interest earned from loans makes up the bulk of overall income for Credit Union Waikato. The lowering of market interest rates has forced Credit Union Waikato to lower their interest rates to stay competitive with the banks, but this has resulted in a drop in overall income for the credit union. While income has dropped, expenses (of which overheads make up a large portion) have remained relatively static. This situation provides Credit Union Waikato with a significant challenge to 'break even'.

Janet Hodgson sees the challenge as one of increasing overall income and reducing overall expenditure. She firmly believes that this can be achieved through the growth of Credit Union Waikato. This is because higher levels of business in terms of mortgages and loans add little to the overall expenses, so by increasing the proportion of income to expenses, a kind of 'economies of scale' can be attained. Furthermore, Janet Hodgson suggests that current members are the best target for increasing business in the short to medium term, for the reasons mentioned earlier in the case. Credit Union Waikato has long-term plans of reaching new customers, but Janet Hodgson is concerned with the moral responsibility of marketing a financial institution that has not yet achieved or has the potential to achieve 'greatness' or excellence. She stated: 'I can't go to the community and say we are great until we truly are great.'

While Credit Union Waikato remains opposed to charging fees, some level of fee charges is likely to be necessary in the long term in order to stay afloat. The concern is how to recover transaction costs through fee charges while retaining the characteristics of a 'not-for-profit' organisation.

As stated earlier, Janet Hodgson believes the key to profitability is organisational growth. Credit Union Waikato continues to come under pressure from smaller credit unions (with asset values of approximately $100,000) to take over their business activities. This happens because statutory requirements on credit unions and the financial implications of these (as already mentioned in the case) have made profitability an immense task for small credit unions with their small member and asset base.

While this added business to Credit Union Waikato may appear to be ideal for growth, the reality is that the minimal contribution to finances (approximately $100,000 from each small credit union) is often just sufficient to cover the additional costs of servicing the new members. Additionally, these new members are likely to require special services, adding costly administration time. The moral and emotional feeling is that it is right to help these firms, but the business perspective stresses that more work for the same level of profit makes little sense to an already struggling organisation.

However, there is the prospect of future mergers with other credit unions whose business is in excess of $1 million, and the feasibility of such acquisitions is currently being assessed from both a financial and a philosophical viewpoint.

A merger with one or more credit unions with combined assets of three to four times the level of Credit Union Waikato would make it the biggest in New Zealand. A credit union of this size in New Zealand may also be sufficient to gain recognition for the credit union as a sizeable and influential financial facility which offers real alternatives to the banks. Such an organisation may then have the ability to boost the credit union movement to a size thus far unseen in New Zealand.

However, the emotional implications of a merger with another credit union of significant size are considerable and must be given consideration. Employees become highly concerned over their job security and changes in hierarchy and lines of authority. The thought of being answerable to someone who has traditionally represented the interests of another rival credit union creates a large amount of disturbance in an organisation marked by loyalty to 'your own people'. Janet Hodgson states: 'If you think you can get through life as a manager without emotional dealings then you're not being realistic.'

While the emotional implications of any business decision are given considerable attention at Credit Union Waikato, Janet Hodgson stresses that a merger proposition of a considerable size requires much more emphasis on a 'financial decision' than an 'emotional decision'.

It is 1996 and Janet Hodgson, the manager of Credit Union Waikato, is looking for a strategy to provide direction in the midst of the uncertainty and changing identity of the union. She believes that the business decision must eventually supersede the emotions. But, she thinks, 'Whatever is done must be for the ultimate benefit of the members!'

Appendix 1

(A) Profit and Loss Statements

Statements of Financial Performance as at 31 August 1993 to 1995

	1995	1994	1993
Operating Income			
Interest Income	815 367	669 707	609 322
Commission	4 501	4 756	3 667
Entrance Fees	7 706	1 167	398
Other	1 649	613	546
Bad Debts Recovered	9 938	16 634	15 033
	839 161	692 877	628 966
Expenses			
Operational and Administrative	310 090	202 979	232 099
Salaries/Wages	259 330	213 116	155 635
Scholarships	9 981	14 588	
Bad Debts Written Off	9 895	10 497	17 611
	589 296	441 180	405 345
Net Operating Surplus	**$249 865**	**$251 697**	**$223 621**
Non recurring items			
City Centre set-up costs	(9 072)		
Gain on Sale of Fixed Assets	1 528		12 222
Gain on Mergers with other Credit Unions		27 997	
Net Surplus before Appropriation	**$242 321**	**$279 694**	**$235 843**
Total Appropriation to Members	257 197	201 056	199 088
Balance to Retained Earnings	(14 876)	78 638	36 755

(B) Balance Sheet Statements

Statements of Financial Position as at 31 August 1993 to 1995

	1995	1994	1993
Term Liabilities			
Members' Term Shares	62 825	25 627	317 824
Current Liabilities			
Members' Fund			
On-Call Shares	4 775 124	4 627 308	4 384 676
Christmas Club Shares	328 564	302 142	
Term Shares	557 040	609 337	
Total Members' Funds	5 723 553	5 564 414	4 702 500
Accounts Payable & Accrual	167 194	80 821	119 703
Total Liabilities	5 890 747	5 645 235	4 822 203
Retained Earnings	689 513	704 389	625 751
Total Liabilities & Retained Earnings	$6 580 260	$6 349 624	$5 447 954
Represented by:			
Fixed Assets			
Leasehold Improvements	41 665		
Office Equipment & Furniture	81 211	48 042	40 936
	122 876	48 042	40 936
Term Assets			
Loans to Members	5 349 668	5 005 016	3 813 703
Investments	925 000	867 770	1 252 956
	6 274 668	5 872 786	5 066 659
Current Assets			
Cash & Bank	136 232	410 197	54 014
Interest & Other Receivables	46 484	18 599	286 345
	182 716	428 796	340 359
Total Assets	**$6 580 260**	**$6 349 624**	**$5 447 954**

Source: Annual Reports.

Appendix 2: Analysis of Credit Union Waikato Accounts

Loan Accounts
Mar-93

Number	Percentage	Average Balance
10	1.1	33
7	0.8	75
26	2.9	145
26	2.9	247
23	2.6	345
34	3.9	449
119	13.6	741
179	20.5	1 492
132	15.1	2 492
80	9.1	3 436
74	8.5	4 511
41	4.7	5 440
31	3.5	6 467
17	1.9	7 372
12	1.3	8 350
11	1.2	9 457
5	0.5	10 770
2	0.2	11 452
41	5.7	97 042

Fixed Term Deposits
Mar-93

Number	Percentage	Average Balance
2	4	500
6	12.2	1 000
17	34.6	1 556
9	18.3	2 462
3	6.1	3 266
2	4	5 000
2	4	6 168
1	2	8 536
1	2	10 000
1	2	11 700
1	2	13 000
1	2	15 023
1	2	17 500
1	2	23 000
1	2	30 000
49		148 711

Average Savings Account
Mar-93

	Dollars	Number	Percentage	Average Bal
Under	$50	1825	32.5	16
$	100	593	10.5	71
$	200	681	12.1	147
$	300	362	6.4	243
$	400	309	5.5	348
$	500	171	3.0	448
$	1 000	554	9.8	715
$	2 000	544	9.7	1 421
$	3 000	260	4.6	2 432
$	4 000	111	1.9	3 425
$	5 000	60	1.0	3 425
$	6 000	52	0.9	4 526
$	7 000	27	0.4	5 417
$	8 000	13	0.2	6 420
$	9 000	7	0.1	7 408
over	10 000	38	0.5	8 694

Appendix 3:

(A) Historical Comparison of Credit Unions

Year	Number of Credit Unions	Number of Members	Total Assets $ (000)
1985	312	138 748	102 774
1986	310	142 034	117 912
1987	268	140 519	138 284
1988	235	139 883	167 792
1989	217	151 957	221 947
1990	210	153 584	243 983
1991	196	158 485	265 819
1992	188	161 996	289 315
1993	177	171 644	317 322
1994	160	179 714	335 999
1995	149	Not available	Not available

(B) Credit Unions: Asset Size

Asset Size	Number of Credit Unions		Total Assets $ (000)	
	1994	1993	1994	1993
up to $100,000	5	14	342	993
$100,000 to $250,000	24	21	3 950	3 570
$250,000 to $500,000	19	25	7 105	8 637
$500,000 to $1,000,000	21	24	15 428	17 540
$1,000,000 to $5,000,000	43	40	95 737	87 487
$5,000,000 to $10,000,000	8	8	59 281	61 044
Over $10,000,000	9	8	151 951	135 056
Total	**131**	**142**	**335 999**	**317 332**

(C) Credit Unions: Loans

	Percentage of Loans		Percentage of Loans	
	1993/94	1992/93	1993/94	1993/94
Purpose of Loans				
Home Purchase	1	1	15	17
Home Improvements	6	6	17	16
Cars	13	15	24	23
Chattels	13	12	6	5
Other	67	66	38	39
Term of Loan				
Up to 1 year	65	49	28	23
Over 1 year and up to 5	33	49	28	23
Over 5 years	2	2	22	22

The average amount of new loans in 1993/94 was about $1641 (1992/93 $1826).
Loans outstanding in 1994 averaged $4990 (1993 $3642) for each borrower.
Average savings for each member in 1994 amounted to $1655 (1993 $1639).

Source: 1995 Annual Report of the Registrar of Friendly Society Credit Unions.

Appendix 4: Comparable Credit Unions

New Zealand Association of Credit Unions
Twenty largest affiliated credit unions 30 June 1995

	Name	Assets	Shares	Loans	Members
1	Sydenham Money Club	20 498 805	18 320 801	17 534 398	4 812
2	Baywide Credit Union	16 215 601	14 045 401	13 786 956	8 264
3	Credit Union Hamilton	15 926 295	14 461 462	11 117 277	7 611
4	Credit Union Otago	13 081 554	11 388 647	9 680 350	6 118
5	Southland Credit Union	11 687 682	11 188 260	11 263 192	5 059
6	East Bay Credit Union	11 344 275	7 511 633	9 632 321	3 868
7	Canterbury Port & Province Credit Union	10 099 950	9 689 534	8 696 453	6 423
8	Credit Union Mt Maunganui	7 182 000	6 559 000	5 989 000	3 651
9	Credit Union Waikato	6 546 220	5 617 391	5 190 342	6 114
10	Credit Union Auckland	6 471 223	5 653 758	5 637 823	4 141
11	Harbour City Credit Union	5 848 164	5 220 086	5 314 939	2 355
12	Hastings & Districts Credit Union	4 582 803	3 844 632	3 252 827	5 280
13	Credit Union Taranaki	4 409 097	3 721 707	3 218 641	3 919
14	Fisher & Paykel Credit Union	4 408 326	3 990 720	2 996 519	1 628
15	Credit Union Central	4 186 264	3 852 960	3 226 499	2 213
16	Steelsands Credit Union	4 168 300	3 486 673	3 519 835	1 200
17	Fletcher Challenge (Ak) Credit Union	4 132 561	3 460 534	3 662 386	1 325
18	Nelson Credit Union	3 644 695	3 169 028	233 086	3 080
19	Credit Union Rotorua	3 169 825	2 849 604	2 805 495	2 735
20	Credit Union Bay of Plenty	3 090 828	2 770 805	2 294 925	2 407

Source: Registar of Friendly Society Credit Unions.

4 Fisher & Paykel Electronics

We spend a lot of time talking rather than exchanging bits of paper. Talking improves relationships inside the company and with our customers and gets them what they want.

(Henry van der Heijden, Fisher & Paykel Electronics, 1994)

Introduction

This case is about a culture that promotes innovation. Fisher & Paykel Electronics Company General Manager, Henry van der Heijden, believes it is innovation that has led the F&P company group to a turnover of $670 million and provided the New Zealand stock exchange with a star performer, generating 40 per cent of its income from exports.

Woolf Fisher and Maurice Paykel founded their household electrical appliance import company in 1934. Within five years they were manufacturing domestic and commercial refrigerators and washing machines, under licence from overseas companies, in Auckland. Sales agreements, followed by manufacture in New Zealand of a range of whiteware products and vacuum cleaners from a number of US companies, characterised the first 20 years of operation. Not until 1956 did the first home-grown product, a patented rotary clothes dryer, go into production at Mount Wellington. The following year, Allied Industries was set up to manufacture radios, radiograms and television sets, forming the basis of Fisher and Paykel Electronics.

F&P has achieved international leadership through adding electronic management systems to household appliances and healthcare products. An example is the integrated motor and control system in the Smart Drive automatic washing machine. This gives designers considerably more flexibility to offer manufacturing and user benefits not possible with traditional electro-mechanical systems. These innovations and resulting product improvements have been achieved through a company culture that has promoted open communication, empowerment of staff and provision of the best of physical resources.

Acknowledgments This case study was developed for teaching by Bob Mills and is based on interviews with Henry van der Heijden, General Manager, Fisher & Paykel Electronics and Healthcare, and invaluable contributions from David Grant. This case was originally commissioned by TRADENZ for an Innovation Leadership Programme for CEOs in the Food and Beverage Industry held at Hotel du Vin, 6/7 March 1995. The authors would like to thank Fisher & Paykel Electronics for their time and their willingness to share their experiences and philosophies. The case is to be used for classroom discussion and not to illustrate effective or ineffective handling of a strategic or administrative situation.

Since the 1970s the electronics industry has changed rapidly and F&P have moved with equivalent speed. Innovative ideas for new products and improvements have come from employees and managers alike. For example, managers study and report on advances in products in the international marketplace as a result of face-to-face customer contact. Ideas are incorporated into product development by the continual interaction of marketing, engineering, production and quality staff who are increasingly being housed together in open-plan offices bounded by glass-walled meeting rooms. Managers also encourage perceptive and creative staff to explore how new and contemporary technology might provide extra value to F&P customers. Individuals in the firm have access to all other departments in pursuit of any information that may affect the potential new product. Promising ideas followed through in this way have a greater prospect of success. However, failure can and does happen and is accepted as a reality. Strategic leadership from top management in promoting and encouraging innovation has proved to be a vital ingredient for success. An emphasis on innovation and product improvement is a matter of long-term planning, not just tactics or chance.

Henry van der Heijden is adamant that 'for a New Zealand company to grow beyond the local market it must have unique products the world wants, not a product made under licence or a "me too" product'. Innovative strategy at F&P has been built on its early foundation of long-term strategic alliances as well as its own special culture that emphasises technical leadership, design flair and a wide range of competencies.

The Company and Its History

Fisher & Paykel is a publicly listed New Zealand group of companies turning over $670 million in the 1994 year, mainly from the sales of whiteware, consumer electronics, healthcare and production machinery. The structure of the group is indicated in Appendix 1. Overseas sales for the group increased by 19 per cent in 1993. F&P Electronics General Manager, Henry van der Heijden, is responsible for both the electronics and the rapidly growing healthcare products, which are sold in 65 countries. Significant growth has been experienced in Australia where F&P, encouraged by the proximity to a growing market and the 150 per cent tax incentive for R&D write-off, established a manufacturing unit in 1989 at Cleveland, Queensland. F&P is now a significant whiteware supplier in that market with sales of 220,000 units in 1994. F&P freezers are even being sold to Japan where the importation of relatively bulky consumer products would not seem to be the easiest accomplishment for a manufacturer. Altogether an additional 140 people were employed in New Zealand and 50 in Australia in 1994. The Mission Statement is shown as Appendix 2.

The corporate view is that F&P is a technology-driven company which relies on innovation to satisfy customer needs in its international markets. In fact F&P brand themselves as 'The Innovators'. Adding value by innovation is seen as the best way to export kiwi ingenuity in practical and consumer desirable packages. But how has innovation become embedded in practices at F&P?

Strategic alliances were a hallmark of the company from its beginning. In the 1960s and 1970s linkages were established with local companies like Shacklock (electric ranges) and Bonaire (domestic freezers) of Dunedin as well as the multinational giant Matsushita Electric of Japan (consumer electronics).

Long-term business relationships were strengthened, culminating in 1971 with an agreement to sell Matsushita Electric's National Panasonic products in New Zealand, nine years after F&P purchased its first product from Japan. The assembly of National Panasonic television receivers started some years later and continued until the late 1980s, when it stopped as a result of changing government policies, specifically, the removal of import licence/production tariffs.

The most recent enterprise area, the healthcare business, grew out of the established electronics core competence and had its roots in the respiratory humidifier. The humidifier has now become standard medical operating theatre equipment and was developed in conjunction with Auckland Hospital and the Department of Scientific and Industrial Research (DSIR) over a period of 14 years. The humidifier has been manufactured since 1971 and now forms the flagship product for F&P Healthcare. In 1985 Baxter Pharmaseal Division was appointed as Fisher & Paykel's humidifier agent in the United States, a reversal of the company history of buying in technology. In 1987 the healthcare business acquired an Australian company, Medcare, which formed the start of F&P's own distribution network in Australia.

National Panasonic and F&P Electronics emerged from Allied Products as two distinctly different businesses in 1985. National Panasonic focused directly on New Zealand consumers and developed into a sophisticated agency with externally sourced products. F&P Electronics, however, changed from television and radio manufacture to producing customised electronics for F&P's whiteware divisions. It absorbed the healthcare business, whose products were also based on electronics. By the mid-eighties technological innovation had been recognised as a necessity in the business world.

The Industry and the Environment

In New Zealand F&P has developed an exclusive dealership arrangement during the last 40 years. The strength of the arrangements were tested and validated in the courts in 1990 when overseas competition tested the provisions of the Commerce Act. However, the market is limited by the relatively small number of household replacement products and the need to furnish new homes with consumer/whiteware items. A market five times the size is available in Australia alone. Sales growth has therefore been almost solely due to the dramatic rise in exports from $81 million in 1990 to $265 million in 1994 (see Appendix 3). Exports have increased from 16 per cent to 40 per cent of Group revenues over the same period. By 1994 F&P had increased Australian market share to 23 per cent, 22 per cent and 16 per cent for washing machines, dryers and refrigerators.

Fisher & Paykel are in the business of exporting 'applied New Zealand brainpower' as Henry van der Heijden puts it, wrapped up in highly differentiated products generated for demanding and individualistic international markets. For example, Europeans have small, quiet washing machines in their kitchen while in the US the laundry is in the basement where noise level is not a priority and consumers have been used to larger appliances. Both requirements are different from a range of intermediate norms found in New Zealand. Some sophisticated consumers like high spin dryer speeds and ecological features to save water and energy, while others believe fast spinning damages clothes and that washing cannot possibly be as clean if less rinsing water is used. There are also changing international trends such as the recent demand for CFC-free gas usage in refrigerators. As well, there has been a trend toward providing a wider range of customised products which has posed product design and assembly line automation challenges.

The small production runs required for the local market and the demand for a wide variety of models is a natural advantage for the F&P production line providing the desired flexibility for the developing export markets. A single production line in New Zealand already had to produce a wide range of models, preferably in an unconstrained sequence. Production engineering companies in the United States could not supply economic equipment for the task and indeed contended it could not be done. In devising innovative automated process solutions to meet this challenge, F&P not only proved it could be done but established a clear lead against its larger competitors already resident in target markets.

The domestic deregulation reforms of the 1980s meant it was easier for European whiteware manufacturers to gain access to New Zealand. To compete with up-market Euro-appliances, the New Zealand-made product had to be more appealing and more appropriate for local needs. Features were added that related to the New Zealand way of life (for example the butter softener compartment for 500-gram blocks and a vegetable cool bin in the refrigerator). More significantly, because the adoption of computers and electronic gadgetry by New Zealanders is extraordinarily high (as is witnessed by the rate of uptake of the fax, cellphones and internet), consumers naturally expected new appliances to have electronic controls. The impetus towards electronics resulted in not merely replacing existing electro-mechanical devices but, in the case of the Smart Drive washing machine, having electronics operate the motor at the heart of the machine.

The geography, infrastructure and small population of New Zealand offers other natural advantages for innovation, particularly in the consumer durables industry. For example, in New Zealand it is practical to service the whole country from one manufacturing site and possible to meet, talk to and influence the country's leaders without resorting to underhand or costly lobbying tactics. American and European competitors, in the past, could argue that they achieve advantage through economies of scale brought about by access to large markets. The F&P experience, however, suggests that this may no longer be an essential advantage since it has been able to grow and thrive in a deregulated market with a home population base of just over three million. Indeed, since product differentiation and attention to the demands of each customer for individual products provides the same constraints for both large and small manufacturers, then cost-effective flexibility of manufacturing holds the key to widening the profit margin.

Easy access to decision and policy makers also provides New Zealand companies with advantages in terms of developing international trade relationships. The queues at important New Zealand government office doors are shorter and not subject to the cost and influence of bribery encountered in some other countries. As well, easy accessibility to policy and law makers can help speed and smooth inevitable changes in national and international legislation that characterise world trade today.

Technological Innovation at F&P Electronics

Woolf Fisher realised the necessity for developing export capability when the UK elected to enter the European Common Market in 1973, even though F&P operations were not directly affected by the move. The dismantling of international trade barriers had begun and exposure of local industry to global market forces was inevitable and squarely faced for the first time. Until the early 70s there had been no need for F&P to export to secure profits, as most manufacturing in New Zealand was heavily protected. The first attempts at trying to prepare for export, however, generated both quality and quantity problems. These problems generated company-wide quality awareness, culminating in the achievement of ISO 9001 accreditation for F&P Electronics in 1994.

Technical Director Julian Williams championed the highly automated flexible manufacturing system for refrigerators put in at the new Tamaki plant in 1973. Models of different shapes and sizes are assembled on the same production line, giving customers the specific model they want, when they want it. The novel production system provided the desired competitive advantage as well as becoming, in due course, an export product in its own right.

Breakthrough innovation occurred in both the production processes and in the creation of new products. An example of how a concept can generate, not just a new product, but a focus on an underdeveloped market, is provided in the medical gas humidifier. It was Dr Matt Spence of Auckland Hospital who recognised and drew attention to the need and patient benefit in providing warm, humidified gas to patients during operations and in critical care. With the scientific support of DSIR he developed a demonstration prototype humidifier in an Agee jar (a popular household glass jar normally used for preserving fruit). DSIR approached F&P to turn this device from an invention (a demonstrable idea) into an innovation (a demonstrable idea that can turn a profit). The device took an unexpectedly long 14 years to commercialise, as much because the whole concept of medical gas humidification was new to the global healthcare industry as because of the reliability and sterile environment required of the product.

Another example of new paradigm thinking, which led to product innovation at F&P, is the Smart Drive automatic domestic washing machine. The Smart Drive has an electronically controlled, purpose-designed and built motor directly fixed to the agitator to eliminate the need for more wear-prone mechanical actuators. The development of the design led to the use of a high-tech thermoplastic polyester resin casing called Rynite. The simple concept of a direct electric drive, with software controllable speed, acceleration and direction, has required extensive effort but has projected F&P into world leadership in its industry. A tangible recognition of the extent of technological leadership is that a Canadian company paid F&P $3 million for the rights to examine the Smart Drive's technology and have an option to manufacture it for the North American market.

The days of importing product design for local manufacture have now gone completely for F&P. All new whiteware and healthcare products are set to be of New Zealand origin.

In addition to the current core business areas, there have been many others which have been explored over the years, like electric fencing, petrol pumps and meat quality meters. In each case there was the potential to further develop existing technology and establish national if not international leadership. The willingness to 'test the waters' in new areas reflects the responsive 'on-line' company attitude to evolving a portfolio of potential future directions.

Other excursions into profitable areas have resulted from technological capability as much as innovative capacity. A prime example is yacht keel machining for Admirals Cup and Whitbread Round the World boats, which started as an opportunity to utilise equipment capacity and has resulted in corporate association with world class yachting.

The results of innovation have been dramatic. But what are its special features and why has F&P been successful at creating valued products?

New Product Development

All of F&P's research and development is done in New Zealand but surprisingly there is no acknowledged 'formal' procedure for the screening and management of new ideas. Rather, project teams, including engineers, purchasing, production, quality and marketing staff, are established to explore opportunities which have emerged from the 'people network'. Recognised techniques like brainstorming and business venture check lists are used, however, at appropriate points in the idea development process. Incidental resources like the company-wide computerised product information system for development histories and fault report histories have proven helpful in both generating and assessing the value of new ideas. Computers are used to facilitate all aspects of business: engineering, accounting, stock control, communication, forecasting and so on, but applications do not have a high level of integration. F&P make available tools adequate for specific functions of new product development but do not appear to provide frameworks for the assimilation or analysis of options or of interactions between the people who are charged with progressing the idea. By this means, time spent in unproductive office work and administration is minimised and attention is focused on only the communications that bring potential products to points where they can be evaluated for further work or be consigned to the 'interesting ideas' shelf.

The most difficult aspect of new product development in the broad consumer market is obtaining useful customer feedback and incorporating it in products to satisfy customer needs and desires. To assist the understanding of customer wants in the generic sense, F&P's industrial designers meet three or four times each year to coordinate the design of product families. Decisions about shapes, colours, types of push button and the like are made and discussed with project teams. The customer perception about how the product looks and how it is controlled can then be integrated into the functional design.

In spite of the constraints that inevitably control the design of any corporate product, the innovators in project teams are given considerable freedom to explore possibilities for potential products. Mistakes and failure are accepted as worthwhile risks and acknowledged as likely to occur. A handful of people who are prolific idea generators has emerged. These innovation leaders feature regularly in the *New Zealand Patent Journal* and are encouraged to maintain their creativity and develop any of their ideas toward new products.

Product or process improvement is somewhat easier than product or process development. Improvement is more frequent and common across all departments but usually involves fewer people and tends to be concentrated in only one or two functional areas. Quality systems and the resulting quality circles are well suited to providing the vehicle for managed small change. Again, however, the existing good verbal communications network in the F&P culture makes this textbook approach particularly efficient and effective.

In summary, the establishment of innovation at F&P can be seen as stemming from the development of stable, long-term international alliances in a protected environment. Thrust into the global business environment F&P worked from a base of 40 years of corporate learning to satisfy local customers and of understanding the technical details of both their own products and those of the overseas competition. The production base for economic operation in a small market like New Zealand required a major advancement in process innovation to allow automated multi-model assembly line operation. Throughout the years prior to 1973 a set of technological core competencies was gained or acquired. The translation of concepts and practical application of new technology into successful new products has emphasised uncluttered communications, including direct access to customers by designers. For F&P this is an unstructured process, based on multi-disciplined teams, well supported by access to computerised information and data manipulation tools.

The Company Structure

'Getting the right people together and providing the right environment for the exchange of ideas' is the recipe for innovation at the company level according to Henry van der Heijden, general manager of F&P Electronics.

Innovative ideas are sourced by staff through contact and discussion with suppliers and customers throughout the world. The company theme for 1993/94 was 'Learning to satisfy our customers' and it emphasised that 'knowing customers' was a prerequisite to successfully satisfying them. One successful opportunity for interaction occurs where sales and marketing teams, which include company engineers and healthcare nurses, attend international shows with F&P products on display. Both good and bad feedback is analysed for ways to satisfy potential clients. Likewise, exploration of new concepts can be used to gauge general customer appeal and product features at the functional level. The participation in Domotechnica in Cologne, Germany, in February, for example, was reported by chief executive, Gary Paykel, to have generated several significant opportunities. Ideas also come from technology push concepts from the product designers as in the case of the Smart Drive and the use of new technology like surface mounting of electronic circuit board components. But how do these ideas from various sources get selected and processed? What environment nurtures innovation at F&P?

Henry van der Heijden believes that the culture and success of F&P have derived from direct communications, at and between all levels in the company. Relatively few memos are sent around; instead people talk to each other regularly. To make direct communication happen efficiently and effectively requires close proximity and access to colleagues and information sources. Offices at F&P sites are therefore structured in a true open-plan arrangement with a deliberate mixture of marketers, engineers, sales and technical staff located physically adjacent to each other. Spacing between staff is sufficient for phone and deskside conversations not to intrude heavily on adjacent workspaces, and furniture is low enough for people to see others, perhaps with complementary skills, who can provide professional help. The conviction is that an office arranged like this prevents functional elitism, avoids specialist information being inadequately estimated or ignored and thereby facilitates a properly considered innovation process.

At F&P Electronics' Carbine Road site a forest of almost 30 glass-walled meeting rooms, aptly named after native trees, is provided at the periphery of the open plan work spaces. The meeting rooms provide the opportunity to reduce disturbance to other staff while focusing on issues that require a number of contributors. The sense of resources being 'hidden away' at meetings is reduced and knowledge about when a meeting has finished is available at a glance. Ideally all the offices would have been located on one level next to the factory floor, but space constraints have divided Carbine Road office space into two levels.

Formal quality improvement meetings and in-house staff training sessions add to the communication regime as do the 250 personal computers with e-mail for a site of 430 staff. Each staff member has an allocated two hours training per week where interaction with others outside normal work patterns can be incidentally developed. Two full-time staff trainers are employed at the Carbine Road site and the opportunity for skills improvement is taken seriously by staff at all levels.

The organisation structure at F&P Electronics is flat and everyone is accessible by decree. 'You don't need authority, you need leadership. Authority comes out of leadership,' says Henry van der Heijden. Growth or fluctuation in staff numbers has not been seen as a problem or a driver for organisational change in itself. Diversity of business focus has, however, brought regrouping of staff as production has increased and product lines matured. There are now more staff involved in non-production work than on the assembly line. Linkages with Japan have helped secure automated assembly equipment which enables manufacture on a worldwide competitive basis. This kind of automation helps greatly in producing quality product on repetitive work. Where possible personnel work arrangements, particularly hours of attendance, have been tailored to match the preferences of both those staff who prefer routine and others who enjoy challenge and flexibility.

The production area reflects the same open style, clean lines and seating as the office space. It is a comfortable, light, air-conditioned and quiet environment. Colour schemes, selected by staff, are pleasant and allow for important safety, quality and instructional information to be read easily.

Fisher & Paykel have enviable staff/union relations based on efforts made in communication and common understanding of company goals and progress. Explanation about company performance is presented at the same time as rewards. Good results provide rewards for all staff, not just for winning teams. Sales staff do not work on a commission basis, nor are individual bonuses awarded. As a policy commitment 15 per cent of profit after tax and dividend paid is distributed to staff on a pro rata basis twice yearly. Response to company performance works both ways, bad years have seen staff and salaries cut. Share issues are also made available to staff. Staff development is assessed and career progression reviewed at least once a year, not by just the immediate supervisor, but by a number of work associates. Altogether staff retention under this regime is very high and F&P is well recognised as a good employer in the industry.

But above all, Henry van der Heijden contends that innovation needs the right mix of people, in the right environment, with the desire to be best in Australasia.

The Future

The corporate F&P view of the future is to capitalise on its innovation and people to capture niche positions around the world. The company's willingness to innovate, coupled with a strong balance sheet and a commitment to involve all its employees, positions it for future growth in both whiteware and healthcare products. F&P has strong international alliances, particularly in Japan, but its real strength is claimed to be its independence resulting in the ability to blend the ideas of its people with the best from around the world to provide 'F&P solutions' to international customers.

The level of success for F&P has been extremely high, but there are other questions and challenges which still need to be addressed. Is it likely that a New Zealand company can foster an international industry in its whiteware when even international companies have failed to develop a domestic automotive industry? How should F&P address static local sales revenues? What competitive advantages are sustainable? Where are key niche markets and with which products should they be penetrated?

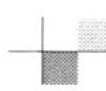

Appendix 1: Group Structure (Wholly Owned Companies Unless Otherwise Stated)

*** Fisher & Paykel Industries Owns**

* Fisher & Paykel Ltd
* Fisher & Paykel Pacific Ltd
* Fisher & Paykel Steel Ltd
Fisher & Paykel Finance Ltd
* R.L. Morris Ltd
Cellnet Mobile Services Ltd
Cellnet Paging Services Ltd
Cellular Communications Ltd
Screencraft Manufacturing Ltd
Chapco Twenty Three Ltd

*** Fisher & Paykel Ltd Owns**

* Allied Industries Ltd
Bonaire Industries Ltd
* Fisher & Paykel Production Machinery Ltd
* Fisher & Paykel Electronics Ltd
Fisher & Paykel Healthcare Pty Ltd
Fisher & Paykel Security Systems Ltd
* H.E. Shacklock Ltd

Fisher & Paykel Finance Ltd Owns

Commercial Finance Ltd
Consumer Finance Ltd
Consumer Finance Corporation Ltd
Equipment Finance Ltd
Consumer Industries Ltd
F & P Executive Services Ltd
CFC Advances Ltd

Fisher & Paykel Finance Ltd Group Operates Under its own Debenture Trust Deed

*** Allied Industries Ltd Owns**

* Fisher & Paykel Australia Holdings Ltd
* Fisher & Paykel Australia Pty Ltd
* Fisher & Paykel Customers Services Pty Ltd
* Fisher & Paykel Manufacturing Pty Ltd

*** Fisher & Paykel Pacific Ltd Owns**

Topsearch F & P (H.K.) Ltd 50%
Topsearch Industries Ltd 10%

*** Companies Operating Under a Negative Pledge Deed**

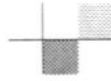

Appendix 2: Fisher & Paykel Mission Statement

Vision

- To be principal provider of the full range of quality lifestyle appliances for New Zealand families.
- To be a significant provider of quality appliances and related products for Australian families.
- To be a growing provider of quality appliances, healthcare products and other related products to the people of the world.
- To provide services and pursue an investment strategy which realises this vision.

Values

Customers
Our future existence relies on understanding and satisfying our customers' present and future needs. Our goal is to be recognised by our customers as a high quality, innovative and cost efficient supplier, and the best to do business with. We recognise that 'the next person in the process is our customer'.

Our People
We value our family of employees as essential to the success of our company. We aim to develop a long-term trusting relationship with each employee, encouraging their contributions and assisting in their personal development and education. In all dealings we will be fair and consistent.

Quality Improvement
We believe in step-by-step continual improvement of everything that we are engaged in, including our administration, marketing, sales, design, service, distribution and manufacturing. We will encourage cross-functional communication and cooperation to aid this.

Suppliers
We view suppliers of goods and services as an extension of our company, with whom we wish to develop long-term trusting relationships. We expect our suppliers to embrace our Quality Improvement philosophy in their dealings with us.

Shareholders
We aim to be a company in whom our shareholders have trust and pride. We will keep our shareholders properly informed of our company's performance and prospects. We recognise the need to provide our shareholders with an excellent return on investments, consistent with long-term growth.

Planning
All short-term decisions will be consistent with long-term objectives that balance the needs of our people, customers, suppliers and shareholders. Each year these objectives will be widely communicated within our company.

Products and Services
We are viewed at large by our end products and services. We will endeavour to produce technologically advanced products and services that offer superior value. Continued innovation and improvement are critical to our survival and growth.

Environment
Reflecting our commitment to a cleaner world we aim to develop products and manufacturing processes which are as friendly to the environment as practicable.

Society
We will conduct our business at all times on a fair, ethical, consistent and professional manner. We accept our responsibilities to be a responsible community neighbour, and will continue to support community affairs.

Combined Unions Commitment

With regard to the company mission statement the combined unions commitment is to job security and quality of life for its members and their families. We pursue these goals through:

- Continuous improvement in all aspects of our work and working life
- A common intention to work together from a consultative basis of cooperation and goodwill
- Input into the decision-making processes of the company.

Appendix 3: Five Year Financial Summary

Revenue

Years ended 31 March	1994 $000	1993 $000	1992 $000	1991 $000	1990 $000
Sales					
New Zealand	374 885	349 886	331 108	359 617	390 062
Overseas	265 963	222 750	144 269	103 381	81 769
Finance Company	28 713	25 183	29 453	37 685	39 922
Depreciation					
Trading	22 091	18 695	14 595	13 011	11 861
Finance Company	3 740	3 622	5 099	7 344	7 949
Interest					
Trading	5 216	5 390	13 185	15 005	13 949
Finance Company	10 684	8 706	11 946	16 733	17 088
Abnormal costs	-	-	4 041	7 792	-
Net Operating Profit Before Taxation	41 370	30 351	11 464	7 130	30 208
Group Profit after Taxation	41 370	30 351	11 464	7 130	30 208
Group Profit after Extraordinary Items	26 950	28 005	6 908	4 439	22 029

Financial

Years ended 31 March	1994 $000	1993 $000	1992 $000	1991 $000	1990 $000
Shareholders' Funds	267 465	251 772	225 933	224 987	218 738
Issued Capital	52 384	51 087	49 240	48 378	46 142
Total Assets	417 008	387 451	380 412	414 905	386 478
Net Asset Backing per 50c share	$2.55	$2.46	$2.29	$2.33	$2.37
Current Ration	219%	251%	355%	253%	215%
Shareholders' Equity	64.1%	65.0%	59.4%	54.2%	56.5%

Dividends & Earnings

Years Ended 31 March	1994 $000	1993 $000	1992 $000	1991 $000	1990 $000
Dividend	16 684	16 228	7 868	9 424	14 649
Dividend per Share	16c	16c	8c	10c	16c
Earnings per Share	26c	19c	8c	4c	23c
Group Profit to Average Shareholders' Funds	10.4%	8.0%	3.5%	1.9%	10.3%

Source: Annual Report, Fisher & Paykel Electronics Ltd.

5 The Gallagher Group

We like to try to get people to operate at 110 per cent of their capability, which works out at about 150 per cent of what they think they can do!

(John Walley, Group Operations Director, 1994)

Introduction

This case describes the way the Gallagher Group Ltd redefined its culture and implemented a strategy to focus on technological innovation for the 1990s.

The Gallagher Group is an international leader in the conception, design, manufacture and distribution of animal containment systems. However, their products alone are no longer seen by Gallaghers as the key ingredient for successful innovation. The company claims the key to success is to establish focused capability to address and simultaneously achieve five key attributes: speed to market, lowest variable cost, multiple product features, quality, and range (to satisfy diverse markets with different product requirements).

These key attributes are usually accepted by manufacturing companies as ideals rather than norms, conflicting aims rather than positive necessities. But Gallaghers believe that company culture must promote the simultaneous and synergistic development of each key attribute. The culture must also allow for centralised vision and global capability while accepting the need for decentralised local market activities and strategic development.

The Gallagher Group has been trading for 56 years and the redesign of the culture presented in this case study was started in 1990. This reshaping of the culture has been a core part of the business plan since 1992 and its adoption has changed the organisation's structure, marketing channels management, operations and innovation strategy. The Gallagher Group now sees itself as a multinational company, as opposed to an international one.

Acknowledgments This case study was developed for teaching by Bob Mills and is based on interviews with Neil Richardson, Group Managing Director and John Walley, Group Operations Director of The Gallagher Group and invaluable contributions from John Gallagher, Bill Gallagher and Steve Hoffman. The case was originally commissioned by TRADENZ for an Innovation Leadership Programme for CEOs in the Food and Beverage Industry held at Hotel du Vin, 6/7 march 1995. The authors would like to thank The Gallagher Group for their time and their willingness to share their experiences and philosophies. The case is to be used for classroom discussion and not to illustrate effective or ineffective handling of a strategic or administrative situation.

The Company and its History

Gallagher Group Ltd has four manufacturing divisions:

- Power Fence Systems (animal containment) – electronics based
- Security Systems (perimeter security) – electronics based
- Plastics and Sunplas Engineering – tool-making and injection moulded plastics
- Franklin Machinery, Pukekohe – fencing hardware.

The Gallagher Group employs 300 staff and has two New Zealand manufacturing locations (at Hamilton and Pukekohe). Over the last 50 years, the company has progressed steadily and is now the largest electric fencing systems manufacturer in the world. It believes it has the largest R&D commitment on electric fencing anywhere and is universally recognised as the international market leader. In 1994 exports represented 70/80 per cent of the Gallagher Group's NZ$45 million turnover. Exports fully utilise a distributor network established over many decades of pioneering endeavour by father (Bill, senior) and son (Bill) in more than 100 countries. The distribution network has a turnover at dealer level in the order of NZ$120 million.

The Gallagher Group is a private family company that has been trading for over 50 years. By the late 1980s Bill was fully involved with the company side of the business while brother John had started to deal more with property and corporate citizenship affairs. However, in the late 1980s the Gallagher Group seemed to have lost momentum as well as its ability to innovate. Something had to be done. In a bold move by Bill and John Gallagher, John Walley and Neil Richardson were appointed (Operations Manager and Group Director respectively) to re-engineer the culture and drive the company into the 90s.

John Walley joined Gallaghers in 1987 as R&D Manager. He is an electrical engineer by training with a background in domestic appliances, motor vehicles, electric motors and medical physics. His management experience is in innovation, operations and logistics with a particular emphasis on management information systems, quality systems, R&D and purchasing. John's initial role was as an internal change agent, a role that necessarily extended into the distribution channels.

During a trip to the United States in 1989, Bill met up again with Neil Richardson. Neil had worked with the Gallagher Group as a management consultant to their Australian agent in order to improve performance in earlier years and was then lecturing at a New Orleans university. They were working together on new arrangements for the major US distributorship which was on the verge of bankruptcy. Bill offered him a three-year contract to put into practice some of the management theory he had been teaching. Neil agreed and started in May 1990. Neil has focused on developing group strategy and driving change external to the main Kahikatea Road, Hamilton site.

The three personalities of Bill, Neil and John Walley have provided the company with complementary strengths. Bill was amenable to the radical proposals of the other two men for a culture change, and together the team have developed a company well equipped for the future.

The Industry and the Environment

The electric fence was a US invention in the 1930s and its potential as a farming aid in New Zealand was soon recognised by Bill Gallagher (senior) and Hubert Christie of Speedrite. Bill (senior) applied for his first electric fence patent in 1939. The problem of these original designs was that long grass touching it could put an electric short in the circuit and render it useless!

The government funded Ruakura Agricultural Research Centre in Hamilton has long been internationally regarded as a leader in optimising animal farming systems. Grassland farming is practised year round in New Zealand and grazing management systems is a research focus. It was Dr Doug Phillips from Ruakura who assembled the first unshortable electric fence energiser unit for animal enclosures, although it was never an official government research project. Dr Phillips was able to demonstrate the effectiveness of pulsed power electric fencing using capacitor-based controllers (patented in 1962) and plastic insulators (patented in 1965). The original licensees, Plastic Products of Hamilton, established the new product locally but failed in its bid to create an export market. Plastics Products was so confident about the reliability of the solid state energiser that it did not provide overseas product support. However, a large shipment to Ireland exposed the vulnerability of the system to lightning strikes and the company failed. Meanwhile agricultural researchers at Ruakura went on to quantify the financial benefits of unshortable electric fencing when used for intensive animal grazing.

By the early 1970s up to eight New Zealand firms were in intense competition for the local market and the Gallagher Group were the first to restart exporting electric fence systems and have continued to dominate the industry.

In 1989 the world market in electric fencing was estimated at $200 million and New Zealand companies made 20 per cent of the products. In 1990 four New Zealand companies, the Gallagher Group, Speedrite, Donaghys and PEL Industries, generated over 50 per cent of the international electric fence export trade.

International competition from the US is regarded as limited by its dated technology and from key players in Germany and Denmark by their focus on energisers rather than complete farming solutions.

A resurgence of interest in electric fence systems research in the 1990s has been the result of the explorations of Waikato University technology research students employed by the Gallagher Group as part of their degree training. Interest has included the concept of the electric fence becoming a conduit for all types of farm management information.

A useful short history of the New Zealand electric fencing industry is included in the book *Upgrading New Zealand's Competitive Advantage* written in 1991 by Crocombe, Enright and Porter.

Innovation Philosophy

The acknowledgment and utilisation of 'chance' events plays a significant part in the new Gallagher philosophy. 'Chance' events and those with an unpredictable outcome are bound to occur from time to time and some will make a significant impact on company operations and fortunes. The situation is always changing and potential for company benefit must be reviewed constantly as part of routine business. For example, while every endeavour was made to appoint management team members for their potential contribution to the company, their capacity to work as a team could not be predicted.

Using the new management team start-up as an example, a series of stages is evident. Firstly the event was recognised, then a compatibility of mindsets was discovered and finally a common determination to succeed was established. The energy from management could then be channelled through staff to effect changes. Naturally there was a need for balance of views and moderation as well as willingness to allow each partner to fulfil his function.

It is therefore argued that a set of random occurrences had been harnessed and channelled into a process that was not random. This, the company believe, is the secret to Gallagher's reformed innovation strategy which has led to success and growth.

The development of a new product at Gallaghers follows the same pattern. An unpredictable sequence of circumstances and decisions generates an idea that must be captured and tamed into a financially viable and saleable item. At Gallagher's the management team sees itself as providing the environment for the process to take place while the staff are free to do the processing. It is expected that from time to time, and in spite of well-directed effort, circumstances will divert a project in unpredictable directions and it will therefore need regular reassessment. Scheduling and costing estimates for innovative projects are therefore seen not as rigid and preordained constraints, but as guidelines which inevitably need review. Clearly there must be early warning to the market if delays to the availability of a promised product are likely, and more importantly the reasons for the delay must be made clear throughout the distribution chain.

Management at Gallagher believe they provide innovation leadership to staff by:

- focusing vision
- building capability
- leveraging aggressively
- operating good processes.

Neil Richardson describes innovation as being rather like a football match with the new product as the ball. No one knows which way the ball will bounce but both the players (staff) and the coaches (management) are vitally interested in winning the game. When the game starts, management retires to the sidelines and watches. The players matter more than the ball. The product will be changed in the future but the team, and how it plays the game, are more important for successful long-term outcomes. An aim for the coaches at Gallagher is 'to get 110 per cent performance from their staff – which is 150 per cent more capacity than the staff believe they have!'

Product Attributes

Traditionally, new products need to have the desired performance, be delivered on time and meet allocated production budgets. These constraints are now taken for granted and form the basis of consideration for selection.

The Gallagher Group believe it is also necessary to address and simultaneously achieve five additional key product attributes:

- speed to market
- lowest variable cost
- multiple features
- quality
- range (for many markets with different product requirements).

These attributes are normally held to be conflicting, but company culture today must be pragmatic and allow for their simultaneous and synergistic development. This requires senior management to focus on the development of corporate capability and functional management must utilise that capability.

Picking Winners

Development projects in each of the three product groups are subject to a formal monthly 'focus review' by the corporate, operations, technical and product managers. The status and recent progress achieved on each project is discussed at these meetings. The meeting outcomes are decisions about changes to project priorities and resource allocation for future work.

Four stages of new product implementation are recognised by the Gallagher Group: (1) specification, (2) test, (3) release and (4) launch.

The specification simply defines what the product will be, what it should do and when it should be available. For the test phase a fixed and limited manufacturing volume is produced (typically 10 to 100 units) and placed with lead-users into specific markets. These units are placed on an 'information or sales' basis, and aggressive follow-up is done in the field to solicit a critical response. Problems and improvements to the test models are analysed and modifications are developed and applied for further evaluation. The release phase involves limited manufacturing on a continuous basis (up to 10 per cent of final market sales could be manufactured at this time). Sales are made in planned volumes, and again a response from users and dealers is aggressively pursued. Upgrades are applied where necessary.

Not until the launch phase is reached are production runs sized to meet market demand. Volume production is pushed and products are sold into any market. A series of planned incremental improvements are phased in as part of the ongoing process of upgrading all 'release' products.

This iterative approach to product development has its risks. Competitors find it relatively easy to find out what new product is being developed. This approach therefore relies on strong branding, product support and patent protection to carry it through to a successful commercial conclusion. The risk of sending an inadequately trialled product into the international marketplace is considered too high to shortcut the adopted implementation. Also, the procedure is intended to create a constant process of 'channel upgrade', because it allows distributors and key dealers to be gradually educated about a product before it is actually launched.

Changes at the Kahikatea Drive Site

The Hamilton site produces:

- electric fence energisers and accessories (over 600 product lines)
- security fence systems based on core electric fence technology
- toolmaking products
- contract moulding
- consumer plastics (clothes pegs).

At this site there are 13 professional engineers, 10 technicians, 20 trades people, 14 professional marketing, accounts and purchasing staff. The remaining employees are production staff. All electronics products are made in New Zealand except where tariff regimes in Argentina and India have demanded licensing arrangements. A second New Zealand manufacturing site was acquired in 1993 in Pukekohe, which manufactures metal accessories including fence and farm gate hardware and farm gates.

The internal changes since 1989 have been most evident in four areas:

- introduction of operations software
- improved staff interaction
- expansion of the R&D capability
- remodelled electronics manufacturing lines for surface-mount technology.

Firstly, the planned and structured business now uses MRPII, which is a comprehensive manufacturing and business control software, for manufacturing resource planning. Since its introduction, stock levels have been reduced, more working capital has been made available and financial information is real-time. Product development makes extensive use of three-dimensional computer aided design (3-D CAD) and numerically controlled (NC) machining as well as software packages for circuit board design, circuit simulation and production.

Secondly, staff interaction and contribution have been actively encouraged. The business plan, for example, was explained directly to all staff meeting in groups of about 30 people.

At one meeting a production worker said he could not do what was required because he had not had the training. In the past it had been accepted that supervisors were responsible for, and had the ability, to carry out training. However, during this meeting it became evident that with the introduction of new methods and techniques, supervisors could not necessarily be expected to have the appropriate experience, knowledge or skills. This incident helped both the company and staff to appreciate the benefits that interaction brings and brought acceptance of the need for active participation in the change process. All staff are now trained to understand more about the business and can find their way around the site to the departments and broadly understand their different functions.

Another example of change has been with R&D staff attitude and image. Staff in the research laboratories have been made aware of the high profile they give the company and are therefore now more sensitive to meeting expectations of that role, particularly when visitors are being shown the facilities.

The third visible change is in the opening of a new R&D suite in November 1994. It can house up to 25 staff and is already over 60 per cent utilised. Good links with local Waikato University post-graduates have developed and continue the strong association with local research agencies that bring mutual benefit to the region.

Over recent years an industrial chaplain has been visiting the site, giving independent support for staff and providing feedback to management about general social issues. The chaplain's contribution has proved to be 'an enormously positive influence', much bigger than was ever anticipated when he was first invited to the site three years ago. Many staff could not visualise what change would mean and really appreciate the help made available through the service of the industrial chaplain.

Changes in Marketing

A major strength of the Gallagher Group has always been its extensive overseas distribution network. By setting in place distribution channels, and the structures and systems to service them, the Gallagher Group became more of a small multinational company rather than an international one. These distributors are sometimes set up under existing agency companies but most often companies were set up under local control with a minority Gallagher shareholding.

The manager of each distribution outlet is selected for knowledge of the local market. Good margins are made available from Gallaghers as an incentive for vigorously pursuing sales. A great deal of trust and training is essential, but the benefit is that markets are seen through the eyes of locals who can respond more appropriately to opportunities. In Peru, for example, a multi-million dollar contract was recently won to provide the fencing for a new development setting up 1000 ten-hectare farms for indigenous people. Local knowledge and worthwhile incentive combined well to secure the sale and provide the mutually beneficial outcome.

Each year in November a major international distributor event is held in either Hamilton or Europe to show products coming through the innovation process and develop marketing strategies for the coming season. To support the innovation process, meetings are held each year in May with all the major market groupings in their own geographical area (Europe, North America, Latin America and Australasia). These meetings closely examine new products, distribution channel upgrades and product issues. The meetings provide invaluable opportunity for feedback and discussion with local farmers trialling new equipment and with other agents. A strong distribution agreement and ownership helps to reduce the risk of distributor defection or poaching by competitors. The 'metered and phased release' of new products allows better opportunity for distributors and their dealers to contribute to changes and upgrades prior to mass release.

The technology for electric fencing was considered to be mature by the many market participants at the end of the 1980s. There was a strong disincentive to make systems more automated, flexible and sophisticated. For this to be overcome and to promote sales of new high-tech equipment, Gallagher's recognised that a steep learning curve was required for both end users and dealers. This was done by first promoting the benefits of built-in intelligence dealing with inadequacies of existing systems. This then enabled confidence to be built up around the added value of new high-tech products and has provided a pathway to supply new families of products like integrated farm information system technology which uses the electric fence as the information highway. The confidence is reflected in the 'Competive Advantages' that Gallagher's claim (see Appendix).

A realistic attitude to implementing a desired innovation culture at the company corporate level has resulted in better products for end users. Better products have also been produced through the intensification of R&D. Strong channels now exist for the development of new ideas in response to customer needs and harnessing technological capability.

The Results So Far

It took three years to work through major change issues and, two years after the changes have been largely in place throughout the organisation, effects can be reviewed.

New Zealand sales have increased from $4 million to $11 million in a period without the help of external factors like strong national economic growth. This reflects a small improvement in the farming sector economy but more significantly Gallagher's ability to meet market needs. The New Zealand distribution channel does have extra R&D involvement, but in many ways the market approach used locally is duplicated in 30 countries in the over 100-country Gallagher network. There is new staff and customer confidence that the animal containment business is far from mature. Staff are given a share of about 15 per cent of company profit each year. A future new product development path to provide intelligent fencing and farm information systems is being assembled and promoted. The distributor/dealership network is well acquainted with forthcoming products which allows them to have confidence and to project that confidence to clients.

The Gallagher Group management team firmly believes that creativity is generated in direct proportion to the gap between aspirations and existing resources. Therefore the Gallagher Group is committed to a culture that fosters and manages creativity right through to the time it can generate tangible returns. There is the perception that the Group has adopted innovation strategy for both survival and prosperity – and 'Perception is Reality'.

Appendix: Competitive Advantages of Gallagher Power Fence Systems Ltd (August 1994)

Complete Product Range
- Total animal containment system

High Quality Product
- Supported by comprehensive warranties (30 day satisfaction, 1 year, 2 year, 5 year, 10 year, 15 year).

10-Year Guaranteed Parts Supply
- Hold stock of parts 10 years after product discontinued.

Exclusive Product Range
- Range of value-added products exclusive to Gallagher, i.e. turbo tape/wire, insultimber, smart fence range.

New Generation Smart Fence Energizers
- Leading-edge technology designed to take power fencing into the future and grow the existing market.

Complementary Product Range
- Franklin gates and gate hardware.

Second Brand Options
- Ability to manufacture and distribute under another brand.

International Brand Identity
- Marketed in over 100 countries around the world.

International Market Leadership
- Recognised as market leader around the world
- The largest manufacturer of power fence products in the world.

Innovation and Technology
- Most comprehensive research and development department in the world
- Returning large percentage of turnover back into research and development.

C.A.D./C.A.M.
- Computer Aided Design
- Computer Aided Manufacture.

Field Staff's Expertise and Attitudes
- In excess of 120 years' combined experience servicing New Zealand rural industry.

High Quality Management Team
- Core competence.

High Profile International Sports Person
- Mark Cooksley
- Available for promotional activity.

Profit Driven
- Committed to providing realistic margins.

Management Advice and Profitability Assistance
- Account management to achieve profitability satisfactory to both parties.

Business or Customer Requirements Planning
- Ability to plan customers' special requirements.

Joint Partnership Plans
- Jointly planned marketing activities.

Partnership Account Management

- Working as partners to achieve a common cause.

Promotional Calendars

- Preplanned activities
- Proactive in market
- Assistance in planning promotions.

Promotional Activity

- National promotions
- In-store days
- On farm field-days
- Canvass days
- Co-op mailers.

High Quality Merchandising and Point of Sale Material

- Shelf merchandising
- High impact displays.

Advertising

- National Press
- Regional Press
- Radio
- Co-op Mailers
- Television (?)

Product Information

- High Quality
- Educational videos (x10)
- Original Power Fence Material
- Mailers.

Testimony, Editorial Reinforcement

- Existing end user
- National press coverage.

Product Training

- End user
- Dealer
- In-house
- External
- On-farm practical
- Product knowledge evenings.

Strategic Demonstration Farms

- Demonstration of product in use by end user.

Free On-Farm Assistance

- Trouble shooting
- Planning advice
- Sales generating.

Display Trailers Available for

- In-store days
- Field-days
- Canvass days
- Training days.

Attendance of National Field-days

- Promoting product
- Staff training.

Convenience Packaging

- Display outers
- Realistic quantities.

Service & Delivery

- National contracts to provide most efficient dispatch and delivery of orders.
- Highly efficient warehousing to allow fast turnaround of orders.

E.D.I.

- Electronic data interface
- Capable of linking to computer ordering systems.

Toll Free Order Phone

0800 Hotline

- Advertised to end user
- After-sales service back up.

6 Healtheries New Zealand

'Thank you' would go a long way to improving things around here.

(Managers and employees of Healtheries New Zealand Ltd, 1992)

Introduction

Healtheries New Zealand Ltd (Healtheries) is New Zealand's leading supplier of vitamin and mineral supplements. Healtheries exports to more than 20 countries from its own food packing and supplements manufacturing plants located in Auckland. The product range boasts three major categories: health foods, nutritional supplements, and skin care. (See Figures 6.1(a) and 6.1(b) for examples of Healtheries' products and informational promotion.)

The company goes back to 1904 when it was first established as a small flour mill. 1904 to 1966 saw little change. But, in 1967, the company went through a transformational development when Bert Macartney bought the company. Macartney had a background as a food technologist with a pharmaceutical interest. His vision was to offer health foods and nutritional supplements of a high quality at a reasonable price. His major goals were to encourage growth and to expand the business through innovative products.

Macartney managed his vision and these goals successfully from 1967 through to the 1970s. He expanded the range of 'healthful' products to become New Zealand's largest supplier of vitamins and nutritional supplements. During this time of development, the company flourished.

Acknowledgments This case study was prepared by Bryan Poulin from various sources, including long interviews with Mark Mathews and other key employees of Healtheries New Zealand Ltd. Special thanks go to Mark Mathews, managing director, and all those people at Healtheries for their input and cooperation in the preparation of this case study. Parts of this case study were previously reported by Manzurul Alam and Bryan Poulin in *Pacific Accounting Review*, vol. 8, no. 1; and in the Department of Accounting and Finance Working Paper Series, University of Waikato, December 1992. This case study is to be used for the purpose of classroom discussion and not as an illustration of effective or ineffective handling of a strategic or administrative situation.

Figure 6.1(a) Healtheries' products

Healtheries
•SPECIALIST•

A unique range of nutritional supplements that recognise your individual needs.

Healtheries
•SPECIALIST•
VERY SPECIAL, VERY PERSONAL.

B-PLEX

The B Complex vitamins are considered to be the single most important factor in the health of the nerves. They are also essential for the metabolism of carbohydrates, fats and protein.

WIDESPREAD VITAMIN B DEFICIENCY

Yet Vitamin B Complex deficiency in the western population is widespread. First because we eat many processed foods from which the Vitamin B has been removed. Secondly, because our sugar consumption is high. Sugar, a pure carbohydrate, is devoid of vitamins, minerals and enzymes to aid its digestion and simply draws for its metabolism upon B Complex vitamins from elsewhere in the body. This may jeopardise the health of the nervous and digestive tracts.

Regular alcohol and caffeine intake adversely effect these vitamins, particularly Thiamine (B1) and Folic Acid. As do times of infection, emotional or physical stress and periods of increased growth such as during adolescence and pregnancy.

STRESS A MAJOR CULPRIT

Finally, our modern, high stress, over-indulgent lifestyles demand a high intake of B Complex vitamins to avoid the deficiency symptoms of fatigue, irritability, nervousness, depression and lack of appetite.

These are not the only effects of Vitamin B deficiency. Hair loss, early greying, cracks at the corner of the mouth and an enlarged red shiny tongue which is full of grooves are all symptoms that have been linked to low levels of these vitamins.

HEALTHERIES SPECIALIST B-PLEX

Is a balanced, High Potency Vitamin B formulation, using Sustained Time Release technology to assure a slower, more natural rate of absorption of the B Complex vitamins. This is important as B Complex vitamins are water soluble and cannot be stored in the body.

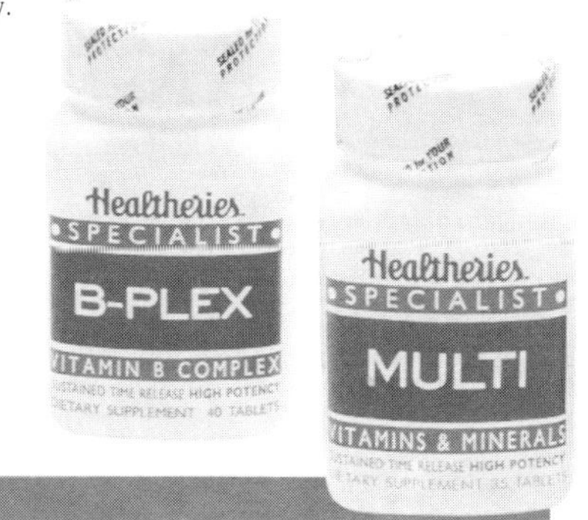

STRESS

Stress is a part of our everyday lives, whether we are hosting a party or living through a divorce. Stress is not the external pressures, however, but our bodily responses to these situations.

STRESS — THE PROS AND CONS

Stress is not necessarily negative. It can give you energy and supply that zest for living. However, if your daily nutrition is inadequate, stress can turn into distress, which manifests itself through feelings of tension, irritation headaches or fatigue. The body's response to stress sets off a chain reaction in which the adrenal glands are stimulated to produce hormones responsible for our 'fright and flight' response. Acute or prolonged stress can lead to exhaustion of the adrenal glands, causing lethargy and susceptibility to infection or allergies. Stress can also affect cholesterol levels, the heart and digestion.

REDUCING STRESS

It is impossible to make our lives stress-free. But we can prevent its long term detrimental effects to the body by eating a nutritious wholefood diet, practising relaxation techniques and expressing ourselves creatively. Ideally you should eliminate from your diet sugar and over-processed foods deficient in nutrients, and stimulants, such as coffee and cigarettes, which rob the body of Vitamin B Complex and C.

HEALTHERIES SPECIALIST STRESS

Has been especially formulated to meet the added demands stress places on the body. It provides both Vitamin B Complex and non-acid C, both of which play a key role in stress management, in a balanced High Potency, Sustained Time Release formulation. This ensures a slower, more natural rate of absorption of these water soluble micronutrients, which would otherwise be excreted rapidly.

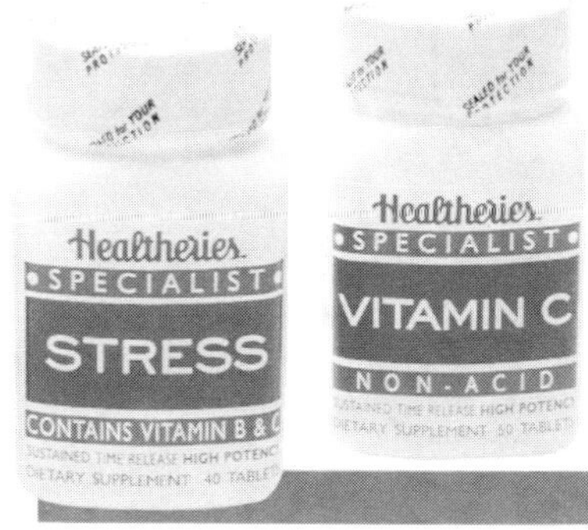

Figure 6.1(b) Healtheries' products

What is Cholesterol?

Cholesterol is a fatty white substance essential to health. It is important in the production of hormones, Vitamin D and bile acids. It forms part of every organ including the brain, nerves, heart and skin.

Healtheries Brown Rice

Where does it come from?

Most cholesterol present in the body (approximately 80%) is manufactured by the liver and other tissues, by using fats, proteins and sugars in the diet. A small amount of cholesterol (approximately 20%) is absorbed from the diet when eating animal products.

Healtheries Wheat

What other factors affect cholesterol levels?

Stress, anxiety, overeating, lack of exercise and a high consumption of refined carbohydrates and saturated fats have all been linked with high cholesterol levels. Some people also have an inherited susceptibility to producing large amounts of cholesterol when they eat fatty foods.

What is the danger of high blood cholesterol levels?

It is believed that when blood cholesterol levels are high, fatty deposits of cholesterol and calcium accumulate in the arteries including those of the heart, increasing the susceptibility to coronary heart disease which is the leading cause of death in New Zealand.

How is cholesterol measured?

When the cholesterol level is measured, the figure refers to the total amount of cholesterol found in the blood. This amount is measured in millimoles per litre (mmol/l). At present, it is thought the desirable level is less than 5.5 mmol/litre.

Healtheries Rye Corn

Total cholesterol comprises of the following proteins which carry cholesterol.

LDL – low density, lipoprotein cholesterol. Although essential in the body, carries cholesterol through the blood vessels and can deposit it on the artery walls causing atherosclerosis. The more LDL there is in the blood, the greater the risk is of developing heart disease.

VLDL – very low density lipoprotein cholesterol is used by the liver to make LDL. The more VLDL there is, the more LDL can be produced by the liver and therefore increasing the risk of heart disease.

HDL – high density lipoprotein cholesterol has the opposite effect to LDL and actually protects our arteries by drawing cholesterol away from the walls. The higher the level of HDL, the more protection there is against heart disease.

What can I do to lower my Cholesterol levels?

When embarking on a cholesterol lowering programme, the following factors should be considered:

1. Reducing the intake of foods high in cholesterol and saturated fats.
2. Replacing refined carbohydrates with high fibre foods.
3. Increasing the intake of fish.
4. Commencing an exercise programme.
5. Lowering your stress levels.
6. Inclusion of specific dietary supplements found to affect cholesterol levels in the body.

Healtheries Soya Beans

FOODS THAT RAISE CHOLESTEROL

Animal Products

Cheese, whole milk, butter, dripping, egg yolks and meat all contain cholesterol or saturated fat, both of which are capable of increasing the body's cholesterol level.

Healtheries Whole Millet

Non-fat milk and margarine can replace whole milk and butter in the diet. Hard cheeses should be avoided as they have a high saturated fat content, although cottage cheese, quark and ricotta can be used sparingly. Avoid the use of egg yolk.

Reduce your meat intake to no more than three meals weekly. Before cooking, trim off all visible fat and only bake, broil or grill using an oven rack, allowing any fat to collect in the lower pan. Skin chicken and bake in an oven bag.

Healtheries Pearl Barley

FOODS THAT LOWER CHOLESTEROL

Fish

Fish is an excellent source of Omega-3 fatty acids which have been found to lower cholesterol levels. Fish 2 to 3 times weekly is advantageous. Fish high in Omega-3 fatty acids are Blue Mackerel, Skip Jack Tuna, Silver Warehou and Kahawai, although it is present in all species to a lesser degree.

Fibre

Wholegrain foods such as muesli, wholegrain flakes and breads provide essential nutrients necessary for fat utilisation within the body. The high fibre content has an effect on reducing the cholesterol level.

Foods high in water-soluble fibre have been found to be most effective. These include all dried beans and lentils, particularly soybeans. Fruit is high in pectin which is also a water soluble fibre. Wheat bran, rice bran but particularly oatbran, should be used regularly in the diet. Half a cup of oatbran (100gms) daily is recommended. This can be added to muesli or eaten as muffins on a daily basis. Healtheries comprehensive bean range can be made into tasty soups and dips as well as main meals.

Healtheries Rolled Oats

Macartney enjoyed a high reputation in the business community. This was reflected in the comments collected in 1985 when a group of Auckland University researchers were preparing an 'excellence' book. These researchers reported:

> (The CEO) is the company. He has entrepreneurial knack, intuition and vision ultimately translated into action to look ahead and position himself to be in balance with the customer's needs at an appropriate future time and ability to communicate the vision. He is the dynamo, his people see him leading from the front. Others reflect his energy. He is an enthusiast, a believer. Where the company is today is largely a result of his entrepreneurial skill and effort. (Inkson, K., Henshall, B., Marsh, N., and Ellis, G. *Theory K: the key to excellence in New Zealand management.* Auckland: Bateman, 1986, p. 31.)

Soon after this positive report, Macartney was to resign for reasons other than 'his entrepreneurial skill and effort'. However, as the pioneer of New Zealand's supplements and vitamin industry, he is rightfully referred to as one of New Zealand's 'great entrepreneurs' by the present management of Healtheries.

The Dietary and Supplements Industry

Current trends in dietary supplements suggest that New Zealanders and Australians are becoming increasingly conscious of the need for vitamins and dietary supplements as part of their health regime.

For example, the use of vitamins and dietary supplements doubled in 'key account supermarkets' over the three years 1990–93. This strong upward growth trend is expected to continue. Nutritional (dietary) supplements and vitamins exceed $40 million dollars annually in New Zealand. The estimated annual sales of dietary supplements and vitamins in each distribution category is indicated in Figure 6.2.

Figure 6.2 Dietary Supplements and Vitamins In New Zealand Estimated Annual Sales ($ million NZ) 1993

Sub-Category	Sales
Supermarket Grocers	$ 17.0
Pharmacies	$ 16.0
Health Stores	$ 5.0
Other	$ 3.0

Source: Estimated from past issues of *Grocer's Review*.

Dietary supplements, vitamins, and personal care products are made from (mostly) natural or organic materials. Brandon Wilcox, marketing manager for Red Seal, one of Australasia's leading health supplement providers, recently noted three major factors which account for the growth of the market:

1 An increasing consumer preference for a more personal and active role in caring for their own health, as consumers feel they must rely on the health system less and less; New Zealanders are taking more responsibility for their own health and so are looking for more preventative remedies.

2 People are willing to spend more on supplements as the economy improves.

3 There is an increasing trend that has seen consumers moving away from pharmacies towards supermarkets for their health care needs.

The supplements and vitamins industry contributes high profit margins for supermarket grocers, pharmacies and health stores. The dramatic growth in this market is attributed to the introduction of new products and information campaigns aimed at purchasers. Vitamin and dietary supplement products are highly priced and offer superior margins compared to ordinary supermarket products such as a bottle of milk or a loaf of bread.

Three companies are the main players in New Zealand's dietary supplements and vitamins industry. They are: Healtheries, Red Seal and Blackmores. Overall, Healtheries has the leading position with about a 35 per cent market share. Red Seal and Blackmores together account for a combined total of another 40 per cent of the market. A host of smaller companies share the remaining 25 per cent of the market.

Healtheries dominate only among supermarket grocers with Blackmores leading in pharmacies and health stores. Some health stores prefer to distribute Blackmores and imported brands because they perceive Healtheries' emphasis on the mass distribution supermarket channels as a threat to them. Over the past 30 years, dietary supplements and vitamins (and personal and skin care items) have experienced growing sales, especially in grocery supermarkets. But it took until 1993 for the grocery sector to overtake pharmacies in the sales.

In 1993 grocery sales of such products grew at a 30 per cent annual rate while pharmacy sales stagnated with no growth in 1993. Similar trends exist overseas, including the US, the UK and Australia. The trend has helped some companies and hurt others. For example, the larger international competitors have chosen to continue to use pharmacies as their major distribution channel. Pharmacies are most loyal to those company brands which do not actively seek presence in supermarkets which tend to offer discounts on fast-moving lines.

The basis of competition is not primarily price but one of value (quality for price). Therefore companies fiercely promote and protect their brand. The highly specialised nature of many of these 'healthful' products necessitates information that promotes attributes and benefits. These products must also be readily available, attractively packaged, and of high quality. Misleading information, for example, information which overstates the benefits of a product, can have a negative, long-term impact on the image of the brand.

Image is considered very important because it helps establish and remind health-conscious customers of desirable attributes over an entire range of branded products. If branded products and remedies are to continue to do well in the competitive arena of supermarket grocery aisles, advertising and marketing strategies must continue to be attractive and convincing. This is because shelf space and shelf positioning are crucial for vitamins and nutritional supplements. The small packaging of most nutritional supplements means that they must have 'linear facing' on the shelf and 'near eye-level' positioning, otherwise the customer may overlook them.

A leading retail grocer suggested the following practice to overcome the shortage of such shelf positioning:

> One way to get around the space problem is to put them (the small packages of vitamins and supplements) next to sun blocks and expand the section when the sun block section shrinks in winter.

However, the greatest single influence on consumer purchase decisions is from family and friends. Other key factors which influence purchasing behaviour include trust and 'heritage' (length of time in the market, reputation and brand attractiveness).

Generally, the market is fiercely competitive with an increasing array of products offered in all groups (vitamins and dietary and herbal supplements) to meet ever more selective customers. Overall, demand continues to grow. Industry spokespeople surmise that the reasons for these increases are:

1 increased disposable income
2 more attractive packaging and
3 'smarter' groupings of related products.

The battleground is seen to be for 'the mind of the consumer' who must discriminate points of difference among all the competing products on offer.

The Influence of Government Policy on the Industry

Historically, successive governments in New Zealand promoted exports by providing export incentives. However, incentives were not seen as an important part of Macartney's or Healtheries' original strategy. For example, the company did not respond to a 1962 government announcement of an Export Market Development Taxation Scheme which allowed exporters to 'write off' export market development expenditure at 150 per cent. However, as time went on, the export subsidies began to look more and more attractive to the industry, and especially to Healtheries.

Economist Wooding wrote this in 1987:

> Additional (government) schemes were announced at various stages, including Development Grants for New Markets, Export Suspensory Loans, an Export Manufacturing Investment Allowance and exemption from sales tax on machinery used in export production.
>
> (Wooding, P. (1987), 'Liberalising the International Trade Regime', in A. Bollard and R. Buckle (eds) *Economic Liberalisation in New Zealand*, Allen and Unwin. p. 89.)

The cumulative effect of these schemes was to make increased exports an almost irresistible temptation. This was because almost any expenditure in export effort would be made 'profitable' by the subsidies paid by the government of New Zealand. It did not seem to matter if the items could be manufactured at a profit without subsidy; the subsidy would make the item profitable. Export was seen as a 'licence to print money'.

From the mid 1970s through to the mid 1980s, Healtheries managers and Macartney focused more and more of their effort on maximising profits through the government subsidies. Unfortunately, one result was that Healtheries began to stray further and further away from being an efficient manufacturer and distributor of high-value health food products and nutritional supplements.

Matters became more problematic when, beginning with a 1982 announcement of economic reforms, the government quite suddenly began to reduce the subsidy payments. At the same time, the government removed much of the tariff protection enjoyed by local manufacturers in the New Zealand market. Together, these policies changed the environmental circumstances considerably and New Zealand manufacturers then had to face international competition and world prices. Amazingly perhaps, Healtheries continued to expand product lines in this new environment of vanishing government subsidies. The situation was unsustainable.

Sadly, all the pioneering effort of Healtheries under Macartney appeared to be in vain as the company skidded down the slippery slope towards bankruptcy. However, the extent of the impending crisis was not fully appreciated until 1986 when year-end financial statements were being prepared. By then it was too late. Confidence within the company collapsed when the financial manager informed Macartney that losses in 1986 would exceed 10 per cent of total sales. The Board of Directors were alarmed. They demanded a change in leadership and management.

Events Leading up to the 1986 Crisis

During the mid 1970s and up to the mid 1980s, the company showed consistent growth and profitability under the direction of Bert Macartney. Macartney maintained an informal control system, made up of industry committees and personal contacts, to help guide his decisions. Accounting was used only to provide information required by external parties such as tax authorities and bankers. The organisation was flexible to the extent that it was simple and directive.

In 1985 the owner-manager did make one notable change when he greatly increased overheads by hiring a number of new managers. Perhaps the decision to increase overheads in the face of an impending crisis is not so paradoxical when the style of management is taken into account. The chief accountant of the time, who in 1994 served as export manager, made these comments on Macartney's narrowing of vision that led up to the 1986 crisis:

> The owner-manager [Macartney] was after short-term profits and did not consider the risks involved. Since the export market was profitable at the time, emphasis on cost was not the main focus. The behaviour can be described as opportunist and short-sighted.

The export manager went on to report that organisational direction in 1986 became incoherent as management style became dominated by this philosophy of opportunism:

> Let me give you an example about how far our activities were fragmented. Suppose all of a sudden people became very conscious about 'cholesterol'. The owner-manager would identify this development and immediately 'ask' the technical and marketing manager to 'go for it'. Maybe that went on for a few weeks until another development took place.

Fragmented decision making meant that the regular product lines suffered as new products were introduced. Without systematic planning, costing or budgeting, large stocks of unwanted products accumulated. The inventory situation was made worse by poor quality control, even for proven products, with some production batches falling short of health standards.

Subsequently, these deficient products had to be discarded and 'written' in the accounts as a 'loss'. This is the way that the export manager described the fragmented decision process under the direction of the previous owner-manager:

> The capital budgeting was patchy. Let me give you an example. One time the owner-manager went on an export trip and there he saw a new type of machine. He bought it [the machine]. His decision did not go through any capital expenditure approval process nor was any feasibility analysis done. Since we had no immediate use for the new machine, it sat idle for some time.

It is not surprising that the enterprise was heading for trouble. By the time the government started to withdraw export incentives in 1984, Healtheries had already run into cash flow shortages. The lack of a sound management accounting system and poor record keeping meant that reasons for poor financial performance were difficult to identify. In short, there was no way for the company to see that it was heading for serious trouble. The current export manager also reflected on the period leading up to the 1986 crisis:

> During the crisis period we did not have any budget reporting, let alone an operating system to control costs. Even after the changes in the economic policy of the government, the owner-manager continued to emphasise exports and diversity.

Mark Mathews and the 1987 to 1991 Turnaround

In 1985, Mark Mathews was hired by the Board of Directors as financial director. Mathews had graduated in the late 1970s with a management degree in accounting and marketing from the University of Waikato. Mathews had about seven years experience working for a large Australian-based firm, where he had acted as financial controller and trouble-shooter on many projects, including marketing. Mathews said, 'Whatever needed doing, I volunteered.'

With the shock of the 1986 financial report, and at the suggestion of the Healtheries board, Macartney agreed to sell the company to outside investors. The Board of Directors then appointed the young financial manager of Healtheries, Mark Mathews, as managing director in early 1988 following a period of management by a short-term contractor. Mathews comments, 'There was nobody else who wanted the job.'

The Board of Directors and the new managing director had arranged that the company be sold to a group of investors with no experience in the food industry. The investors gave to Mark Mathews, as managing director, complete authority and responsibility for the turnaround of Healtheries. The investors made it very clear that profitability was to be restored as soon as possible.

But the future of Healtheries was far from certain. For about one year, until Healtheries could be sold, Mathews managed the business on the basis of 'self-managed receivership'. That is, the managing director reported frequently to the bankers of the enterprise who had to be convinced of the company's viability. Otherwise, the banks would call for the company to be 'wound up'.

Figure 6.3 Healtheries of New Zealand Ltd Organisation Chart in 1992

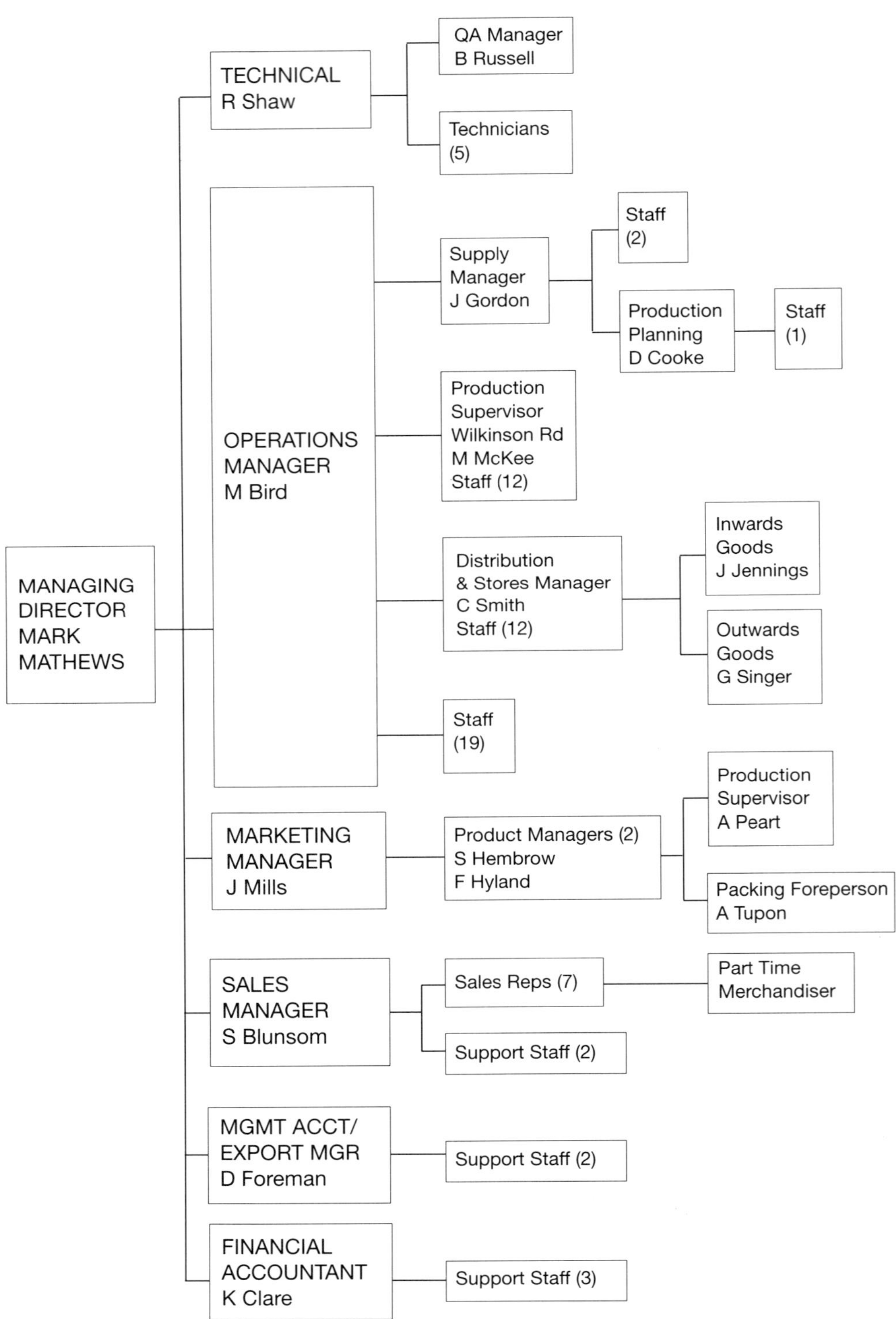

Measures to Restore Profitability at Healtheries

For about the first six months of 1988, the new managing director directed what he called a purely survival strategy. He used control systems as the main lever in implementing this turnaround strategy. More specifically, the new managing director sold or otherwise disposed of unneeded assets; he established formal control procedures to reduce costs through budget control; and he introduced quality assurance procedures. Control of expenditures was considered crucial. The managing director insisted that spending be in line with budgets. He also controlled the company's inventory levels to see that they matched sales forecasts. A cost accounting system was implemented, based on historical data and absorption costing. As these professional control systems were put into place, all other department managers were made directly responsible to the new managing director for quality and cost control. (See Figure 6.3 for Organisation of Healtheries.)

The company retrenched by selling its overseas and domestic retail distribution outlets and by reducing the number of upper and middle managers by half. Of some 200 employees, 70 were transferred out of Healtheries with the divested retail outlet; 30 people were laid off in one day. The announcement became known as 'the day of long knives'.

In this shaken environment, the Chairman of the Board and Mark Mathews moved quickly to reassure the remaining 90 employees that the company needed them and that the company had a good future. The managing director also coined this simple, three-word encapsulation of his survival plan for the enterprise: 'profitability, accountability and flexibility'. Accountability meant people would set out to achieve realisable targets and deliver on their commitments; flexibility meant that the systems and the structure of the organisation were generally consistent with the new direction; and profitability was to be the result.

Non-core products and activities were dropped. Of those managers and employees who were retained, some of them shifted positions while other chose to leave or retire. This is the way that Mathews reflected on the importance of cost control during the retrenchment phase of the turnaround:

> We addressed every cost and we made do with what we had. We reduced people and tasks, focused on key products and marketing areas, and changed people. We put extra effort into all external relationships and over-compensated on stocks to ensure delivery. And we worked through a priority list of what was most important to do at this time.

This new approach inspired confidence. As the employee representative stated in a 1991 interview: 'He [the managing director] kept us up to date with what was going on.'

Management was truthful and people 'felt better'. The managing director described his approach in a similar way: 'I think you build trust by informing people.' Success became measured in terms of doing the 'little things' right: sticking to budget and reducing costs and increasing production efficiencies and delivering quality products on time. Action and analysis were carefully conducted. For example, as product lines were rationalised, emphasis among distribution channels was changed and efficiencies were realised in what the enterprise did best.

The company also changed its relationship with its distributors and new control systems were installed to track distributors' sales more closely to manage the company's inventory system and to adjust to the manufacturing schedule. In concentrating on domestic rather than export sales, exports went from 40 per cent to 20 per cent. Changes in distribution are shown in Figure 6.4.

Figure 6.4 Distribution Channels of Healtheries in 1986 and 1990

(Sales Split by Channel)

Channel	Before Reorganisation **(1986)**	After Reorganisation **(1990)**
Supermarket	30%	65%
Health Food	40%	19%
Pharmacy	26%	12%
Others	4%	4%

Source: Company Records.

Healtheries stressed high volumes in targeted distribution channels rather than a spread among the channels. By 1990, less than four years after going to the brink of receivership, Healtheries regained profitability and the enterprise held onto market leadership in its key products.

Key products and core competencies were then used to promote branded products, with the company realising efficiency gains in marketing, production and distribution as smaller effort was necessary at each unit sale. Inventory control, product and packaging improvements were key initiatives. Each decision was measured against budget forecast and it was controlled at points of production and distribution.

The net result of the introduction of this professional management system, emphasising budget and cost control, was a dramatic increase in product quality, delivery timeliness and profitability. The turnaround strategy also became more sophisticated with time. The managing director summarised the turnaround strategy in this way:

> We utilise our strength – brand name, distribution coverage, accumulated knowledge of industry and flexibility for production, marketing, sales, and investment – to focus on core businesses of natural health products, and to maintain and market a wide range of niche products. The focus builds upon unique skills and our own brands. We pursue opportunities while maintaining margins appropriate to the effort involved.

Prior to the 1988–91 turnaround, the misfortunes of Healtheries led to a lack of confidence among its external stakeholders (distributors, customers, and bankers). Regaining the confidence of stakeholders was seen as a priority by the new managing director. However, regaining confidence was not an easy task, as Mathews acknowledged:

> Some important stakeholders held the idea that if you don't have at least 10 years' experience in the industry it is impossible to run a health food company.

Mathews did not have 10 years of experience in the industry. But he was able to take a number of steps to regain the confidence of the stakeholders. For example, with the 1988 introduction of costing, budget control and quality control systems, management had already made some progress in controlling costs, improving product quality and in delivering these products.

Budget analysis also helped management to understand what was feasible and possible in the turnaround situation. Such an understanding also helped management negotiate with the company's stakeholders. Again in 1994, the managing director reflected on the turnaround approach that he first conceived in 1988:

> For a start, we could give them [the stakeholders] some positive view for the future based on budget calculations. We had a shareholder who would support whatever plan management wanted to put. So it was really back to the responsibility of management to come up with a plan of what the company was going to do.

Communication was maintained with the customers by informing them what the company planned to do in terms of product development and product quality. Local sales representatives who covered the country were charged with preparing market reports for management. The stakeholders also benefited because they saw how their involvement affected Healtheries' prospects. In other words, they had a more direct stake in the company. The managing director added these further comments about stakeholders:

> We told them what we had in mind, showed them things we had done already as a proof that we were not just talking. So we didn't just approach them unless we had something to show them what we were about.

External relationships were also helped by changing the organisational structure as management decided to involve more experienced people. For example, the company appointed sales representatives who had a background in health food. These sales representatives were able to provide detailed costing and budgeting information on a product and market basis, and to negotiate future sales with customers. All this led to a return to profitability.

Mathews stated that not only was financial performance profitable in 1990 and 1991 but the average return on net assets (RONA) exceeded 10 per cent for 1992 and 1993. Figure 6.5 is a summary of financial indicators from 1983, three years before the 1986 crisis, to 1991, five years after the crisis.

From 1983 to 1985 Healtheries enjoyed a positive return as a result of government subsidies in the form of export incentives on sales value and refunds for export-related expenses such as marketing and advertising. According to Mathews one of the serious problems with Healtheries during 1983 to 1985, the time period before the crisis and subsequent turnaround, was inaccurate financial reporting. Also, there existed a time lag between claims made to and revenue received from government subsidies. This delay would further confound the interpretation of the financial results.

It is striking that overheads are reported to have increased in the 1985 to 1986 period leading up to the crisis. Mathews stated that the persistently high overheads of 1987 and 1988 were due, in large measure, to the design, purchase and commissioning of new management control systems.

Figure 6.5 Financial Results at Healtheries (1983–91)

Financial Indicators	1983	1984	1985	1986	1987 ($000)	1988	1989	1990	1991
Sales	9503	13378	13404	13168	13490	11925	11590	12223	12976
Prime Cost	6751 2752	9611 3767	9623 3781	10510 2658	11320 2170	8914 3011	7824 3766	8094 4129	8525 4451
Gross margin	29.0%	28.2%	28.2%	20.2%	16.1%	25.2%	32.5%	22.8%	34.3%
Overheads	2759	3400	**3739**	**5513**	**5566**	**5366**	**4105**	**3970**	4221
Other income	361 354	346 713	311 **353**	879 **-1976**	809 **-2587**	408 **-1947**	178 **-161**	281 **440**	280 510
Profit before taxes (% on sales)	3.7%	5.3%	2.6%	N/A	N/A	N/A	N/A	3.6%	3.9%
RONA average for the period		+7%			-35%			+6%	

It took until 1989, four years after the rapid rise in overheads, for overheads to be brought down to near 1985 levels. Consultants' reports and the installation of the improved information and control systems tended to keep overheads high, in spite of the savings due to reduction in managers and improved operating efficiencies that were in place as early as 1987.

The Present Condition of Healtheries

In 1991 and 1992, a comprehensive cultural study of Healtheries was undertaken. Interviews with key people throughout the organisation and a questionnaire administered to all employees and managers at Healtheries largely substantiated the views of Mathews. The advantage of the interview and questionnaire data is that it allowed a rank ordering of the issues. These issues were classified into the three dimensions: strategic vision, control systems and structure.

From approximately 100 issue-statements identified from interviews with people throughout Healtheries, the 23 most highly valued settled ones (10 strategy, nine control and four structure) are shown in Figure 6.6. (For a full description of the process of the research, see 'The Successful Turnaround of Healtheries New Zealand' by Manzural Alam and Bryan Poulin, *Pacific Accounting Review*, Volume 8, Number 1, June 1996, pp. 66–95.)

The settled issues of Figure 6.6 have been listed in order of the value people place on the issues. For the sake of efficient presentation, the issues are shown in Figure 6.6 rather than the full issue-statements contained in the questionnaire. For example, the actual statement on 'pragmatism' in the Healtheries case is this: 'We are not market leaders for the thrill of being market leaders, but to make money'. It is also apparent that in 1992, some four years after the turnaround began, budget control continued to play an important role at Healtheries. This is reflected by the importance given to such settled issues as: 'production and budgets targets' and 'a computer system for budget and operations control'.

Figure 6.6 Settled Issues at Healtheries in 1992

(Rank-ordered by Perceived Importance)

Strategic Vision	Control Systems	Structure
Manufacturer for health	Production and budget targets	Authority by position
Profitability, growth and competitiveness	Computer system for budget and operations control	Personal responsibility
Market and product development	Customer support system	Positional responsibility
Reputation	Progress and budget comparison	Respect for CEO
Success	Product improvement	
Survival	Budget control of expenses	
Customer acceptance	Overhead control	
Flexibility	Performance	
Pragmatism	Financial control (decision making)	

The prevailing management style of directive authority is reflected in the issues of structure at Healtheries such as 'authority by position'. In short, the settled issues in 1992 have most to do with professional competence: identity and profitability, budget and operational control, and the direction from the top. But, just as interesting are the issues which were unsettled at Healtheries in 1992. The most important issues that people would like settled but remained unsettled are shown in Figure 6.7.

Figure 6.7 Unsettled Issues at Healtheries

(Rank-ordered by Perceived Importance)

Strategic Vision	Control Systems	Structure
Appreciation	Market knowledge	Leadership by example
Competence	Understanding success and failure	Serving and leading
Excellence	Supplier relations	Managers loyal to subordinates
Truthfulness	Customer feedback	Teamwork
Positive behaviour	Communication	Clear line of responsibility
Commitment and hard work	Minimum waste	Helping one another
Future direction	Listening to and valuing people	Competence of authority
Positive relationships		
Product value		
Self-improvement		

Interestingly, the majority of the unsettled issues have to do with such social or interpersonal perceptions and behaviour, especially in the vision and structure dimensions but also, to a lesser extent, in the control dimension. From Figure 6.7, it is also apparent that other issues will play an important part in the future. This is reflected in the importance given to such unsettled issues as: 'appreciation', 'market knowledge', and 'leading by example'.

Again, the issues rather than the full issue-statement have been reproduced in Figure 6.7. For example, the full issue-statement on 'appreciation' is this: '"Thank you" would go a long way to improving things around here'.

Challenge for the Future

The majority of unsettled issues at Healtheries are social, not technical, in nature. In other words, the issues which managers and employees see as unsettled, but desire to be settled, mostly concern social competence. This is because technical competence has, to a large extent, been accomplished during the turnaround period.

Managers and employees all agree that people at Healtheries should ideally appreciate each other more, work better in their teams and aspire to excellence. In short, the evidence at Healtheries suggests that social competence is viewed in these terms:

1 **strategic vision**, as a desire and a means to achieve excellence
2 **control systems**, as a means of appreciation of people, competence in understanding the market, and building positive relationships inside and outside the company
3 **structure**, as a means to provide direction, and to learn how to work better, individually and in teams.

Mark Mathews' reaction to the study is generally positive. He is both heartened and challenged by the results of the survey. He believes it is good to have solid confirmation of the things he and his team have been trying to achieve over the past five years. But, as the survey results show, there remains much to be improved.

The old manufacturing plant has 'seen its day' and it is showing its age. Also the present manufacturing and distribution facilities have been outgrown. The existence of two manufacturing sites, one dominated by the management team, does not generate a sense of 'one company together'. This might be part of the reason there exists a 'them and us' attitude between the people at each of the two sites. Mathews thinks that a new location and a new facility offer unique opportunities to address these challenges, including an opportunity for 'a new lease of life for Healtheries'.

But Mathews is concerned beyond the perceived weaknesses that the survey has uncovered. For example, he wonders, 'How will people view the new move?' He also wonders, 'How might commitment be increased? How might teamwork be made more attractive?' He knows these are not easy questions, and the answers will take some time to work through the company.

So while Mark Mathews is somewhat concerned with the future, he is also quietly enthusiastic about 'the possibilities'. He already 'sees' some new ideas that may suit the challenge for the future. He foresees a time when there may even be many more opportunities ahead for a 'renewed' Healtheries. Surely there will be many interesting and exciting times ahead for the company called Healtheries New Zealand Ltd.

7 Mills Reef Winery

If you treat people the right way in this business, you've got a customer for twenty or thirty years. That is what time and effort and being creative can bring, loyal customers and their personal ownership to the brand.

(Warren Preston, Managing Director,
Mills Reef Winery Ltd, 1996)

Introduction

Mills Reef Winery Ltd produces a range of quality grape wines for the New Zealand wine market from their new premises on Moffat Road, near Tauranga in the Bay of Plenty. Mills Reef Winery is a wholly owned subsidiary of Preston Group Ltd, a family business owned and run by family members.

Tauranga is generally unsuited to grape growing, so grapes are brought in from their own vineyard and from contract growers in the Hawke's Bay region and processed in Tauranga. Hawke's Bay, on the other hand, is renowned for its climatic and soil conditions which are ideally suited for growing grapes. With a combination of such quality grapes and the special skills of the Preston Group, Mills Reef have been able to win top awards for their premium wines.

Background

The Preston Group was initially founded in 1981 with the creation of Preston's Kiwifruit Winery. The company produced kiwifruit wines under the wine making of Paddy Preston (father) and Tim Preston (son), and achieved remarkable success with only limited experience. Warren Preston recounts the origins of the winery:

> When our company first started, there were three people: My brother [Tim Preston], my father [Paddy Preston] and myself, with perhaps one production member. It stayed at that level of employees until about 1984 when my two sisters joined us. One was involved in administration, the other in sales.

Acknowledgments This case was prepared by Michael Dance and Robert Kelman under the supervision of Bryan Poulin. Special thanks go to Warren Preston and Paddy Preston and other members of the Preston group for their input and cooperation in the preparation of this case study. This case study is to be used for the purpose of classroom discussion and not as an illustration of effective or ineffective handling of a strategic or administrative situation.

> My brother and father began by making their own kiwifruit wines. We've had help with the production methods, but we've never employed a wine maker because this is where my father's interest lies and is the reason for the company's growth to what it is. He [Paddy Preston] has been fascinated by wine making as opposed to the sales and marketing side. His expertise or interest is in the production side and I suppose that I am more from the business and sales side. It's been a reasonably good mix with everybody working in their own area without too much overlap. But, as I say, the company is sort of run on that joint basis of a committee of three.

Kiwifruit was sourced from local orchards and the wine was sold through local markets. In 1984 the company made its first export shipment to Japan, and today export and duty-free markets account for over 90 per cent of the kiwifruit wine sales. Preston's Kiwifruit Winery remains a vital part of the Preston Group, contributing over 4 per cent of total sales. Warren Preston comments that the kiwifruit wine continues to be 'the best performer at the annual kiwifruit wine makers competition, where our kiwifruit wine has been judged New Zealand's best fruit wine, not quite every year since 1983.'

Mills Reef Winery Ltd was formed in 1989 to diversify from kiwifruit wine into grape wine production. Warren Preston describes the events leading to the development of Mills Reef Winery:

> The Mills Reef or grape wine side of the business developed from my father's interest in wine making. Once he had perhaps mastered the kiwifruit wine side of things, his interest then spread as the company was more established and we had made some money from the kiwifruit wine. He then turned his attention to grape wine and expanded his interests into that, thinking it would be a good thing to do.

Mills Reef Winery Ltd (Mills Reef for short) operates as a separate business, but under the umbrella of the Preston Group organisation. There were two reasons for the development of the Mills Reef range of grape wines. First, with the experience gained from making kiwifruit wine Paddy Preston was motivated to try his skills at grape wine making. Secondly, kiwifruit wine sales had become very reliant on volatile export markets for sales. It was hoped that by selling the bulk of the grape wine on the domestic market and the kiwifruit wine on the export market this would tend to reduce overall fluctuations in demand, thus stabilising returns to the Preston Group. This new venture also allowed for greater efficiencies in production by using the same plant and equipment for making both kiwifruit wine and grape wine.

Until 1995, Mills Reef operated from the Preston Group premises in Belk Road on the lower Kaimai Range in the Bay of Plenty. But, in 1995, the scope and scale of the business had increased considerably and operations were moved to the current 20-acre (8.09-ha) site on Moffat Road in Bethlehem.

The new complex houses the company's offices and both the grape and kiwifruit wine production as well as bottling facilities. When the winery moved to Moffat Road, Mills Reef added a restaurant and a tasting room to the winery and increased the range of wines produced by Mills Reef. However, the increase in the variety of wines and the scope of operations has brought increasing complexity into the everyday management of Mills Reef. The family members are now dealing with a much broader range of issues and responsibilities and they see a requirement for new management skills and capabilities. Warren Preston comments on the development of Mills Reef from a small to medium-sized business:

> Previously when things weren't going right somewhere or you were a bit behind on something it didn't matter that much because we were a much smaller tighter-knit business, whereas now we are relying on various people to make different things work.

The new restaurant was opened in 1996 to complement the new tasting room. Together the new restaurant and tasting room have increased demands on management in terms of time and resource allocation. The restaurant is particularly resource intensive as achieving success in the restaurant industry is a difficult and demanding task. Experience is essential to success in all three areas: restaurant, kiwifruit wine and grape wine. The Prestons have had little experience in the restaurant industry. It also remains to be seen whether a significant increase in demands on time and resources is worth the modest profits and market prominence earned by the restaurant.

Staff numbers at Mills Reef have increased from an initial group of 13 people at the previous site (before 1995) to a current level of 30 at the new site. Personnel issues are now a major component of the family duties, so much so that Warren Preston has considered employing a sales-marketing manager to take on sales and marketing so that Warren can concentrate more on the role of personnel manager.

Moving to Moffat Road has also raised the profile of the company within the local wine making industry. Consequently, a need is perceived for a company figurehead to deal in high profile areas like wine tastings, national wine awards and production generally.

Reputation

The Mills Reef brand has a good reputation for a number of reasons. The combination of name, labels, awards and trophies, and the association with the picturesque Tauranga region create an inimitable set of attributes that few other wineries can match. The location and site qualities do have a number of unique features that create identifiable advantages. The Bay of Plenty is not a wine growing region, therefore there are few local competitors. This helps to differentiate Mills Reef from other New Zealand wineries in the main wine centres.

Quality of wine is determined by the quality of grapes and the wine making style. Grape quality is determined by a variety of factors including soil quality, hours of sunshine, and the maturity and condition of the grapes. Mills Reef are very good at sourcing quality grapes, and their experience, history and skills in making kiwifruit wine have been successfully employed to achieve a high level of competence in grape wine making. Many skills valuable in Prestons' Kiwifruit Winery were able to be transferred to and developed in the grape wine production under Mills Reef. In other words, the competencies which helped achieve recognition and consistent quality in kiwifruit wine making were applied to the grape wine making. The combination of these factors enable Mills Reef to produce high quality wine and gain recognition as a quality wine producer.

As consumers continue to have an increasing selection of wines to choose from, methods of differentiating Mills Reef wines from the rest of the market are becoming increasingly important. Wines must develop a strong reputation if they are to stand out from their competitors. As Warren Preston states: 'Somehow that label has to be able to stick out above the rest.'

The company sells wines under three different labels: the standard Moffat Road range; the middle-tier Reserve range; and the upper-tier Elspeth range. Distribution of the wine to the local market has been contracted out exclusively to National Liquor Distributors since 1990, with sales going to a wide variety of supermarkets and liquor stores throughout the country. International sales of Mills Reef wines began in 1991 distributing through different wine merchants in each overseas market. Today Mills Reef wines are enjoyed by consumers around the globe. The United Kingdom purchases the majority of exports, just over 70 per cent of the total. However, new markets are also being developed in Canada, Hong Kong and most recently in Japan, with the first shipment to Japan in August 1996.

Industry Information

The New Zealand wine industry is growing. Both the number of wine producers and the area of land planted in grape vines are on the increase and have been for a number of years. Membership of the Wine Institute of New Zealand is voluntary, but has increased from 131 producers in 1989 to 238 in 1996 (an 81 per cent increase in six years).

Total vine area in New Zealand has increased from 5800 hectares to 8293 hectares in the period from 1989 to 1996. Total production has increased from 54.4 million litres in 1990 to 56.5 million litres in 1996. The implications of these figures are important because vines are not harvested for grapes until at least five years after planting and the early yields are significantly smaller than yields from matured vines. Consequently, harvests from newly planted grape vines will not have an impact on the industry for a minimum of five years after planting. This implies that the dramatic growth in vine planting experienced in recent years is yet to have its full impact on the industry.

The expansion of grape vines leads to the issue of oversupply. While domestic production of wine has been steadily expanding, domestic consumption per capita has been relatively static and even declining in recent years. With no projected increases in population, consumption is unlikely to increase in the foreseeable future. So with increasing production and relatively static consumption, our domestic wine market will be oversupplied with wine.

A further consideration is trade liberalisation which has increased the volume and variety of imported wines available in New Zealand. In 1996 just over 21 million litres of wine was imported into New Zealand compared to just under 8 million litres in 1990. The prevailing strength of the New Zealand dollar means that this trend is set to continue. Foreign wines are expected to become increasingly more competitive in price against New Zealand wines, and becoming increasingly more attractive to the domestic consumer.

The overall outcome of these three forces of increasing domestic supply, static domestic consumption and increasing foreign supply is the oversupply of wine to the New Zealand wine market. Given the trend for New Zealand wineries to increase their production of wine and the oversupplied domestic market, many wineries are likely to have stocks of wine which cannot be sold in New Zealand. Furthermore, wineries are no longer allowed to hold stocks of wine tax free, and income tax is now due when the wine is produced not when it is sold. These tax changes place increasing pressures on wineries, already operating with cash flow problems, to access other wine markets where there is a demand for New Zealand wine.

An option for New Zealand wine producers is to export wine overseas. More than 250 million hectolitres of wine are produced for the international market, with New Zealand contributing less than 1.25 million hectolitres. The encouraging aspect of this for New Zealand wine producers is that exports to overseas markets have increased significantly since 1986, and these exports have extensive potential for increase. Further overseas trends indicate that the current exports are being supplied to premium segments of overseas markets.

Exporting more New Zealand wine may be one possible avenue to alleviate the effects of overproduction within the New Zealand wine industry. An especially attractive export option appears to lie with the Japanese market where the Preston Group already achieved success with kiwifruit wine and has a degree of familiarity in terms of contacts, experience and branding.

Vision, Goals and Performance at Mills Reef

The Preston Group is finding it difficult to define a shared understanding of the strategic operations of Mills Reef. Warren Preston describes the development of Mills Reef Winery and its product:

> We have never been formal goal setters with a business plan or a strategic plan written down to cover a period. Everything has just gone on and on and things have developed as we went. In the beginning it was more a case of trying to produce all the styles of wine possible and the company struggled like mad for the first three to five years. Different styles of wines were just produced, again because my father was interested in making them. Before we knew it we had too many products and the company had lost a bit of its focus.

While the main product of Mills Reef continues to be their wine, the winery has also moved into other supporting areas like the restaurant and the tasting room. Mills Reef have further plans to embark on entertainment and accommodation ventures including a motel and maybe a ballroom to add to the appeal of Mills Reef as a venue, not just a winery. While these aspirations may have a place in the firm's strategy, wine is still the basic revenue-earning unit for the company and determines the long-term success or failure of the business. Mills Reef must agree on which areas of the business are important to their long-term survival and then focus resources and energy on these areas to achieve organisational goals and obtain the greatest long-term success.

Mills Reef have two primary organisational goals. The first concerns product quality and the recognition of Mills Reef Winery as a skilled and experienced establishment. Gold medal or trophy awards are desirable as a symbol of Mills Reef's achievement of quality in wine making. The second goal is to increase the financial returns from Mills Reef to the family. Family members would like their personal incomes to reflect the success of Mills Reef in the New Zealand wine industry.

Separate from these primary goals, Mills Reef need to identify specific organisational objectives. These objectives must be derived from a sense of identity and organisational definition. Warren Preston asks, 'What is our business, what will it be and what should it be?' Once these objectives have been set, Mills Reef will be better able to increase their level of strategic awareness and envision a future direction for Mills Reef Winery. Then it will be easier to determine where resources are to be concentrated to produce the greatest success for Mills Reef.

While Mills Reef have difficulty with setting focussed objectives, management are aware of specific issues they would like included in organisational goals. Such issues include wine quality, communication, effective operations, delegation of authority, skill development and increased profitability. The financial performance of Mills Reef for the past four years (1994 to 1997) is indicated by Appendix 1 and Appendix 2.

Personnel

Mills Reef are now recognising the responsibilities of managing a group of approximately 30 employees. Warren Preston has even considered handing over other responsibilities so he can concentrate on human resources issues. Up until recently, Warren Preston has dealt with employees in an informal, ad hoc manner. However, with the increase in the number of employees, Mills Reef require some policy and procedure for dealing with routine staffing issues including job descriptions, staff training, promotion and reward systems, discipline and dismissal procedures.

It is not economical to employ a full-time human resource manager at Mills Reef because the company doesn't have the size to warrant such a position. One alternative is to hire a consulting firm for advice on hiring policy and training of employees, including an orientation programme for inducting newly hired employees into the organisation.

Structure

The fact that Mills Reef is a family business owned by family members is a very important element of Mills Reef Winery. Warren Preston attributes the success of Mills Reef to the extraordinary commitment from the family:

> It's a real sort of family business, everybody is involved with everything. The prime reason for our success was the commitment to the family company. We've had three initial key staff at the beginning and they're still all here after years where we've taken a minimal amount out of the company, perhaps just enough to live on, as opposed to being the employee of a new company who requires a full salary and everything that goes with that. It's the ability to be in survival mode for four or five years in the mid eighties that ensured our success.

There is no doubt that the family involvement is responsible for the ongoing commitment to the success of Mills Reef. However, this family atmosphere where everyone does 'what is needed' whether it is part of their formal responsibilities or not, has implications for the Mills Reef structure. The structure is very informal and unclear at the top level, and a job description for Warren, Paddy or Tim would be so broad it would be of little use to anyone. Warren Preston has many cases where employees perceive this lack of formal structure and take their concerns straight to either Warren or Paddy, rather than to their supervisor. Of course, there are many advantages of this type of structure, as Warren Preston tells us in these next words:

> Paddy, Tim and I individually get lots of calls from friends and acquaintances saying, 'I'm thinking of having this party or function at the winery.' We never say, 'You've got the wrong department,' and refer them to someone else. We take all their details and try and help them out and it gives them the feeling that they are dealing with the owner and the lines are open.

The formal structure of Mills Reef Winery is shown in Appendix 3.

Marketing

As already indicated, Mills Reef offer three different lines of wine. These are the Moffat Road range, the Reserve range, and the Elspeth range, with the Moffat Road line more affordable and the Elspeth range more of a deluxe product.

Warren Preston has identified three sets of issues relating to the marketing of these three different lines.

1 Product related issues concern the actual wine product in terms of the range offered, the variety of wines in each line, the production of a small number of specialist wines and other ways of differentiating Mills Reef wines from those of the competition.
2 Price related issues have been identified as deciding how each Mills Reef line of wines will compete on prices in their respective price brackets.
3 Promotion: where the wines will be supplied is extremely important in creating the desired image for Mills Reef. The ideal is to supply Mills Reef wines only to places which are consistent with the Mills Reef image and identity.

The distribution of the product is an area of concern highlighted by both Warren and Paddy Preston. In the past Mills Reef have sold their wines through only one distributor, and the family now wonders if they 'have been far too restrictive on where we want to be selling'. Paddy Preston says: 'I think our distribution could be improved. In fact, we are working on that right now as it has become an important issue.'

Mills Reef wines compete in a number of market segments within the grape wine market and, as Paddy Preston states, 'We can make more or less anyone happy.' While this may be true, Mills Reef needs to be able to tell whether or not buyers really are happy. Warren Preston has a clear perception of the typical buyer of Mills Reef wines but he is unable to accurately monitor the company's success in reaching these customers.

Warren Preston describes his customers this way:

> I would say the average customer is over 25, middle to high income bracket, with a definite interest in wine. This observation is due to the fact that we don't make wines in casks or provide a generic style wine, for example a 'dry red' or 'medium white'. We are selling premium quality varietal wines, so we're in a smaller market area than other producers.

However, with increasing foreign and domestic competition Mills Reef need to know not only the nature of the market for different kinds of wine, but whether the customers are satisfied and how to further satisfy these different market segments. Warren Preston identifies the lack of feedback the winery receives from the customer as an important marketing concern of Mills Reef.

Warren Preston has shown interest in the employment of a marketing manager who would be responsible for marketing strategy and brand maintenance for Mills Reef. Tasks such as organising advertising campaigns, labelling details, point of sale displays and establishing a system for market and customer research are roles which have the potential to define and improve the Mills Reef image to customers, distributors and the industry.

The Future

When Paddy Preston first came to Tauranga he did not have a clear vision of his future direction. As he said: 'We had a motel but we found that we didn't like that much.' While the family didn't like the motel business in the past, the restaurant business remains one way to increase the profile of Mills Reef wines, at least locally. But the question remains as to the compatibility of a restaurant with the long-term direction of Mills Reef Winery.

Mills Reef Winery has developed over the years from a small winery to a potential 'tourist complex', as Warren Preston tells us: 'At the former premises there wasn't a lot happening in and around the winery, it was more of a factory or production plant in comparison to this.'

Warren estimates that 30–40 per cent of the people that visit over the summer months do so because it is an entertainment alternative rather than for the love of wine. The consequence of catering to both 'tourists' and 'wine lovers' is the ongoing complexity of trying to please customers who have very different expectations of a winery. Warren Preston describes the vision:

> We have quite a bit of land here close to town, and that lends itself to all sorts of things. At the moment we have functions and weddings here consistently which interrupt the restaurant facilities. We've got an idea to build a ballroom that can take two to three hundred people, and a motel to accommodate the people who come to the functions. Only Mills Reef wines are served at the functions, and having the extra facilities around the winery enhances the whole story or concept behind the Mills Reef brand.

Distribution is another area which needs attention in the future. The first Mills Reef vintage was released in 1990 and since then the winery has sold exclusively through one national distributor. If a wine shop from Wellington was to contact Mills Reef directly for some wine they would be referred to the distributor. Warren Preston voices his concerns on this matter:

> We've been reflecting on the last four to five years and we're thinking that this has been far too restrictive on where we want to sell and what we want to be doing. A real improvement would be to change our distribution to enable direct dealing with the winery in some way.

At present, a major limitation at Mills Reef is the lack of time. Warren Preston lacks the time to perform general management duties because he finds himself continually having to deal with staff-related issues. Warren often considered employing someone else to do the job of export and sales management so he could try to become the personnel manager.

> I've listened to people over the years in different businesses say that their biggest problem was staff and it never really occurred to us in our old site with 13 employees. Now if anyone asks me where the biggest headache in the business is I say staff and training, staff expectations, what they expect from us and what we are looking for from them. This is a major area where we could do with improvement and real assistance. Finding the right people for the right job.

An opportunity for Mills Reef has arisen out of an almost accidental situation where stocks of wine have been unintentionally put away and then sold as aged wines. Most New Zealand wineries are selling current vintage wines for the sole reason of cash flow, so there are not a lot of aged New Zealand wines available. Mills Reef unintentionally put aside some 1992 Chardonnays and they were found and sold in 1997 'like a rocket'. This uncovers a potentially valuable market for aged wines, but Mills Reef face the same cash flow problems as the other wineries and aging wines requires further investment. Warren Preston outlines his intentions:

> We are trying to build a stock of older wines. When we get down to two or three hundred cases of a nice wine we'll put it down in the warehouse and just forget about it and bring it out later as a limited release.

But this is just part of the picture ahead. Warren Preston and the other senior partners of the Preston group wonder what long-term directions they should take. As Warren Preston asks, 'What overall strategy should we be pursuing and how is this to tie in with our need for a complete marketing strategy?'

Appendix 1:
Profit and Loss Statement Preston Group Ltd Years to 31 March 1994–97 ($000)

	1997 (31/3)	1996 (31/3)	1995 (31/3)	1994 (31/3)
Sales	6 505	6 251	4 812	4 260
Less				
Cost of Sales	4 251	4 280	3 300	2 919
Marketing Expenses	147	154	118	166
Vehicle Expenses	22	21	23	21
Administration Expenses	485	450	334	310
Bad Debts	7	0	0	17
Foreign Exchange Losses	6	5	13	16
Insurance	24	25	20	10
Interest	337	320	137	97
Legal Fees	1	1	8	1
Repairs & Maintenance	23	34	26	27
Depreciation & Allowances	207	200	119	117
Add				
Sundry Income valuing people	15	16	12	16
Bad Debt Recovered	0	0	14	0
Foreign Exchange Gains	8	0	0	0
Earnings Before Tax	748	776	741	565
Taxation	247	256	252	165
Net Profit	**501**	**520**	**489**	**400**

Some of these figures have been factored, for confidentiality. The ratios remain valid.

Appendix 2:
Consolidated Balance Sheet
Preston Group Ltd
Years to 31 March 1994–97 ($000)

	1997 (31/3)	**1996** (31/3)	**1995** (31/3)	**1994** (31/3)
Current Assets				
Bank	173	26	244	423
Debtors & Prepayments	683	665	638	621
Debtor – Property Sale	0	0	0	473
Inventories	1 829	1 880	973	829
Work In Progress	11	0	0	0
	2 696	2 571	1 855	2 346
Current Liabilities				
Bank Overdraft	53	255	0	4
Creditors & Accruals	714	726	1 109	631
Loans	103	102	34	21
	870	1 083	1 143	656
Fixed Assets				
Land & Buildings	3 281	3 561	2 925	1 265
Vehicles	15	19	25	33
Plant & Equipment	710	750	883	372
Investments	105	23	23	19
	4 111	4 353	3 856	1 689
Term Liabilities	1 157	1 579	552	284
Net Assets	4 780	4 262	4 016	3 095
Represented By:				
Paid Up Capital	300	300	300	300
Retained Earnings	2 605	2 104	1 584	1 095
Reserves	320	326	322	307
Shareholders Advances	1 555	1 532	1 810	1 393
Shareholders Funds	4 780	4 262	4 016	3 095

Some of these figures have been factored, for confidentiality. The ratios remain valid.

Appendix 3: Organisational Structure: Mills Reef Winery Ltd

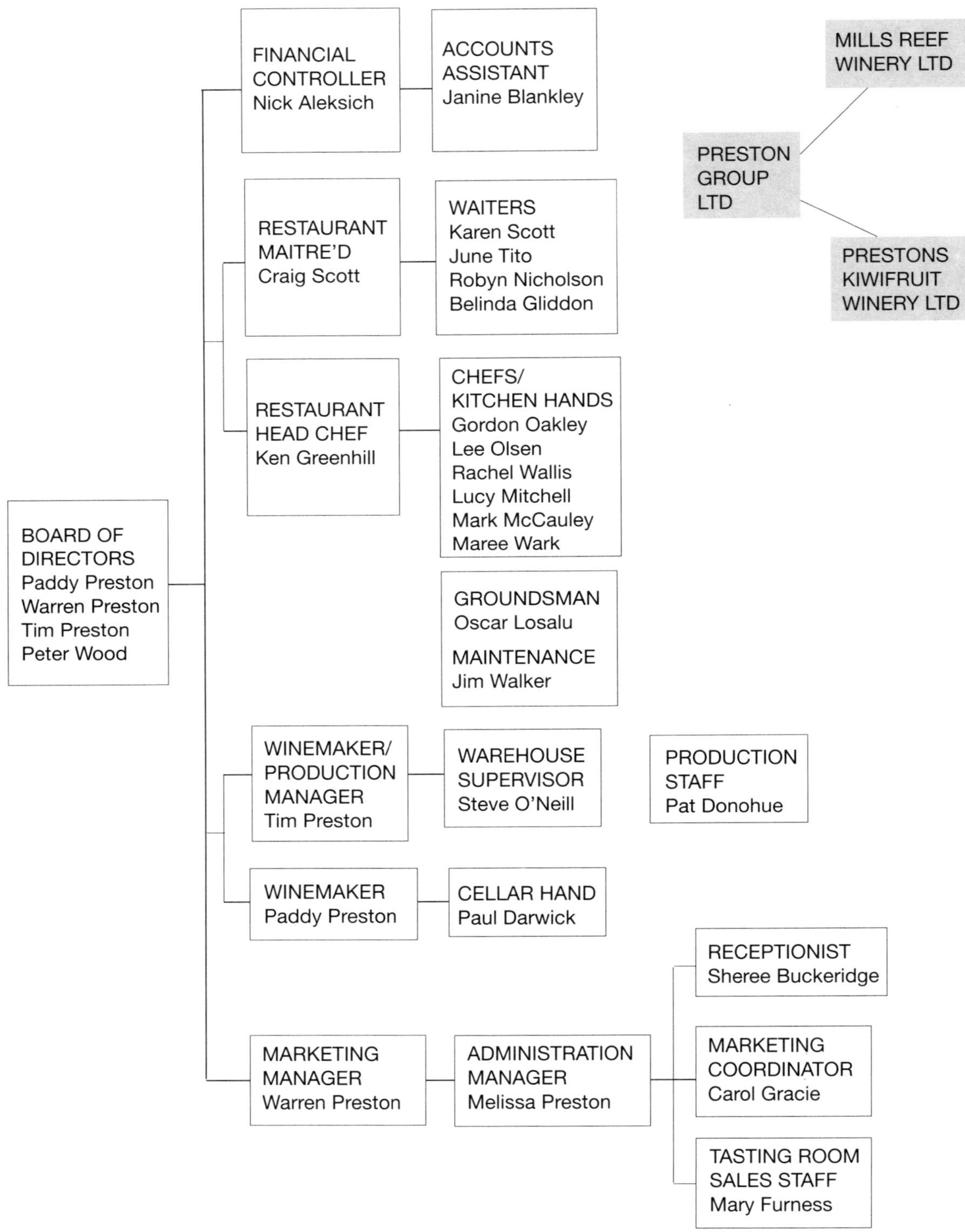

8 PEC (New Zealand)

Leadership is dynamic and could (from time to time) work against Innovation. But Culture is in the walls of the place, and we have an Innovation Culture.

(Kevin Low, 1994)

Introduction

PEC (New Zealand) Ltd is an exporting manufacturer located in the small rural town of Marton, in the south of the North Island. This case examines PEC's internal environment and its global outlook. It demonstrates how these factors enable the company to develop innovative new products and successfully compete in some of the world's more difficult markets. New product development process is at the heart of company strategy. This case study uses the 8850 project as a practical example of the strategic approach of the company.

The project is formally known as the 8850 Service Station Retail Automation System. A service station retail automation system provides 'Point-of-Sale' (POS) terminals as well as a full 'Office' management system. The product is comprehensive, suited to high traffic and multiple transactions processing for service stations and convenience stores both in New Zealand and overseas – sites that pose more challenge than a supermarket or other conventional retail situation.

The 8850 project started early in 1988, and the first trial system was installed in a Marton service station in December 1990. By 1994 annual sales of the system exceeded $17 million, and included export shipments to South Africa, Brazil, Hong Kong, Philippines, Malaysia, Singapore, Thailand and Australia. This has placed PEC near the top of the specialised management systems market worldwide. How has a small company in rural New Zealand become a global player in this part of a giant industry? The case explores company origins and examines the PEC vision, core values and beliefs, objectives and mission. The case study concludes with the explanations offered for PEC's success by Managing Director, John R. Williams.

Acknowledgments This case study was developed for teaching by Bob Mills and is based on interviews with John Williams, Managing Director, PEC and invaluable contributions from Kevin Low and Tony Dobbs. The case was originally commissioned by TRADENZ for an Innovation Leadership Programme for CEOs in the Food and Beverage Industry held at Hotel du Vin, 6/7 March 1995. The authors would like to thank PEC for their time and their willingness to share their experiences and philosophies. This case study is to be used for the purpose of classroom discussion and not as an illustration of effective or ineffective handling of a strategic or administrative situation.

The Company and Its History

The Second World War provided the impetus for PEC's first product, munitions for the Allies. The production of instruments of war was followed by the manufacture of rice ploughs for China under a United Nations contract. In 1947, oil industry products were introduced, and petrol pump manufacture followed in 1955.

John R. Williams, son of the founder, joined the company in 1963. In 1965 his father appointed him as the company's senior executive. After a few years he came to realise that the company was not in control of its own destiny, because it was a follower rather than a leader. He decided to assume a leadership role by diversifying into the new technology of solid state electronics.

In 1969, PEC introduced the coin-operated petrol pump using a design which led the world at that time, and which would significantly shape the company's future. Self-service petrol dispensing systems were launched three years later with early export sales to Australian oil companies. This initiative also helped PEC's growth over later years.

By 1975, PEC realised that microprocessors (or computers on chips) were likely to become the building blocks for future industrial products, and the company decided to introduce microprocessor technology into its products. Two years later PEC introduced the world's first microprocessor-based petrol pumps and associated self-serve consoles.

Further diversification followed when PEC's microprocessor expertise was introduced to personnel access control and alarm monitoring with the launch of its CARDAX system – now sold throughout South East Asia, the United Kingdom, Hungary, Australasia and in the Middle East.

In the UK, CARDAX is regarded as the fastest growing access control system, and its reputation has been greatly enhanced by its extensive use by London Underground and by British Post. In Australia, CARDAX has earned a reputation as the most reliable networked system, and is widely used on university campuses. In New Zealand, Telecom have probably the largest access control and alarm monitoring network in the southern hemisphere featuring the CARDAX system.

The fuel equipment business continued to provide other opportunities for innovation. In the mid 1980s PEC took note that larger service station sales room counters were cluttered with sole purpose equipment including:

- A cash register
- A self-serve console
- A 'zip-zap' plastic funds transfer card machine.

PEC realised that there was a gap in the market for a product that combined the functionality of these three devices in one box, and as a result EFPEC, the world's first integrated Service Station Point-of-Sale (POS) system, was born.

EFPEC was a world leader. Although EFPEC only sold in Australasia with minor sales to South East Asia, it was a highly successful product. A product service feature was the inclusion of a policy to regularly update software to meet the constantly changing needs of the industry, and an offer to customise software to give purchasers specific competitive advantage.

In 1988, PEC faced the option of either further developing EFPEC to extend its sales life, the 'incremental' approach, or the 'revolutionary' step of starting a new product design from scratch. The incremental approach offered a number of attractions:

1 EFPEC was selling strongly, and appeared to have a reasonable sales life ahead which could be prolonged further
2 A number of options were becoming available which would provide more processing power and overcome data storage limitations
3 The design could be re-engineered to improve its aesthetic appearance.

The risk of taking this approach was that PEC would be providing only a limited extension of life to the product. More importantly such a choice did not match PEC's desire to remain at the forefront of the world in its chosen market segments.

The revolutionary approach of starting with a clean sheet of paper required considerably more courage and commitment as well as a much larger investment. But it gave PEC the chance to leapfrog its competitors, a stance that matched PEC's Vision and Identity. The pioneering PEC 8850 System was developed.

PEC's Vision is that its customers can rely on the company to consistently deliver innovative, cost-effective solutions in time to meet their business needs anywhere in the world. All staff members are aware of this Vision, and there is a genuine belief that it influences daily decisions. PEC's Vision Statement is shown in Figure 8.1.

A statement of Core Values and Beliefs, shown in Figure 8.2, was compiled for the first time in 1992, but John Williams, the managing director, and the management team believe that PEC has been influenced by those principles ever since his father started the company in 1939. The statement defines a truly 'family' environment, and Williams firmly believes this to be the ideal (and perhaps only) environment in which the innovative ideas of all staff members can be expressed, fairly evaluated, and the best suggestions incorporated in new products, services and upgrades. Williams emphasises the importance of creating a company structure in which everyone with a good idea will be heard. He wholeheartedly agrees with Penny de Valk, general manager of the New Zealand Institute of Management in Auckland, who said in an article in *Management* magazine: 'Success today requires us to use every scrap of talent, creativity and commitment and that calls for a different kind of management'.

In Williams' opinion the most important factors in ensuring that all those 'scraps of talent, creativity and commitment' are extracted, evaluated and used are:

1 a 'family' atmosphere'
2 the highest quality communications: within the organisation (both locally and overseas), with subsidiary companies and distributors and of course with customers
3 a flat organisational structure.

Figure 8.1 PEC's Vision

To have PEC's customers regard it as the company they rely upon to consistently deliver innovative, cost-effective solutions in time to meet their business needs anywhere in the world.

(1 January 1994)

Figure 8.2 PEC's Core Values and Beliefs

Above all else we value our staff members. We trust and empower them, and accept our responsibility to assist continually with their development.

We are committed to providing such a high quality environment at PEC that our staff members regard the company as one of New Zealand's best employers.

We go to great lengths to build a strong family environment at PEC.

We enjoy hard work, and working in effective teams.

Participative decision making forms a cornerstone of our relationships at PEC.

We expect and reward superior performance from our staff members.

We believe in sharing PEC's profits fairly with our staff members.

We value our customers – especially our existing customers. We strive to ensure that everything we do for our customers always meets, and regularly exceeds, their expectations.

We are committed to quality:

- quality of product
- quality of service
- quality of relationships between our staff members, and with our customers
- quality of our communications
- and the quality of our promises.

We believe in growth for ourselves and for PEC.

Innovation is vital for PEC's growth, and we shall constantly work to enhance our innovative environment that has been, and always will be, a prime reason for PEC's success.

Profit is the life blood of our organisation. Whilst it is not the sole goal of our efforts at PEC, we must be an efficient, productive and profitable business, or else we limit our ability to meet the needs of our staff members, our customers, the company and of society.

We are committed to the highest standards of ethics and integrity. Our interactions with customers, suppliers, governments and the general public must always reflect the high standard we profess.

(1 January 1994)

Figure 8.3 PEC's Objectives

PEC provides a framework to empower staff members to design, manufacture and market solutions which generate sufficient profit for:

Staff members to consider PEC to be one of New Zealand's best employers

PEC's staff members to be provided with the opportunity for:

- innovation
- challenge
- achievement
- responsibility
- recognition
- and advancement

PEC's shareholders to be fairly rewarded.

PEC to be regarded as a good corporate citizen.

(1 January 1994)

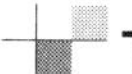

The Industry and the Environment

For some years the New Zealand banking system has provided one of the most secure data transfer systems in the world. This has meant the early adoption of this data transfer route for secure funds transfer by New Zealand's retail systems developers. Early development has given these system developers a commanding position in Australasia and the international market. A further unique feature of Australasia is the actual ownership of petrol station assets by leading oil companies rather than individuals. This means that retail system businesses can land multiple site deals and spread product development over an adequate volume to contain unit costs.

Competition between industry leaders PEC and Task Technology for the business of the four oil industry giants in New Zealand is fierce and has added an edge to the competitive spirit. The business is attractive and is eyed regularly by would-be newcomers.

Until the nineties New Zealand manufacturers had a comparative advantage in export because of the country's relatively low exchange rate. Recently New Zealand currency has been appreciating relative to Australia, the US and European and some Asian countries.

Internationally, New Zealand has enjoyed a good reputation as a reliable supplier. And since the deregulation of the economy, starting in the mid 1980s, New Zealand manufacturers have played a larger role in the Asia Pacific markets.

The PEC 8850 Retail Automation System Development

Market Research

Market research for the revolutionary PEC 8850 Retail Automation System was conducted on several fronts concurrently. Market research included customer research, industry research and technological research.

PEC's staff members have fostered very close relationships with key retail automation people in the head offices of a number of oil companies over many years. These connections enabled PEC to arrange many discussion sessions, both in New Zealand and overseas, with leading thinkers in the retail automation field whose views were respected within the worldwide oil industry.

PEC had to investigate whether it was possible to ensure that the different requirements of the world's major oil companies could be met or exceeded in a single design. PEC's size and scale did not give the company the luxury of providing widely differing product ranges, and considerable ingenuity would be required to satisfy the widely differing requirements within a single basic hardware design. One of the major factors in the success of 8850 internationally has been that PEC marketers were able to convince influential people in the major oil companies that they all contributed important architecture and features of the new product. Some felt real 'ownership' of the design.

John Williams asserts:

> I cannot emphasise enough the importance of implanting this feeling of ownership with key influential people, at the earliest possible stage of a development. There is no better way for a company to demonstrate that it listens to its customers than for it to produce what key customers have asked for. By playing one's cards with care it is possible to have some of these key people believe that you have taken the trouble to develop the product especially for each of them. As an illustration of the effect that one key person's ownership can have on the sales of a new product, I can tell you that we are now selling 8850s in a particular and totally new market to us, solely because a senior person in the international head office of an oil company believed that we designed 8850 to meet his particular needs. PEC's 8850 orders from this new market in 1994 exceeded $3.5 million.

At the outset, PEC recognised the potential for explosive growth in service station stores. This was both because service systems were changing rapidly, moving from selling fan belts and radiator hoses to the wide range of products that are sold today, and because such a shift had been anticipated by PEC staff members. PEC had anticipated that oil industry service station 'shops' would be involved in increased sales of petrol as well as increasingly becoming like sophisticated speciality stores, department stores and supermarkets. Therefore the 8850 system had to deliver the requirements of a comprehensive and efficient convenience outlet which sold increasingly diverse products at higher volumes.

As it was recognised that considerable advances had taken place in the retail sector, outside the oil industry, it was decided that the 8850s 'product champion' Brendon Deere, then Manager of the Retail Division and a director of PEC, should attend the World Retail Conference held in New Orleans in 1989.

The speaker whose presentation made most impact on Deere strongly emphasised that retailers would demand increasingly to have control of their own data and to have access to much more 'open architecture' systems than were available at that time. This address, which had such an influence on both the hardware and software architecture of the 8850, was probably the single most important influence on the success of the product from a technical point of view.

Many other features and ideas were gained and incorporated into the 8850 as a direct result of Deere's attendance at that 1989 conference. This example clearly illustrates the point that companies must be completely aware of what their own competitors and companies in similar industries are doing before embarking on new product development.

The great breadth of experience of PEC staff in many fields, and their knowledge of the latest developments gained from reading selected technical magazines and attendance at seminars in New Zealand and overseas, enabled technological advances and options to be studied that would support, rather than dictate, the 8850s architecture. This was seen as critical to the success of the 8850 which had to be driven by market factors and not just by technology.

The 8850 Cross Functional Team and Its Work

The design specification for 8850 was formulated by a cross functional team of 10 members consisting of a mixture of marketing, hardware and software staff members. Their enthusiasm, innovation, ability, motivation, team spirit and willingness to listen to the ideas of people, within and outside the team, proved invaluable to the project.

One of their starting points was to carry out a detailed SWOT Analysis (Strengths, Weaknesses, Opportunities and Threats) on the older EFPEC product, and this produced some excellent pointers about what to include and eliminate in the new 8850 design.

As an illustration, it was found that the majority of EFPEC service faults in both Australia and New Zealand were caused by faulty connectors, even though PEC had a policy of purchasing the very best quality gold-plated connectors. It was therefore decided to use as few connectors as possible in the new 8850 design.

The 8850 team members thoroughly investigated their own ideas and those suggested by others. The final 8850 design included virtually everything that anyone had ever wished to have included in the new product, even with hindsight. The fact that PEC are today still selling large quantities of virtually the same product, albeit with many added software enhancements, demonstrates the comprehensive nature of the initial design. The team spirit grew.

John Williams observes:

> I never cease to be amazed by the enthusiasm that the majority of teams at PEC have for their projects, enthusiasm that often means that some members work all through the night and weekends, both here and overseas, so that critical project dates or customer expectations (many of which are totally unreasonable!) are achieved. The decision to work these ridiculous hours is theirs alone, not their supervisors' and certainly not mine. The decisions are made, in my opinion, because they have been empowered (a hackneyed word, but there is no other to use) to complete a task on a date agreed with a customer, and they decide that on some occasions making unrealistic demands of themselves and of their families is justified.

EFPEC was basic and functional. It lacked the immediate impact of products incorporating the latest and best industrial design. The aesthetic appearance had taken a distant second place to the clever technology. PEC decided that, since the

8850 was to be a revolutionary product, it had to look revolutionary. A leading New Zealand industrial designer was duly employed in order to bring impact and life to the product's external appearance.

The designer's brief was to design an aesthetically pleasing product that minimised valuable shop counter space and had a modern, perhaps slightly futuristic appearance. A key design element was the insistence on clean lines, an especially difficult constraint given the multitude of attached cables associated with equipment of this nature.

Innovative touches, such as having all cables exit underneath the console, ensured that 8850 was (and still is) the tidiest and most professional looking product of its type in the market, anywhere in the world.

8850 Marketing

The international marketing of the 8850 system was notable for the successful and innovative decisions taken by the team.

The Amazing Effect Achieved By Showing a Customer a Wooden Box!

About midway through the development process, PEC became aware that one of the international oil companies was showing interest in a competitor's system. Unlike the food industry, the high-tech product industry is besieged by suppliers who actively promote what is often referred to as 'vapourware' – new products that are 'about to be released', a good percentage of which never arrive. PEC didn't want to be branded as one of the 'vapourware' brigade, and yet felt it was vital that potential customers were brought up to date with progress on the 8850 development.

The team finally decided to send a member to the other side of the world to meet the customer. To assist with 'selling' the fact that a revolutionary product was well on its way, it was decided to commission a wooden model of the striking console, so that it could be shown during the 8850 discussion.

PEC were amazed by the effect that the block of wood had on the customer. Because the external appearance of the product looked so professional, the customer immediately jumped to the conclusion that the internal electronics and software would also be of the same high standard. It was an assumption that amazed and obviously delighted PEC, and it emphasised something not to be forgotten – the tremendous importance external appearance has in persuading potential customers of the quality of the contents.

Customer selection

Six months away from launching the 8850 a final decision was needed about where, how and to whom the product would be marketed.

This is probably the most important decision that had to be taken in the project. It was felt that the way to make the most informed decision was to send the Team Leader, Brendon Deere, around the world on another fact-finding mission. After spending a month away, his recommendation was that the company should market 8850 only in the southern hemisphere, and focus on only two of the 'seven sisters' (the seven major international oil companies).

The key point to emphasise is that PEC chose where to market its product and to whom it would be sold. PEC selected and focused on potential worldwide customers and markets. John Williams says:

> Many companies do not realise the vital importance that customer selection has on product positioning. I suggest that all new product development teams must be charged with the responsibility to make such recommendations – if not decisions.

John Williams explains that the company selected the southern hemisphere because PEC felt that it would be very difficult to break down the bonds established in developed markets over many years between, say, a German oil company and their traditional German supplier of rudimentary retail automation equipment, even if PEC's product was a significantly superior and revolutionary one.

In the southern hemisphere, however (with the exception of Australasia where PEC were well known and represented), service stations had no automation equipment at all, just simple cash registers. It was felt that the marketing challenge in the southern hemisphere would be somewhat easier.

PEC decided to focus on only two of the major international oil companies because they were very concerned about their own ability to provide a level of professional customer service to more than two customers. Williams recalls that the result was the 'Chaos' that Tom Peters wrote about (in *Thriving on Chaos*, 1988) except that Williams depicted it as a stimulating challenge:

> We were forced to double our Retail Department staff numbers and to increase our overall staff numbers by over 60 per cent within a two-year period. That was not an enjoyable experience because it is not possible to grow at that rate and still have sufficient 'experienced' staff members around.

Company Structure

PEC's management team consists of 11 managers. Below the managers are team leaders and staff members.

John Williams does not always chair the management meetings; chairmanship is rotated among managers and team leaders. Williams sees this as one of the most effective ways to make senior executives and the CEO himself aware that the majority of his or her time is as a coach and not as the Supreme Commander of Operations. Another worthwhile spin-off of this management approach is that it forces much wider dissemination of information among key executives. Meetings are more efficient because everyone, and not just the CEO, has to know what is going on and what the issues are.

In Williams' opinion, a CEO can only be successful if he or she is regarded by their staff members as just another member of the team – an important one certainly, but not one whose view has to be accepted just because it was his or her idea. Consequently, PEC's structure greatly assists the upward transfer of innovative suggestions, and the flow of information in both directions, so that any good idea from any PEC staff member will be given the chance to be evaluated. This means a flat, not a hierarchical, structure.

Williams summarises the PEC attitude to company structure:

> In order to succeed and be more innovative, you have no option, in my opinion, but to abandon hierarchical structures within your organisation with the greatest urgency. It won't be easy, because middle management will resent their loss of authority. In future your staff members at all levels will demand to be listened to, so do it first, before the best of them leave, and before those that remain impose a solution upon you that is not to your liking!

The PEC Way

PEC believe the company leads the world with innovative products in its three product sectors. How does PEC achieve this – and from the small country town of Marton, New Zealand?

John Williams espouses the following reasons:

1 PEC staff members belong to one of the of the most innovative nations in the world – New Zealand. As a corollary, the most discerning and hardest to please customers in the world are New Zealand companies, followed some distance behind by Australians. So, although PEC people find the going difficult in Australasia, they are constantly comforted by the fact that if they are finally able to satisfy a New Zealand or Australian customer, then they will have produced a world-leading product.

2 New Zealand has the fastest growing economic region in the world on its doorstep – South East Asia/Asia.

3 PEC encourages a 'family' atmosphere. Excellent communication, within PEC through its structure and with its distributors and customers worldwide, ensures that every good idea that is around is 'extracted', and fairly evaluated.

4 The company has established a Vision, Core Values and Beliefs, and Mission (or Missions if a company has a number of diverse divisions), and ensures that all staff are aware of these and the reasons behind them. In Williams' opinion, this is the best way in which to have all staff members pulling in the same direction and thinking about ideas that could benefit the company. (PEC's missions are shown in Figure 8.4.)

5 Customer and industry research is crucial, including thorough study of the all important trends in each product sector.

6 An analysis of previous product success or failure is always undertaken. Often teams want to get on with the new challenge and forget that a wealth of information from past success or failure is available.

7 The company should ensure that new products give the first impression that it expects customers to retain. John Williams believes investment in the external appearance of products is always repaid.

8 John Williams believes that innovation behaviour should not be left to product designers. Marketing, distribution and service contribution is becoming increasingly important. It is important to ensure that marketers are fairly represented on the product development teams and are challenged to search for innovative approaches.

Figure 8.4 PEC's Missions

Retail Systems Division
To be in a position to supply our oil industry solutions anywhere in the world by end 1998, to meet the current and future needs of our customers.

(14 September 1993)

CARDAX Division
To ensure that CARDAX is recognised as the world's best professional, integrated security system by end 1995, and that in our chosen markets, profitable sales with annual growth rates of around 30 per cent are achieved until the end of this decade.

(7 December 1993)

Petrol Pump Division
To extend PEC's pump sales beyond Australasia by the introduction of new, innovative designs – profitable sales to these markets to exceed $5 million by end 1996.

(15 February 1994)

The Future

Sales at PEC have gone from $5.7 to almost $19 million in the period 1992 to 1994; the sales trends of products is shown in Figure 8.6. Exports in 1994 accounted for 80 per cent of PEC's sales, and all new product specifications are prepared with the needs and expectations of export customers in mind. The European service station market still awaits the introduction of a system similar to PEC. US banks have found it difficult to securely send financial data through the EFTPOS system, let alone add the extra information that is at the heart of the PEC 8850 system. So the window of opportunity for the world-class 8850 product is still open.

Figure 8.5 PEC's Sales Trends (1992 to 1994)

Product/Services	1992	1993	1994
Petrol Pumps	100	264	233
Point of Sale Equipment	133	300	554
Security Access Control	68	33	208
Totals	**301**	**597**	**995**

The figures used are based on dollar sales value and have been factored to provide an indication of the trends.

PEC chose its core technology, the 486 motherboard platform, wisely and has capitalised on this advantage. But more than marketability and technical merit, PEC stresses that a product should 'delight' the customer to the extent they forget the others. For example, all software written by the company for use in its products must now be capable of being easily modified by the customer so that it can display and print data in any required language. Securing technology patents has been superseded by putting effort into design copyrighting. Software is more difficult to deal with but burying it in the hardware and committing themselves to rapid, continuous development allows the company to stay ahead. The Appendix lists PEC's critical success factors, ranked according to criticality.

New Zealand has the 'toughest market in the world'; PEC have used it to develop products that fuel their future. There is no doubt that PEC products have been successful in the past. The key questions for the future include how PEC is to manage its rapid growth and determine what kind of people, managers included, the company needs to attract to ensure success in the long term.

Appendix: PEC's Critical Success Factors

Critical Success Factors	Criticality
Listening to customers views on their future product needs	5
Atmosphere that encourages and rewards innovation	5
Defined medium-term plan and regular updates	5
Continuous high level of investment in R&D – new products and enhancements of existing products	5
Importance of high quality management	4
Continuous drive for improved quality systems	4
Extensive niche market knowledge	4
Up-to-date technology knowledge	4
Desire to employ and retain high performing staff	4
Knowledge of importance of recognition and reward for discretionary effort by staff members	4
Desire to consistently meet and exceed customer needs and expectations	4
Creation of high quality people relationships – internal and external	4
High quality communications between people – internal and external	4
Commitment to be world's best in chosen market niches	4
Team spirit – family atmosphere	3
Recognition of the vital importance of staff training – inhouse and external	3
Importance of company and product positioning at the 'professional end' of the market	3
Importance of provision of high quality after-sales service and support	3
Insistence on highest quality industrial design – especially aesthetics	2

Subway Hamilton Central

I wanted to get into the fast-food industry but I wanted to get in on the healthy aspect because I felt that was where the eating trends were going.

(Mike Carroll, Subway Hamilton Central, 1997)

Introduction

Mike Carroll is Owner-Operator of the Subway Sandwiches franchise that is located in the central retail area of Hamilton (hence Subway Hamilton Central). Carroll comments on the Subway Sandwiches and Salads (Subway) fast-food franchise operation:

> There is not a lot of planning. Subway is in 55 different countries now and prior to that they were only really in America. Subway outlets are not as well prepared as they should be. There is not the market research that a McDonald's or a Burger King does, and therefore it is left very much up to the Development Agents and the franchisees in each country to make it work. It has grown basically out of interest in the idea. I am not the only one to recognise healthier eating trends.

Subway's 'appetite for growth', both in the domestic (US) market and international markets, has propelled the franchisor to become one of the largest fast-food restaurants in the world. The relative size of fast-food restaurants, by number of outlets, is shown as Figure 9.1.

The phenomenal growth of Subway (see Figure 9.2 for growth of stores) is part of an aggressive mission:

> We feel it is important to gain as much market share as possible. Our mission is to equal and exceed the number of outlets operated by the largest fast-food company in every market that it enters. (Subway promotional material, 1997, http://www.subway.com)

Acknowledgments This case was prepared by Simon Bowers and supervised by Bryan Poulin from personal interviews and other information gathered in an investigation for Subway Hamilton Central. The case is to be used as a basis for classroom discussion rather than to illustrate either effective or ineffective handling of an organisational situation. Cooperation of Michael Carroll of Subway Hamilton Central is gratefully acknowledged in the preparation of this case.

Figure 9.1 Largest Worldwide Fast-Food Restaurants (by number of stores 1996)

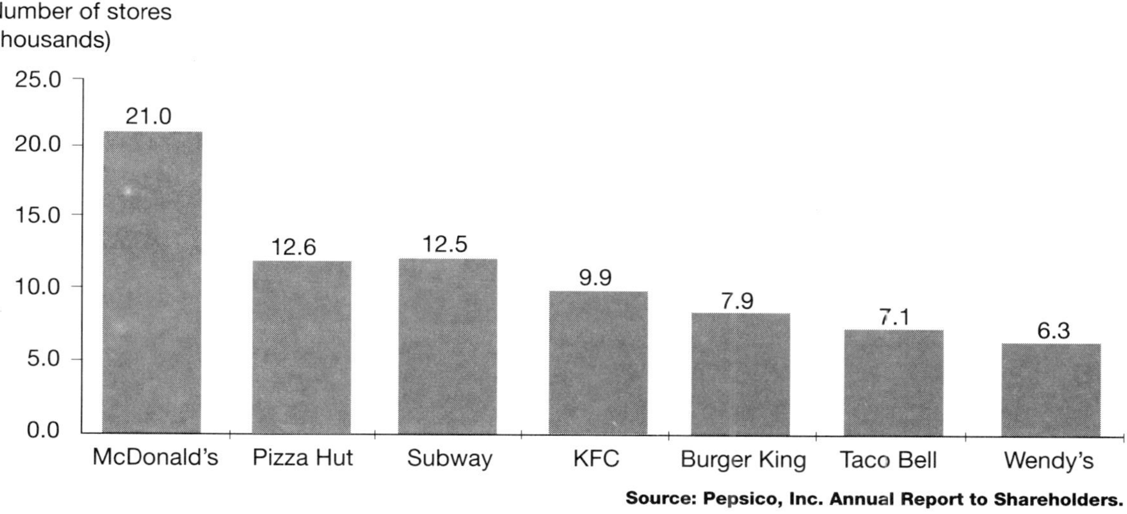

Source: Pepsico, Inc. Annual Report to Shareholders.

Figure 9.2 Growth of Subway Sandwiches and Salads restaurants

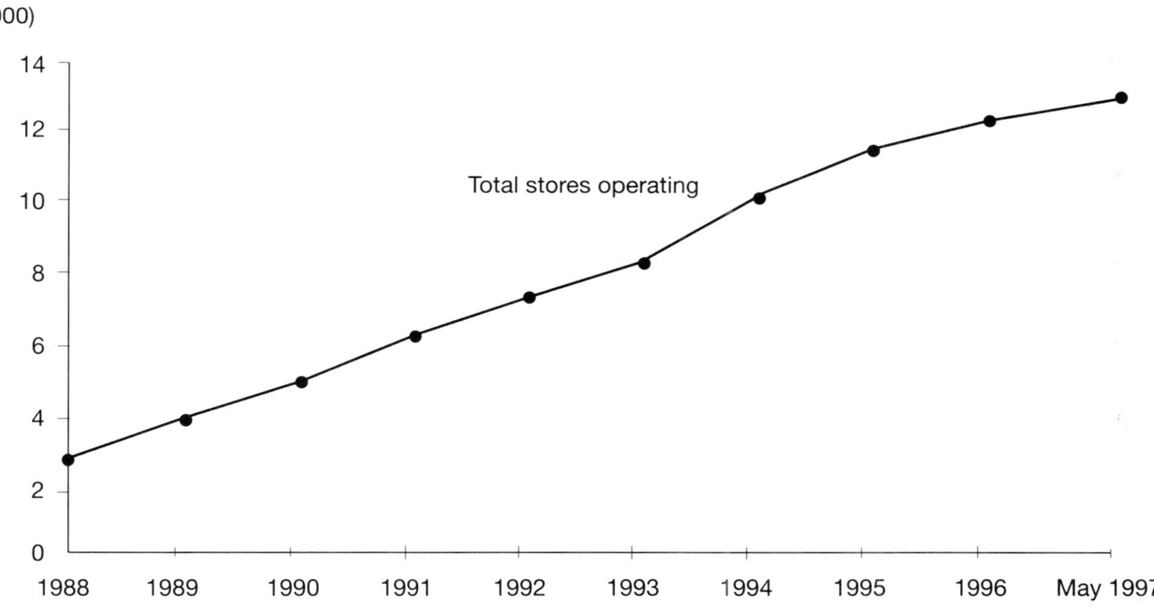

Figure 9.3 International Subway Locations as of 1 May 1997

Country	Stores	Country	Stores
Argentina	2	Jamaica	2
Aruba	3	Japan	154
Australia	112	Jordan	3
Austria	3	Kuwait	1
Bahamas	8	Lebanon	2
Bahrain	1	Mexico	23
Brazil	48	Netherlands Antilles	5
British West Indies	2	New Zealand	13
Canada	1 181	Nicaragua	1
China	2	Paraguay	1
Colombia	3	Peru	2
Costa Rica	8	Philippines	2
Cyprus	1	Portugal	12
Denmark	1	Saudi Arabia	2
Dominican Republic	3	Singapore	2
Ecuador	2	South Africa	1
Egypt	1	South Korea	14
El Salvador	8	Spain	12
England	3	Switzerland	5
French West Indies	1	Taiwan	2
Greece	2	Thailand	1
Guatemala	1	Turkey	1
Honduras C.A.	2	United States	11 044
Iceland	4	Uruguay	2
Indonesia	5	US Virgin Islands	5
Ireland	3	Venezuela	3
Israel	20	West Indies	1
		Zimbabwe	1
Total: 12,747 stores in 55 countries.			

Subway's Early US history

Subway started in 1965 when Fred DeLuca, a 17-year-old high school graduate, was trying to raise money to fund his university tuition. In August 1965, a nuclear physicist and a close family friend, Dr Peter Buck, suggested that Fred open a sandwich shop to help pay his tuition. Dr Buck had seen the success of a sandwich shop in his home state of Maine and he believed that a similar venture could prove successful in Connecticut. Less than one month later, with the help of a $1000 loan from Dr Buck, Fred DeLuca opened the first shop, Pete's Super Submarines. On 28 August 1965, Pete's Super Submarines sold its first freshly made 'footlong' sandwich.

However, the summer business was considerably slower than anticipated. In fact, at the end of one particular business day, Dr Buck and DeLuca stared gloomily at $6.00 in total sales in the cash register. DeLuca saw the obvious solution as cutting their losses and closing the store. Dr Buck had another idea.

He asked, 'What if the way to make the business profitable was to open another store? Then customers would see us growing and the stores would become better known.'

It was at this point that both men realised that market impact and visibility would be as important to their success as the product offering. A second store was opened and, while not yet profitable, the venture looked more promising. Soon a third store was opened, in a more visible location, and the partnership started making money. The trademark yellow logo was introduced and the original name 'Pete's Super Submarines' was shortened to 'Subway'. No longer would they rely on the weekly meetings in the DeLuca family kitchen to form the 'strategic' direction of the business. The company's goals were outlined in a long-term business plan.

The first step of the plan was ambitious. It involved the objective of opening 32 stores in the first 10 years of operation. But with only 16 stores opened by 1974, Dr Buck and DeLuca realised the company would not reach their objective. The partners decided that the best way to increase the number of stores would be to franchise.

The first Subway franchise opened in Wallingford, Connecticut in 1974. Subway soon reached the goal of 32 stores and immediately set the new objective of 200 stores, which was reached in 1981. International expansion began in 1984 when a store was opened off the coast of Saudi Arabia in the island country of Bahrain. The next objective was to have 5000 stores operating by 1994, a target easily reached in 1990.

McDonald's: The Fast-Food Industry Benchmark

International expansion has been part of an internal growth emphasis for fast-food chains since McDonald's Restaurants first began 'exporting' its fast-food restaurants worldwide in the early 1970s. A pioneer in international fast-food retailing operations, McDonald's believed international markets offered a considerable opportunity for their well-developed franchise system. However, unlike those of the US markets which had at least some experience with fast-food restaurants, many international markets had never tasted a hamburger or had an experience at a quick-service restaurant. Therefore McDonald's found itself in the position where their people were 'educating' these markets on the concept of eating out at a fast-food restaurant. As reported in a recent book on McDonald's Restaurants:

> We just ploughed dumbly ahead using the same old system that we had in the US. It was like reliving history. (Cameron, 1995: *McDonald's Behind The Arches*, p. 416.)

Fundamental to McDonald's international success has been the ability to successfully transfer their standardised franchising system. The system is based on a philosophy that stresses four factors: quality, service, cleanliness, and value (QSCV). While initially supported by the US operations, McDonald's International planned and built the infrastructure which is now the basis of their global operations. Their worldwide system enables 'global purchasing' driven by large economies of scale.

In 1996, McDonald's International sales accounted for 59 per cent of total operating income, an increase of 20 per cent from 1992. International sales are projected to grow at a rate of 20 per cent per year compared to only 5 per cent in the US domestic market. As 80 per cent of international income is concentrated in only seven countries, McDonald's believes there is considerable potential for further growth.

International expansion has not only established the McDonald's name in over 100 countries, it also has helped develop an international fast-food market that major competitors such as Subway are rapidly entering.

The New Zealand Fast-Food Industry

Statistics appear to reinforce the relative 'under-development' of the New Zealand market when compared to overseas markets. The current penetration of branded fast-food restaurants in the New Zealand market is one unit per 10,600 people as compared to one for every 7900 Australians and one for every 2700 Americans.

This potential market growth is further supported by the fact that only 14 per cent of all meals in New Zealand are prepared outside of the home as compared to 22 per cent in Australia and 47 per cent in the US. Statistics New Zealand figures report that the ready-to-eat foods market increased by 10.6 per cent in 1995 following increases of 9 per cent and 30 per cent in the previous two years. Consumer expenditure, by year, is shown in Figure 9.4.

Figure 9.4 Consumer Expenditure on Cafes, Restaurants & Takeaways (New Zealand)

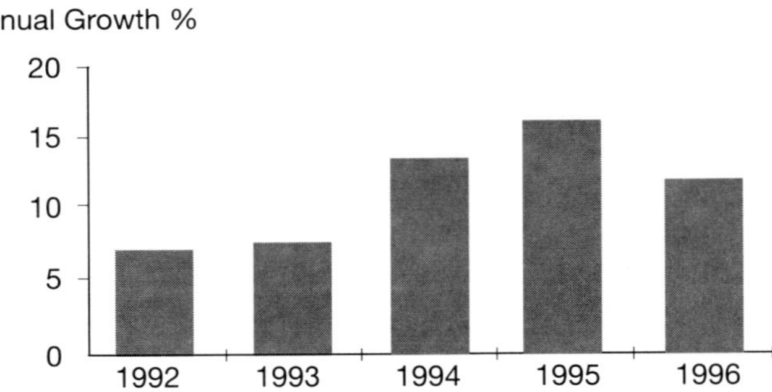

Source: New Zealand Department of Statistics.

Increases and expenditure are encouraging. However, it is interesting to note the following forecast for 1997 by one New Zealand restaurant analyst:

> We don't foresee any major lift in the market in 1997, as many of the same factors are influencing the market as last year; we also expect more direct and indirect competition will continue to emerge in fast-food solutions. We believe interest rates will rise later this year, affecting mortgage rates, and that, coupled with the change to the planned tax cuts (postponed) this year, will certainly serve to put an upward lid on market growth.

Competitors and Marketing

The fast-food market is extremely competitive, with the large franchises spending a considerable amount on advertising, in particular television advertising, to attract customers. For example, McDonald's has spent more on television advertising for the last four years than any other company in New Zealand. It is estimated that short-term sales and product promotions, promotional offers, brand positioning, community support, causes related to marketing and new product launches has cost McDonald's over $12 million in advertising in 1996.

Targeting the family market, McDonald's is unquestionably the market leader in New Zealand with a turnover of approximately $260 million in 1996 from 120 restaurants nationwide. As is the case in many of its markets overseas, the sheer size of McDonald's tends to create its own market, with New Zealand suppliers now exporting over $20 million of food-related goods and services overseas. With such large volumes, McDonald's have considerable purchasing power over local suppliers to make them competitive. Such advantages are not shared by small or new franchisors such as Subway.

However, the relatively recent entry of Wendy's to New Zealand has proven that a large advertising budget and competitive clout are not always necessary to gain market impact. 'Winning gold' in the 1996 retail category for advertising effectiveness, Wendy's employed a strategy of differentiating itself from competitors by focusing on one key attribute, quality. Wendy's thereby avoids a strictly 'pricing' approach to competition. In this way, Wendy's have consistently communicated their strengths without having to spend large amounts of money.

Subway Operations in New Zealand

Subway entered the New Zealand market in 1995 with the first franchise opened by development agents as a kind of pilot project. By the end of 1995, two additional franchise outlets were opened in Auckland. Subway Hamilton Central was the first franchise outside of Auckland and it opened in Hamilton in May 1996. There are now currently 13 stores throughout New Zealand, with a further five stores planned in the next six months. Mike Carroll gives his reasons for opening a Subway franchise in the city of Hamilton (population 100,000):

> I wanted to get into the fast food industry, but I wanted to get in on the healthy aspect because I felt that was where eating trends were going. People are more conscious of the amount of fat in their diets.

Although Subway is now the second largest food chain in the world, by number of outlets (having just overtaken Pizza Hut), the decision to enter the New Zealand market has certainly brought considerable challenges. Carroll explains:

> The key thing affecting our sales is brand awareness and brand recognition. That will come with the number of stores reaching critical mass. When we reach our critical mass, 20 stores, we will have that added purchasing power we need to be able to advertise on national television.

Carroll has found food ingredient costs (in the production of sandwiches) in New Zealand are 38–40 per cent of retail sales. In the US food ingredients are only 28 per cent of sales. Mike Carroll expects an increase in purchasing power over the next year will help reduce these costs to around 30 per cent.

The National Advertising Fund Trust, which takes a levy of 2.5 per cent of each franchisee's sales, will be initially used in television advertising to promote the Subway brand identity. Carroll believes that the New Zealand market needs advertising that 'introduces' Subway to the market rather than 'keeping the brand in the minds of existing customers' which is the focus of US advertising. This difference may be because Subway already has a strong market presence in the US.

McDonald's, Burger King, KFC and Pizza Hut outlets have a significant market presence in New Zealand with large advertising expenditure and numerous outlets. Steve Burns, Research Director of Syndicated Services, a research service, believes that 'the key elements in enticing customers to frequent a chain involve brand image and development.' He suggests that 'the fast food market has developed from being product-orientated to service-orientated'. He goes on to state, 'more specifically, convenience, product value and industry experience are important factors in a chain's success'.

While advertising and market development may help increase Subway's profile, the key determinants of success appear to be the underlying factors for all quick-service restaurants – food quality, menu variety, value, service, cleanliness and convenience and perhaps two energising factors of food safety and nutrition. Such factors have driven fast-food restaurant success around the world. Mike Carroll believes that Subway New Zealand's competitive advantage will exist only when it develops these factors in a way that is different from that of its competitors.

Performance

Because Subway Hamilton Central has only been operating for a year, annual financial reports are not available. Mike Carroll considers his early financial performance could be misleading and, as such, he is not keen to share details at this time. The restaurant is only now approaching profitability at the end of its first year of operation. The volume of sales may not be increasing in Hamilton at the same rate as New Zealand sales nationally. Subway Hamilton Central's location in downtown Hamilton is good from a visibility standpoint, with high-profile stores in the vicinity. Subway is across the street from the Village 7 multiplex cinema and around the corner from discount retailer The Warehouse. Burger King is nearby and McDonald's is just one street away. However, the difficulty with the location is the lack of foot traffic. People simply do not walk past Subway in great numbers. Parking in front of the store is also scarce.

Mike Carroll is committed to making the restaurant profitable, despite the higher than expected costs of running the franchise. His main areas of concern are labour, rent, and food costs, which currently account for about 80 per cent of gross sales as compared to approximately 58 per cent in the United States. Combined with an 8 per cent royalty fee to Subway, and the 2.5 per cent national advertising fee, as well as administration costs such as insurance, New Zealand stores including Hamilton Central are struggling to break even. Ingredient costs are the single most expensive area, and variance is highest against competitors. Carroll is seeking ways of purchasing ingredients at more favourable prices from suppliers but this remains one of two outstanding areas of concern for Subway Hamilton Central. The other is the brand awareness concern already mentioned.

Co-branding Possibilities

One possible way of increasing brand awareness is co-branding. Co-branding is the development of stores in non-traditional locations with the assistance of another branding partner. Presently, the largest partner for Subway fast-food franchises are convenience stores (usually attached to large-scale, branded petrol stations). Over 1700 Subway Sandwiches and Salads outlets in the US have been opened with branded convenience stores in the last three years. This 'partnership' is a form of co-branding, as the following extract from a 1996 newsletter from *Thomas Food Industry Register* illustrates:

> Co-branding is the practice of uniting two businesses with complementary aims for the mutual benefit of both parties. It is a concept that has been around for some time but only recently has it saturated the food industry as a marketing technique.

The advantages of co-branding for fast-food outlets is that they can team up with a convenience store owner-operator who already has prime real estate. The advantage for convenience store owners is that they have a partner franchise which has high brand recognition. Both stores might also benefit from well developed systems and operating procedures since co-branding enables the cost of overhead, labour and management systems to be divided among both partners. The benefit to the customers is the convenience of purchasing fast food while, at the same time, filling their car with petrol.

There are, however, some problems inherent in a co-branding concept. For example, owners of nearby franchises are often not protected against 'cannibalisation' of their sales by a new co-branded franchise. While existing stand-alone franchisees are often offered the opportunity to own the new co-branded franchise, the possibility remains that the market area is simply not big enough to support both a stand-alone and a co-branded franchise in the same area. Co-branding has also led to some generic branding difficulties as noted by Janet Wagner, Associate Professor of Marketing (University of Maryland, 1996):

> The long-term benefit of such close juxtaposition of brands remains to be seen. It (co-branding) has to make as much sense to consumers, too. They need to see that the images are compatible. The stores have to have complementary products, but the brands also have to be on a par in terms of pricing and prestige.

In 1997 *The National Association of Convenience Stores* (US) reported that fast-food now counts for 13.7 per cent of all convenience store purchases which makes it the second most purchased category in convenience stores. In line with such trends in the US market, Caltex Oil of New Zealand has co-branded with Subway in four Auckland sites as part of its convenience store developments.

Subway in the 1990s

With over 12,700 stores in 55 countries, Subway is behind only McDonald's in terms of outlets. But, in terms of sales, Subway's sales of $3000 million or $3.0 billion (US) in 1995 meant that Subway was ranked only ninth in the 1996 top 25 quick-service restaurants (QSR) by the *Restaurant and Institutions* magazine.

But the 1997 *Restaurant and Institutions* survey of America's favourite restaurant chains did vote Subway Sandwiches and Salads considerably higher on other factors. (See Figure 9.5 for results of the survey.)

Figure 9.5 1997 Restaurants and Institutions magazine survey
US Domestic ranking of New Zealand competitors on varying factors

Overall		**Food Quality**		**Menu Variety**	
Wendy's	3.57	Wendy's	3.77	Wendy's	3.69
Subway	3.49	Subway	3.72	Subway	3.50
Pizza Hut	3.42	Pizza Hut	3.71	Pizza Hut	3.47
Burger King	3.41	KFC	3.55	Burger King	3.36
McDonald's	3.36	Burger King	3.55	McDonald's	3.36
KFC	3.30	McDonald's	3.24	KFC	3.33

Value		**Service**		**Atmosphere**	
Wendy's	3.56	Subway	3.53	Wendy's	3.33
Subway	3.49	Wendy's	3.50	Pizza Hut	3.28
Burger King	3.48	Pizza Hut	3.35	Burger King	3.16
McDonald's	3.39	Burger King	3.32	McDonald's	3.15
Pizza Hut	3.29	McDonald's	3.27	Subway	3.15
KFC	3.27	KFC	3.23	KFC	3.05

Cleanliness		**Convenience**	
Wendy's	3.50	McDonald's	3.77
Subway	3.47	Burger King	3.67
McDonald's	3.35	Wendy's	3.60
Burger King	3.31	Subway	3.59
Pizza Hut	3.31	Pizza Hut	3.53
KFC	3.21	KFC	3.49

Each chain was rated on a scale of 1 (poor) to 5 (excellent).
Source: *Restaurants and Institutions* magazine, February 1997, pp. 26–46.

US Industry

Again, according to this 1997 Restaurant and Institutions industry forecast, quick-service restaurant sales are forecast to reach US $110.8 billion this year which is an inflation-adjusted real growth of 3.3 per cent. However, domestically, US fast food chains will find it increasingly difficult to increase their 'flat' same-store sales (e.g. sales in existing stores have not increased). Many industry observers believe that the US domestic market has limited growth potential and may even be over-saturated. According to Hal Sieling, a California-based restaurant industry analyst:

> Over-saturation of the fast-food restaurant segment is a well-guarded secret. A lot of chains have depended upon growth, but with them all chasing the same 'Holy Grail'; sooner or later you come to the point of saturation.

Sieling believes that the traditional strategy tactic of opening new restaurants to increase revenue and drive 'double-digit' (more than 10 per cent earnings on sales) earnings is now a thing of the past. And the supply of ideal locations is dwindling for stand-alone restaurants. To combat these trends, some franchises such as McDonald's have shifted their focus to purchasing other franchise chains which scaled down or were about to close completely. An example of this was when McDonald's brought 184 Roy Rogers hamburger restaurants in the US in 1996 to convert them into McDonald's restaurants. This tactic has also been followed in New Zealand with McDonald's purchasing of 17 Georgie Pie outlets in New Zealand in 1996. However, the fact remains that fast-food restaurants in the US face an ever-decreasing supply of prime locations for stand-alone outlets. Along with international expansion, one strategy currently being used to combat an over-saturated market is the development of stores in non-traditional locations.

The continual development of traditional free-standing restaurants is becoming increasingly difficult in the US. For example, only 10 years ago the US market still had plenty of room for geographical market expansion until its critical market mass was reached. Existing franchisees now believe that their territories are being squeezed as the Subway opens more and more outlets. This has led to a current problem of market saturation for traditional free-standing units. Rising real estate prices and a lack of prime locations create new barriers for domestic US expansion. Increased competition within the industry has driven the need for location and convenience. Subway views development in non-traditional locations as an important part of their growth and has rapidly expanded into new sites.

Non-traditional locations also have one other advantage – the start-up costs for a franchisee is considerably lower than that of a traditional stand-alone store. But symptomatic of the problem of over-saturation is the lawsuits that are being filed by existing franchisees over territorial rights when too many franchisees have been allowed in a limited geographical area or market.

Future Direction of Subway Hamilton Central

In Michael Carroll, Subway has an enthusiastic and dedicated franchise owner-operator. In an industry which is fiercely competitive, with new competitors entering and established heavyweights enjoying 'top of mind' awareness, Subway's advantage could lie in the ability to provide a more personalised service than its high-traffic competitors. Carroll comments: 'Service is what makes Subway so popular. More time is spent with the customer, so you get to know your customer better.'

Mike Carroll is characteristically optimistic for the future. He comments:

> There are a number of things that I personally have learnt in regards to this business and these principles apply in general. These are: (1) the time to develop the business is always nearly double what you expect, and (2) promoting of a business is expensive but in today's business climate in New Zealand it is imperative to success of this type of business.

Carroll sees the future of Subway in Hamilton and in the country as positive. He states:

> Subway will fully succeed nationally when regular TV advertising is in place. Subway is a variation of sandwiches which is staple food in New Zealand and so education is not a huge hurdle. Good promotion will be the key to its future success. Subway will succeed on quality food and service, not price.

But Carroll wonders: 'When is Subway's development to achieve a critical mass?' Certainly the strong similarity to the early difficulties encountered by DeLuca and Dr Buck might suggest that this could indeed be the key to the development of Subway in New Zealand.

Mike Carroll believes that there is also a need for a more strategic approach so that Subway can match or beat its competitors. He also thinks such a strategy must form the basis of development of Subway in this country. Carroll is willing to do his part, but he wonders, 'Is it going to be enough?'

10 Tidco International

Tidco has gone back to specialising in the Barmac [rock crusher] alone. We've cut out all diversification.

(Andi Lusty, Managing Director, Tidco International Ltd, 5 August 1992)

Introduction

Tidco International Ltd, a world leading manufacturer of rock crushers, is an unusual company. For example, Tidco International Ltd (Tidco) is not concerned with glamour, a good thing since rock crushers have never been glamorous.

Tidco's home in Matamata in the North Island is also an unusual location for a manufacturer of heavy equipment that is destined for a world market. Matamata is better know as one of New Zealand's best horse breeding and dairy farming regions. Tidco now has a distibutor/dealer network throughout the world (see Figure 10.1).

Figure 10.1 Tidco International Ltd's worldwide operations

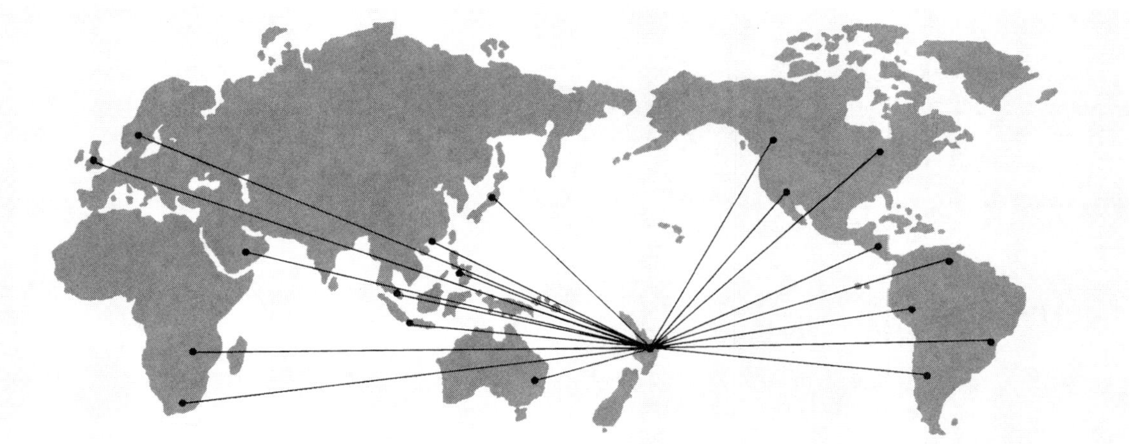

Acknowledgments This case was prepared by Mathew Parkinson and Bryan Poulin from personal interviews and other information gathered by senior students in the Department of Strategic Management and Leadership, University of Waikato. Special thanks go to Andi Lusty and Bob Lowe and many others of Tidco International Ltd for their cooperation and valuable input. The case is to be used as a basis for classroom discussion rather than to illustrate either effective or ineffective handling of an administrative or strategic situation.

Tidco manufactures and sells the 'Barmac', the most innovative rock crusher in the world. International competitors have spent millions of dollars each year in an attempt to copy the Barmac rock crusher. It remains largely unchallenged.

Large primary and secondary rock-crushing machines are required to break rock down to the medium 50 mm (2") size. The Barmac excels from this stage. This is because Barmac tertiary rock crushers are specially designed to break medium-sized, 50 mm rocks down to sand and gravel in sizes ideal both for surfacing roadways and for processing mineral-rich rock into a concentrated form of mineral ('concentrates'). Often it is concentrates, rather than 'pure' forms of mineral rock, that are shipped to final processors and manufacturers located around the world.

The Early Years and the Barmac

The Barmac crusher is as original as the two men behind Tidco's success – founder Paul Tidmarsh and current managing director Andi Lusty. In 1968 Paul Tidmarsh left school at the age of 14. He then built a welder on the back of a truck and, from this mobile base, he began to visit local rock quarries and undertake general repair and maintenance work wherever he could find it.

After about five years of hard work providing welding and related services, Tidmarsh started a workshop and began sub-contracting for manufacturing engineers. He traded under the name P.L. Tidmarsh Ltd. Even at this early stage of the business, Tidmarsh set very high standards of quality, standards that pervade the Tidco operation today. Lusty describes the founder as meticulous: 'He marked the style of the place. He wouldn't let anything out unless it was really good.'

In the late 1970s, P.L. Tidmarsh was offered an opportunity to manufacture and sell a newly designed machine called the MacDonald Impactor. It was a new rock-crushing machine that was soon renamed the 'Barmac' after its developers, Bryan Bartley and Jim MacDonald. P.L. Tidmarsh began to sell these new and innovative crushers throughout North America. (See Figures 10.2 and 10.3 for information on the Barmac crusher.)

Over the next few years the company developed an impressive reputation for quality. The company grew at the rate of 20 per cent annually. Most of this growth is attributable to the success of the Barmac Tertiary Rock Crusher.

Tidco during the 1980s

In an effort to diversify, an expanded range of Barmac rock crushers was developed as well as a range of related products. In 1988, subsidiaries were established in Britain, Hungary (to serve Eastern Europe), and Chile. P.L. Tidmarsh Ltd was then renamed Tidco International Ltd (Tidco for short).

By 1990 the rapid geographical expansion and an expanded product range began to cause problems at Tidco. Problems concerned product development and sales of the newly introduced products. But sales were also affected by a New Zealand dollar which had appreciated dramatically, making Tidco products relatively more expensive for international customers. Other difficulties had to do with a depressed international market which saw sales fall by 35 per cent.

Finished inventory grew rapidly – an expensive process when one machine could retail at up to half a million NZ dollars. Tidco began to seek equity capital

Figure 10.2 Promotional Information on the Barmac Rock Crusher

A high tonnage rock-on-rock Barmac that makes money for you.

The complete range of patented Tidco BARMAC DUOPACTOR vertical shaft impact crushers feature the unique, proven Cascade Feed system. This incorporates wear free rock-on-rock technology that has revolutionised material reduction worldwide. Tidco BARMAC DUOPACTOR crushers, operating as third and fourth stage reduction crushers, can process feed rates to 500 tons per hour. The dual feed Tidco BARMACS offer the additional feature of processing material to 100mm (4") feed size where the circuit and material characteristics allow the combination of secondary and tertiary crushing. The BARMAC'S unique rock-on-rock technology combines high velocity impact crushing with high intensity milling that can process hard, highly abrasive rocks routinely.

The DUOPACTOR crusher is ideally suited for the production of top quality aggregate products for asphalt paving, concrete aggregates or specification sand. It crushes a wide range of materials with low horsepower per ton and higher reduction ratios than can normally be achieved in compression crushers.

The Tidco BARMAC DUOPACTOR is the only crusher that offers the modern operator product grading control by optimising numerous variables:

- ***Selection of several size rotor diameters***
- ***Choice of crushing chamber cavity rings***
- ***Variation of rotor speed***
- ***Adjustment of Cascade Feed ratio***

The high velocity turbulence achieved in a Tidco BARMAC DUOPACTOR crushing chamber beneficiates the material and reduces product moisture, improving the soundness and shape of the stone, easing the screening task while enhancing product quality.

DUOPACTOR Features

- Low capital cost
- Rugged, heavy duty steel construction
- Designed for quick, easy installation
- Adjustable, efficient internal dust suppression system
- Alloy steel shaft and large heavy-duty bearings supported in a rigid cartridge type housing
- Simple, reliable grease lubrication
- Lower service and maintenance requirements
- Rock lining of rotor and crushing chamber reduces the number of wearing parts
- Low power consumption per ton of product
- Excellent product shaping and scrubbing

Figure 10.3 Technical Information on the Barmac Rock Crusher

The patented Barmac rock-on-rock crushing action.

Within the Rotor and the Crushing Chamber.

The illustrations below show the unique rock build-up within the machine which eliminates high wear costs associated with traditional type crushers.

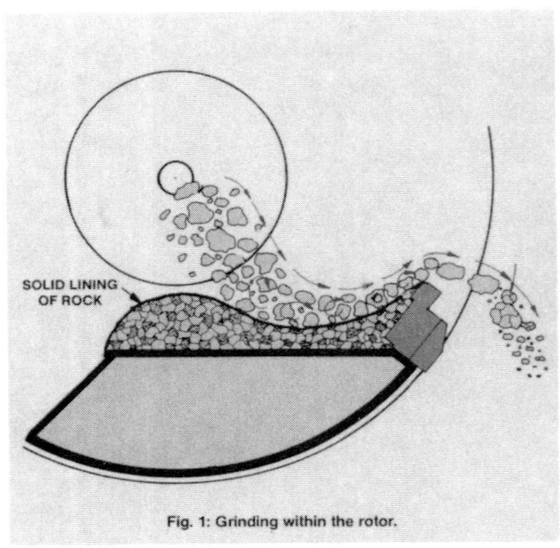

Fig. 1: Grinding within the rotor.

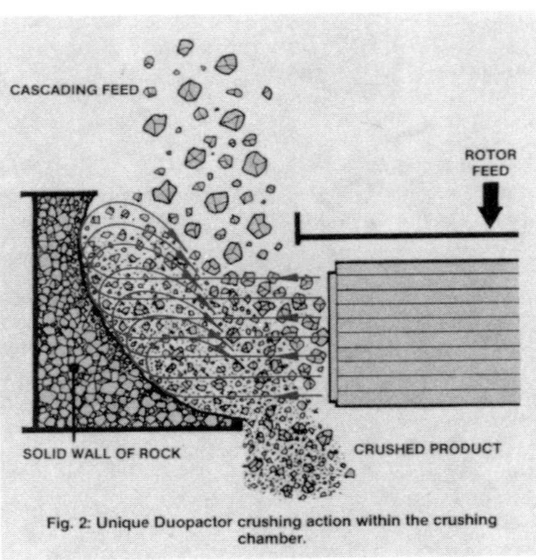

Fig. 2: Unique Duopactor crushing action within the crushing chamber.

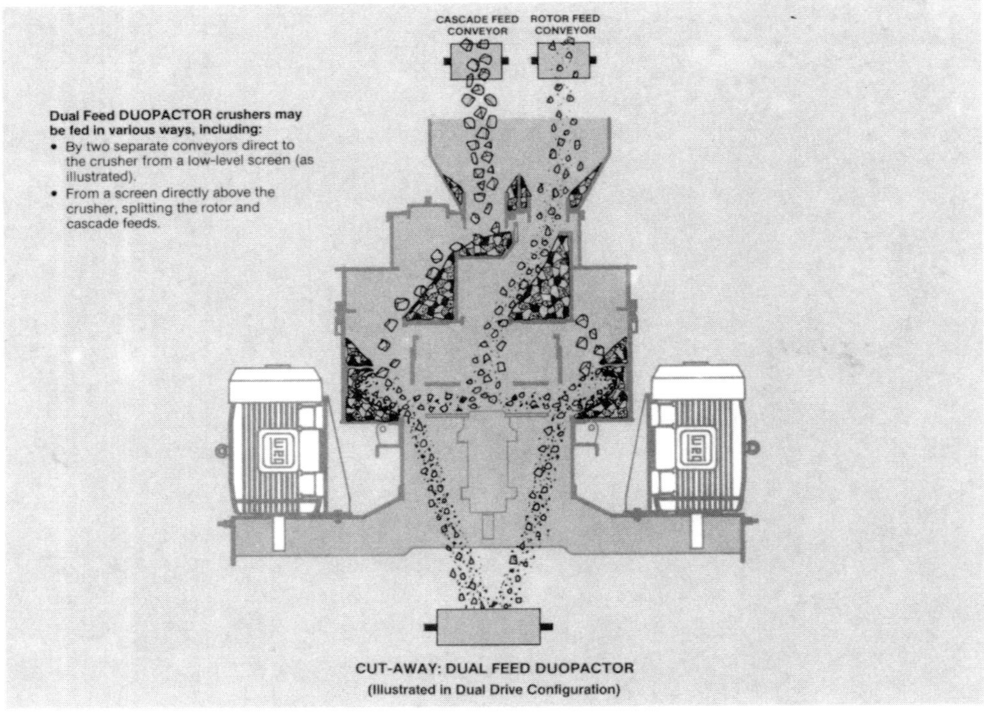

CUT-AWAY: DUAL FEED DUOPACTOR

(Illustrated in Dual Drive Configuration)

to ease the cash flow strains. Later, in 1990, Paul Tidmarsh was forced to consider selling the company. He finally sold it to Allis Mineral Systems (AMS), a subsidiary of a large international Swedish company, Svedala Industri (or Svedala for short).

Svedala is a recognised industry leader in crushing and mining technology, with over $US1.5 billion in annual sales. After joining the AMS group of Svedala, Tidco restructured to concentrate on the manufacture, sales and service of its key product, the Barmac range of tertiary rock crushers.

Management layers decreased from four to two and manufacturing staff at the Matamata plant were cut by nearly two thirds. The staff cuts came in two stages and Lusty concedes that may not have been the best choice, although the end results were positive:

> Through selective cutting of our workforce we kept the best people. We were probably too optimistic about when we thought the market would recover. The final cut was really drastic to give those remaining some sense of security. Quality and productivity have improved.

Production of the Barmac

Tidco's reputation is built around quality of and continual improvements to the Barmac crusher. Promotion manager Bob Lowe sees constant improvement as integral to the company's continued success, stating: 'The pirates and the copiers will always be two or three years behind.'

The Barmac crusher was designed for ease of use and low service requirements. The unique feature of the crusher is that it forces rocks to bang into each other, reducing them to gravel and sand. This produces much less wear and much greater intervals between repairs or replacement of worn components than conventional machines. But, because Barmac crushers are used for smaller size (50 mm) stone, they might be considered 'finishing' crushers or 'shaping' crushers.

Typically, conventional machines use rollers to crush or 'hammer' the rocks, resulting in wear on both the rollers and the drum against which the roller crushes the rocks. Reliability and low parts wear are important considerations in the mining industry, where machines are required to run 24 hours a day.

The Barmac is also popular because of the granular stone products it produces, perfectly shaped for roading and a variety of construction jobs. These quality products, together with the increased output at lower cost by the Barmac, offer incredible value to the purchaser. Lusty claims that, on average, a Barmac crusher will pay for itself in two years of cost savings alone.

Most components of the Barmac are manufactured locally, with 80 per cent of the parts sourced within New Zealand. This hasn't always been the case. Lusty shows some frustration at the attitude of some New Zealand companies towards supplying components to Tidco at prices and quality that are internationally competitive. He also reports that it has taken a long time to negotiate such internationally competitive terms. Parts are supplied by just six local companies.

Tidco has long-term contracts with these six suppliers. Tidco also has a policy and a system of guaranteeing consistent supply of component parts at stable costs. For example, Tidco guarantees to take certain levels of production from suppliers who in turn agree only to raise their prices at the rate of inflation – and even then 'they have to explain these increases to Andi Lusty'.

Parts most susceptible to wear are cast in local New Zealand foundries. It is important that Tidco maintains a close relationship with these suppliers. As promotion manager Bob Lowe states:

> The reputation of our machine can rise or fall on their suppliers' backs. When we ring them and say we've got a problem, they'll get on to it straight away. They will even get staff in over the weekend to fix a problem for us.

Tidco makes up a large share of the business of these suppliers and Lusty has developed strong personal relationships with each manager. The emphasis on improving the quality of suppliers' materials and components has helped Tidco achieve the coveted international standard – ISO 9001. Lusty also credits the relationship with suppliers as crucial to the dramatic financial improvement after the restructuring of the company. He comments: 'The result of that effort has made us one of the most profitable companies within the group again.'

For the future, Lusty aims at further strengthening relationships with local suppliers in an effort to ensure the long-term viability of Tidco's Matamata base. Matamata is where Andi Lusty and his team of employees prefer to stay. However, this must also make long-term economic sense to the parent company, Svedala Industri.

Financial Performance

Savings have been made in several areas. Better quality control on the shop floor has reduced the cost of reworking deficiencies in production by 50 per cent.

Net cash flow is higher in 1992 than it was before the 1990 financial crisis. This improvement is reflected in the financial statements of Tidco shown as Appendix 1 and Appendix 2. These are the simplified revenue statements and consolidated balance sheets for 1990 to 1992 respectively.

Since the takeover of Tidco by Allis Mineral Systems, financial control has tightened considerably, and profits have returned to 1990 pre-crisis levels. Lusty recalls that Paul Tidmarsh did not undertake elaborate financial analysis of business decisions. He is the kind of guy who 'if it feels right, he'll go ahead and do it'.

The Industry and its Environment

The rock products industry is very closely aligned to exchange rate fluctuation and cyclical effects in the economy of this fluctuation in New Zealand currency as indicated by Figure 10.4.

Construction and mining are two of the first industries to slow down with an economic recession, and they are also the first to resume during a recovery. However, the nature of the industry means there is a lag between orders for new equipment and the beginning of economic recovery. This is because construction and mining companies will first use all surplus capacity before committing to the purchase of new equipment. But, as the idle Barmac machines are used again, more parts are required. Therefore, the first sign of an economic recovery is a resurgence in Tidco's spare parts business.

Figure 10.4 Exchange Rate Fluctuation 1989–91 ($NZ v. $US; mid-rate)

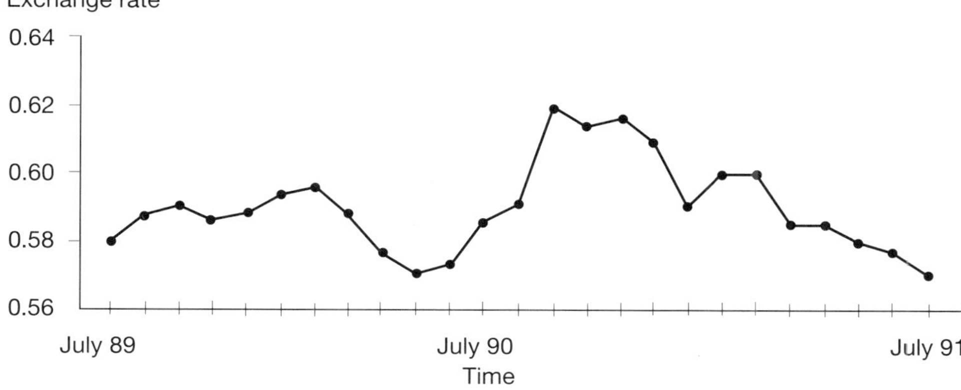

Mineral-rich rock products supplied by the quarrying industry provide the essential inputs for the survival and growth of most countries. End use products from these intermediary rock products affect every area of life. These various end uses include:

1 Personal use – e.g. purified water, toothpaste, cosmetics, tablets
2 Eating – e.g. cutlery, crockery, glassware, plastics
3 Transportation – e.g. pavements, roads, railways, ships
4 Buildings – e.g. airports, houses, schools, hospitals, shops, offices and factories

The importance of the quarrying function to the economies of developing and developed countries must be balanced with social responsibilities such as anti-pollution equipment, financial responsibility of those industrial companies, environmental rehabilitation and sustainability. Mining and processing of mineral-rich rock and non-mineral-rich aggregates such as limestone, rock and sand not only deplete the earth's natural resources but, if not properly managed, these extraction resource processes can effectively increase the rate of environmental deterioration.

The deterioration of the environment has been shown to have long-term effects on both the quality of life and the economic viability of many countries. Taking care of the environment means not only replanting forests, but also minimising the effect of air pollution caused by loose particles in the atmosphere. Atmospheric pollution is a special concern where there are surrounding communities as quarrying operations can affect the long-term quality of the very air we breathe. The industry is therefore interested in environmental issues at both community and processing levels of operation.

The use of advanced technology may help in overcoming these negative effects on the environment. But technically advanced machinery is highly specialised and capital intensive, usually requiring custom-built installation mechanisms and highly technical service. As a result, the decision to purchase and install rock crushers is no longer simple. Sometimes the social and commercial consequences can delay purchase decisions for many years.

No doubt social and political change has forced the industry to take more notice of environmental considerations, especially air and water pollution. Surprisingly, such awareness has already benefited Tidco. This is because not only does the Barmac make the best manufactured gravel and sand products in the world, but the process is also relatively dust and pollution free. With natural sand in short supply due to widespread bans on beach mining, this is a major selling point for Tidco, especially in the US. It is thought that social pressure to maintain the environment will increase markedly in the US with President Clinton's term.

Tidco has already been affected by a strengthening New Zealand dollar, and everyone at the company is aware of the dangers. Lusty sees it as a uniquely Tidco/Svedala problem:

> When foreign companies buy a New Zealand manufacturer, it's generally to service New Zealand and/or Australia. I know of no other situation where a foreign company has bought a Kiwi company to service the rest of the world.

The forecast for the global economy over the next few years is mixed. The New Zealand Institute of Economic Research voices serious concerns for the growth prospects of New Zealand's trading partners. Despite this, the industry remains optimistic about its own fortunes. For example, industry magazine *Rock Products* forecasts positive growth in the huge US market, as is indicated in Figure 10.5.

Figure 10.5 Forecast of US Rock Output (% growth) 1993 over 1992

Crushed Stone	+4.5%
Sand and Gravel	+2.75%
Cement	+6.0%
Gypsum	0.0%
Lime	+4.5%
Aggregate	+4.5%
Construction	+4.0%

Source: Extracted from *Rock Products.*

In short, not only are maintenance and slow-wearing qualities of rock-crushing machinery important factors, so are crushing options, dust suppression, simplicity of lubrication and suitability for the working environment. Here, the Barmac has significant advantages.

Competitors and Marketing

There are two main types of suppliers in the quarry industry. These are international suppliers and small-scale suppliers. Each type of supplier provides a different level of service to the end-user.

International suppliers provide branded machinery, often competing on value – a mix of technical features, overall quality and machinery maintenance attributes. Suppliers of well-known crushing equipment often obtain the large government and industrial contracts. In other words, the smaller suppliers tend to be overlooked for large orders. But the local suppliers can compete if prices are low enough.

Svedala's major competitors in rock crushing are Nordberg (Finland), Komatsu (Japan), Kobelco (Japan), Jacques (Australia), Powerscreen (Ireland), Kueken

(Wales) and Cedar Rapids (USA). No major competitor has manufactured exactly the same, or even a closely similar, crusher to date. Tidco has won seven awards for exporting excellence since 1985. Ninety per cent of Tidco's production is exported around the world and the proportion is likely to increase.

The company estimates the potential worldwide market for crushers such as those produced by Tidco at 100,000 machines. Lusty comments: 'That's pretty challenging, given that there have only ever been 2000 Barmacs sold to date'.

To spread the word of the Barmac story, and the advantages to potential customers, Tidco has a force of agents and associate companies in over 40 countries. Unsurprisingly, the people at Tidco take a special interest in keeping an eye on developments around the world.

> We're in Brazil, Chile, Tanzania, Israel – you name it. I get sick of travelling, but it's unavoidable. Our business is based on relationships and we all have to travel regularly around the world at least three times a year.
>
> You can't tell what's happening just by looking at the figures. One guy might be doing it all wrong but selling lots because his area is booming. Another office might be doing everything right but failing due to a tough market.

So Lusty visits the foreign office and goes into the field with agents who make sales calls. It is all part of the relationship building which seems to be a hallmark of Tidco's operations. Tidco's marketing force consists of two systems: distributors, and the sales offices of its parent company, Allis Mineral Systems (AMS), owned by Svedala Industri. Bob Lowe, Promotions Manager, says it took some time for the AMS sales force to adapt: 'They were so used to competing against us. It took a while for them to realise, "Hey, we aren't fighting this anymore, we can sell it ourselves".'

As the AMS sales force slowly became more successful in making more sales, so the old agent-distributor system has had some trouble. For example, it appears that agents do not have the same commitment as Tidco or AMS sales forces. Tidco has recently severed the contract of an American agent-distributor to sell and service Tidco products.

Marketing efforts are also based on trade magazines in conjunction with the all important personal relationships. Sales offices and agents may hear of a new mine to be opened or a major construction plan that will increase the production from a rock quarry. Established customers are contacted so that they may be impressed with the product and include more Barmacs in their expansion plans. This process is only possible if customers know about Tidco's product line and its capabilities.

Sales agents from all around the world gather regularly at Tidco's Matamata headquarters to learn about new models and new uses for the Barmac line of crushers. The forum is aimed at both education and fostering the kind of 'creative thinking' which could lead to new markets.

Andi Lusty believes Tidco should be interested in taking the concept of exporting 'to the extreme'. For example, he reminds others:

> We had some guys over here from NASA, talking about building on the moon. The first thing to be done will be concreting. Some day we could see Barmacs up there on the moon crushing basalt rock for construction work.

Leadership, Management Style and Structure

Andi Lusty has been part of the Tidco story since 1981 when he joined the company as an accountant. Formerly a professional squash player, he found the sport hard on his body and chose to change careers. This change took the kind of dedication and commitment that Lusty brings to his job at Tidco.

In 1982, Andi Lusty relinquished his accounting function to join the marketing effort at Tidco. The emphasis at Tidco during this time was firmly on selling crushers rather than keeping an 'eagle eye' on costs. Three years later he found himself in the US talking about a joint venture distribution plan with then-owner, Paul Tidmarsh. Lusty explains:

> In those days the company wasn't consolidated. Paul had partners in every division. The 'divisions' would be independent companies owned by Paul Tidmarsh and the local manager. The deal to merge didn't seem very attractive to me personally.

In order to entice Lusty to consent, Tidmarsh 'sweetened the deal' financially and offered him the post of managing director of the combined group of companies. The return to work full time at the factory in Matamata in his new role has seen Lusty forge his commitment to his staff and his community.

Among the company aims listed on a plaque in the reception area is a commitment to helping staff become more capable in their job and to enjoy their lives at work and after hours. There is also a stated aim to help the general Matamata community. These aims are tangible evidence of Lusty's desire to offer others what he considers his 'ideal lifestyle'. He explains:

> I couldn't get a lifestyle like this anywhere else. Our parent company has got a plant with excess capacity in Brazil that could manufacture Barmacs at potentially lower cost and price and be closer to the major markets. For the Swedes to continue their manufacturing base in Matamata, we have to be doing some things right.

One of these things is the motivation to continually seek better skills for workers. This is evident in the attention to detail that extends to the friendly and professional reception staff. Skill development is not an accident at Tidco. For example, the reception staff have undergone the 'Kiwihost' training programme run by the hospitality industry; their certificates are displayed proudly on the wall. New manufacturing staff are trained by the best Tidco workers and all staff are continually learning about all of the different functions in the company.

Tidco also has a social club which is very active. A note in the published accounts reveals Tidco has provided financial help to the social club when necessary.

The present structure of Tidco is conventional (see Figure 10.6). Lusty dismisses any notion that the relationship between Tidco and its employees is unusual. He sits at this desk in a polo shirt, looking as casual a courier van driver, and laughs:

> What we do isn't unusual, it's just common sense. If we want to stay in Matamata we have to perform. The best way to perform is with a happy, educated, productive workforce, and a supportive community.

Figure 10.6 Tidco organisation structure

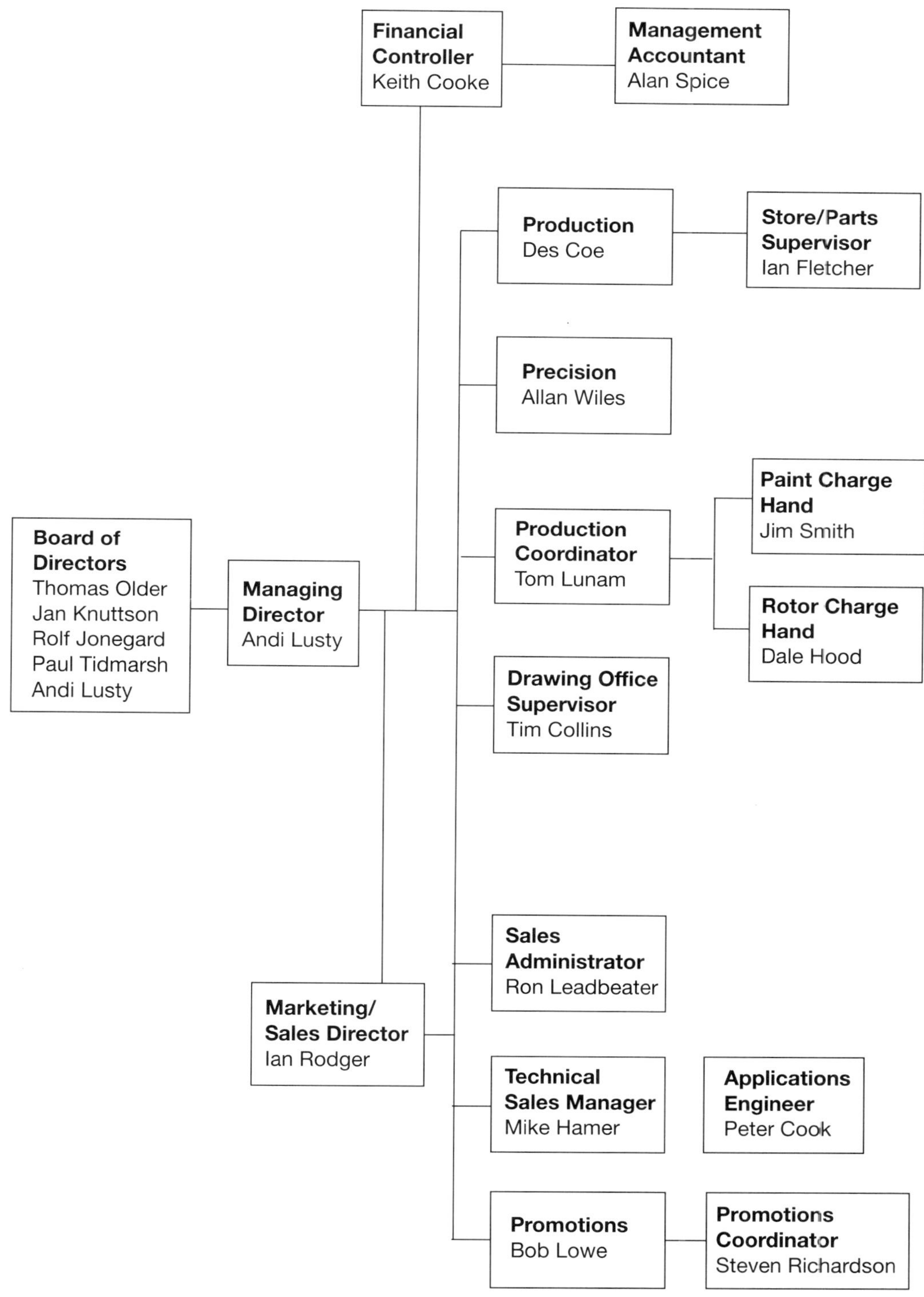

The Future

The way ahead for Tidco appears positive. The company has a unique product that leads its competitors. Tidco employees know how to make quality products and to build lasting customer relationships.

The new accounts are due out: Lusty is pleased to note that sales turnover has doubled over the past two years, that is since 1991. He doesn't want to rest on past achievements, though, realising how dangerous complacency can be. Lusty reflects on the changes over these recent years and the challenge ahead:

> If we hadn't sold the company when we did, it would have got very difficult. We would not likely be here now. Now, it's a matter of production keeping up with sales. We've just had to hire more staff.

The potential market for new Barmacs seems enormous. One new opportunity is to tap into environmental awareness by adapting the Barmac for concrete recycling. Other new uses for existing and extended products are being thought of constantly.

Recently, however, Tidco has become even more aware of the importance of being in closer touch with the market. For example, sales have slowed in America, Tidco's largest market. Tidco suspects the agency arrangements, not the markets, are to blame. Lusty is considering an unscheduled trip to the US to sort out the matter. But, realistically, he wonders, 'How many more trips like this can I take?'

Appendix 1: Revenue Statement (Simplified)

Revenue Statement Tidco International Ltd
Years to 31 December 1990–92* ($000)

	1992	1991	1990 (6 months)	30/6/90*
Turnover	**9 397**	**8 018**	**5 503**	**17 657**
Less				
Audit Fees	25	44	34	63
Directors Fees	12	-	-	8
Depreciation and Allowances	516	582	214	406
Interest Paid	374	1 261	746	1 339
Rental and Leasing Costs	56	64	43	157
Foreign Currency Losses	-	77	-	-
Cost of Sales and Misc.	7 473	11 093	6 034	15 047
Add				
Foreign Currency Gains	99	-	350	134
Sundry Income	56	139	126	72
Earnings Before Tax	1 096	(4 964)	(1 092)	843
Taxation	3	480	(297)	287
Minority Interests in Subsidiaries	(15)	187	109	443
Extraordinary Items	-	-	(109)	455
Net Profit	**1 078**	**(4 777)**	**(795)**	**1 054**

***The financial year was changed from June to December in 1990, hence the 6-month period from 1 July to 31 December in 1990.**

Appendix 2: Consolidated Balance Sheet (Simplified)

Consolidated Balance Sheet ($000)

	1992	1991	1990	30/6/90 (6 months)
Current Assets	**6 059**	**7 544**	**13 743**	**12 519**
Including				
Bank Balances	31	276	67	765
Receivables and Prepayments	2 119	2 062	4 376	4 517
Inventories	3 572	3 078	5 185	7 237
Other Debtors	337	2 128	4 115	
Current Liabilities	**980**	**1 119**	**1 610**	**4 851**
Including				
Bank Overdraft	22	247	1 501	
Creditors and Accruals	980	983	1 347	3 146
Finance Leases	14	16	138	
Other	100	66		
Fixed Assets	**3 404**	**3 558**	**3 542**	**3 894**
Including				
Land and Buildings	1 810	1,845	1 880	1 897
Vehicles	181	207	296	528
Plant/Equipment/Fittings	1 413	1 506	1 366	1 469
Investments	336	24	21	239
Intangibles	423	503	1 217	2 071
Minority/Other Assets	94	117	40	
Term Liabilities	**3 900**	**6 341**	**12 152**	**7 550**
Net Assets	**5 342**	**4 263**	**4 785**	**5 649**
Represented By				
Paid Up Capital	10 000	10 000	5 741	5 740
Retained Earnings	(4 668)	(5 743)	(966)	(509)
Reserves	10	6	10	418
Total Shareholders Funds	**5 342**	**4 263**	**4 785**	**5 649**

Source: Annual Reports.

11 The Tower Group of Companies

I'd like to believe if there's one thread that runs through the group from myself, it is that people know where they stand and they know that they'll get a fair deal, no matter what.

(James Boonzaier, Tower Group, September, 1996)

Introduction to the Tower Group of Companies

The Tower Group of Companies had its beginning more than 125 years ago when, in 1869, the government of New Zealand established the Government Life Office (GLO). The idea of the government was to create in New Zealand an alternative to then dominant English-based life insurance companies. The New Zealand government advanced £4000 Sterling to the fledgling organisation, an advance that was soon repaid from internally generated profits on operations. By the 1950s, the GLO had become the dominant life insurance and retirement savings organisation in New Zealand with a market share of about 40 per cent.

However, in the 1960s and 1970s, competition intensified from larger Australian Life insurers now operating in New Zealand. The GLO's market share began to slide, rapidly. By 1980, the GLO's market share stood at a lowly 10 per cent, well behind the market leaders AMP, National Mutual and New Zealand Insurance. The managers of the GLO decided to diversify.

The GLO purchased assets and shares in other companies to take advantage of the high inflation of the 1980s. These asset purchases included Harcourt's Real Estate, National Insurance, Trustees Executors, and a share broking company called Renouf Partners. Many commercial office buildings were also acquired. Financial results looked promising at first but then deteriorated as the recession of the late 1980s hit the country.

In 1990, the government decided to cut its links with the Government Life Office by privatising it. But the GLO could not be sold because the government did not actually own it. It was in fact owned by its policy-holders as a mutual cooperative. That is, each policy holder was entitled to a share in the mutual cooperative, by way of the original articles of association of the GLO back in

Acknowledgments This case study was prepared by Bryan Poulin from various sources, including an interview with James Boonzaier of the Tower Group. Special thanks go to James Boonzaier, Group Managing Director, and all the people at Tower who contributed in the preparation of this case study. This case study is to be used for the purpose of classroom discussion and not as an illustration of effective or ineffective handling of a strategic or administrative situation.

1869. The government's 120-year direction of the affairs of the organisation ended with the passing of The Tower Corporation Act of 1990 which saw the GLO renamed Tower Corporation. The New Zealand government guarantees on Tower's life insurance and superannuation policies fell away with the passing of the Act.

Progress Since 1990

One of the first things that the Board of Directors did with their new-found freedom was to appoint a new managing director for the Group of companies under Tower ownership. His name was James Boonzaier, a man who was to transform the way that Tower thought of itself and how it did business.

James Boonzaier moved to New Zealand from South Africa on 20 October 1987 to become the chief executive officer of National Insurance, the fire and general insurance company that was eventually purchased by the old GLO. National Insurance then belonged to a construction and development company called McConnell-Dowell. But, two days after his arrival in New Zealand, the share market crashed. Six months after the share market crash, McConnell-Dowell was forced to sell off assets. The Tower Group acquired National Insurance and James Boonzaier carried on as CEO of National Insurance for the next three years, that is until 1990. National Insurance continued to offer fire and general insurance, but now within the Tower Group of Companies. James Boonzaier had so impressed Tower's board with his direction of National Insurance that they chose him to oversee the entire Group of Companies in late 1990.

The deregulation of the 1980s had made it clear to Tower's board and top management team, including Boonzaier, that returns on investments needed to be increased in real terms. This meant that Tower's operation had to become much more productive and efficient if it was to attract and retain investment capital. For one thing, costs were far too high. For example, in 1990 Tower's expenses as a percentage of assets were about 4.6 per cent. But by 1996 expenses had been brought down to 2.3 per cent, a huge difference in the narrow-margin, high-volume and competitive financial services business.

Competition was increasing, not only from other insurance companies, but from the banks. For example, banks were vying for the insurance and retirement business, now that they too were set freer of government regulation. The banks are advantaged by the fact that they are much bigger than insurance companies and could achieve superior economies of scale.

The banks also have more information about their clients: how much people earn, how much discretionary money they have, and how people spend. The way for insurance companies to prosper is for them to somehow offer better services at lower cost than the banks. This is a tall order. But there are at least two options open for the insurance companies. These are:

1 to make existing distribution channels more efficient
2 to find other, more efficient channels of distribution, such as direct distribution.

Fintel (telephone financial services), National's telephone insurance service, started in 1994, Tower's successful answer to the direct distribution channel option.

Recently, Tower has developed a broader range of financial products and services expertise so it could 'lock in clients' by offering them everything they need in the savings and risk management area, short of competing head on with the banks in such specialised areas as cheque accounts. However, Tower management thinks hard about what areas to enter and what areas to avoid. For example, James Boonzaier explains why Tower divested its corporate banking arm and invested in the insurance business in Australia:

> It's not our business; we don't know enough about it. One of the first things I did when I got this job was to start divesting non-core businesses. We sold our corporate bank to National Australia Bank. We got out of computer service; we got out of real estate; we got out of printing – all those things because they were things we didn't understand. But what we did at the same time was to say, 'Well, fine, the New Zealand market is going to become tougher and tougher because of the pace of deregulation.' We still had reserves available. We said, 'Well, what shall we do? We can expand into Australia.'

Tower began to expand into Australia in 1990, using funds generated by the sale of its non-related businesses in New Zealand. This expansion was motivated both by the recognition of Australia's less deregulated market, making the insurance-based savings environment more attractive, and by the desire to learn more about the Australian market. Tower's first acquisition in Australia, Adriatic Life of Melbourne, at a cost of about $NZ50 million was a modest purchase by industry standards. But this was a significant investment for Tower.

Tower doubled the size of the business over the next few years. More significantly, Tower learned much about the life insurance business in Australia, including the differences between the two countries and the value Tower might add to Australian insurance and savings operations. The one obvious difference between operating life insurance businesses in Australia, compared to New Zealand, is that Australian companies are much more heavily regulated. This means that while potential competition from new entrants is less severe, compliance costs remain higher in Australia than New Zealand. Other differences include Australia's more diverse and much larger population (3.5 million people in New Zealand versus 18 million people in Australia) and the very different geographies of the two countries.

But the most significant difference is that Tower Australia customers, unlike Tower New Zealand customers, hardly know anything about Tower. To make Tower's presence felt by more customers in Australia, in 1993 Tower acquired a second life insurance company called Friends Provident, a much larger acquisition. Tower then merged the two together, calling the venture Tower Life Australia. The top managers of Tower as a whole felt confident that Tower Australia could be successful. This confidence was based on the fact that Tower had been successful in a smaller way, with the first acquisition, Adriatic Life. That merger has been one of the most successful mergers in many years in Australia. Tower Life Australia then took this opportunity to relocate its Head Office from Melbourne to Sydney. One of Tower's directors said of the Friends Provident–Tower Australia Merger, 'It went just brilliantly', and it did.

One of the uplifting aspects of the move to Australia has been the awards showered on Tower Life Australia, winning against such industry giants as AMP of Australia and Citibank of New York. However, as James Boonzaier is the first to admit, Tower has a long way to go to enter the ranks of these leading players.

How Tower Stacks Up Against Industry Leaders

In 1990, in New Zealand market leader AMP controlled $655 million (34.4 per cent) of a $1904 million unlisted managed funds industry. However, over the past five years, AMP only managed 73 per cent growth in a market which grew by 467 per cent. A recent private report stated that niche stars such as National Insurance Life & Health (part of the Tower Group) and Sovereign Assurance are beginning to out-perform their larger rivals by offering more customised and more personal service. As a result, AMP is streamlining its operations, taking a more customer-focused approach and concentrating on more specific markets.

AMP is also increasing its activity in another area of business – home loans. Although this is an area traditionally controlled by the banking sector, *The Sunday Star Times*, Section D, reported on 28 July 1996 that the AMP is widening the scope of services offered through its subsidiary Ergo Financial Services. Such operations in the area of mortgages means that insurers can now directly compete with banks. Insurers can offer services such as lines of credit, as well as credit cards linked to Automatic Teller Machine (ATM) and electronic transfer (EFTPOS) services.

The major difference between the banks and insurance companies is that insurance companies currently do not take deposits. A report in the *Dominion* of 7 February 1996 suggested that some insurance companies might well gain 'strategic benefits' in cooperating with the banking sector to sell policies not currently being offered by the banking sector.

One major trend that may continue is expansion through acquisition. Over the last 10 years, through the process of mergers and acquisitions, the current leaders in the life insurance and funds management market – AMP, National Mutual and New Zealand Insurance – all internationally owned, have been able to maintain their market position. These companies have made acquisitions primarily to expand their customer base, to increase the pool of funds available for investment, and to meet the increasing competition that is occurring between the insurers, themselves and the banks. So far, the competition in the investment market is not as intense as it is for the general insurance market.

There still may be many future opportunities for the more innovative companies. For example, Sovereign Assurance is growing fast, having only entered the industry in 1989. Factors which contribute to Sovereign's rapid growth are innovative co-insuring with its reinsurers (an uncommon practice in New Zealand), its respectful treatment of brokers and innovative use of technology. These and other considerations are well within the realm of concerns when time is taken out by busy Tower managers to plan their future strategy. With its change in emphasis away from traditional Life Assurance towards the broader area of Funds Management, Tower has steadily been building its market share. In 1995 it overtook AMP for the first time to become New Zealand's largest Retail Funds Manager. It still holds that position.

Strategy-time at the Tower Group of Companies

Each year around February or March, James Boonzaier travels around New Zealand and Australia, spending two or three days with each of the executives or top management teams. This is the way James Boonzaier describes the strategy process:

> We go to some suitably pleasant spot and reflect on the meaning of life, but according to a very systematic approach.
>
> Our approach to mission is a classical one: Who exactly are our customers? Exactly what business are we in? What is the competitive advantage going to be? Why us? I keep saying: 'Why you, why not AMP?' If we don't answer that, the customer will buy on price. It's as simple as that.
>
> We do a SWOT [Strengths, Weaknesses, Opportunities, Threats] analysis and competitor analysis, which is vital in this day and age. We try to identify between two and four key issues that are fundamental to achieving our mission. At 20 pages, it [the strategic plan] is not a long document. Each year we roll this over for the next five years and look at the last year's to see whether or not we met our strategic objectives.

Managers at Tower compare the performance of their company to the small number of key competitors who are the most immediate and dangerous ones. The basis of comparison is mission, target markets, and uniqueness. Estimates are made of the market shares of competitors for each of the businesses, using publicly available industry statistics and knowledge of Tower's own operations in each of the target markets. This is done according to key performance attributes.

The strategic plan for each operating company is considered very important. This plan emphasises such areas as financial projections, including assumptions and risks. Profitability is viewed as 'an outcome of everything else done right'. For example, Tower considers that one of the factors in their recent success is in leading the market in innovative distribution of its products and services. (Tower's Mission, Key Objectives, and Outcomes are indicated in Appendix 1.)

The strategic plan of each business is not simply a duplication of the Group's strategic plan which is much more general. The main requirement is that each operating company's plans must be consistent with the group plan. James Boonzaier, as group managing director, sits in on the strategic planning at both the Group and individual business levels. The Tower Group no longer considers itself as an insurance company but rather a holding company of businesses related to insurance and investment. The holding company's role is to set strategy for all nine companies in the Tower Group. Tower's rapid growth in the six years since James Boonzaier was appointed Group Managing Director is indicated in the 'time line' that is shown as Appendix 2.

The Insurance Industry

Insurance policies are issued by insurance companies to individuals or organisations as a hedge against loss of life, property or employment. There are two main types of insurance companies:

1 General Insurance companies, offering Fire and General Insurance

2 Life Assurance companies, offering Life Assurance and Superannuation.

Superannuation is the general term given for a range of retirement schemes and retirement savings plans.

Life Assurance companies generate funds by charging fees or premiums for offering insurance, particularly life insurance products (policies), investment and pension plans (superannuation schemes), and some accident and income security products. General Insurance companies generate funds by offering insurance on domestic houses, motor vehicles, commercial buildings and marine vessels. $400 billion worth of New Zealanders' assets are protected by general insurers.

The recent decline in superannuation policies could change with the new government's plan to make superannuation compulsory for New Zealanders. And the decline in profitability of general insurance, due to increased competition, could also be reversed in the longer term trends of population increases due to immigration to New Zealand by overseas peoples, a return by New Zealanders from overseas, and a growing number of elderly people in New Zealand. The trend in the aging population of New Zealand is indicated in Figure 11.1.

Figure 11.1 Elderly Population (000) by Sex, 1951–2031, Aged 65 and Over

Year	Men	Women
1951	83	92
1961	92	125
1971	103	128
1981	120	180
1991	170	220
2001	180	275
2011	250	340
2021	380	415
2031	410	500

Source: ***New Zealand Now 65 Plus*****, Statistics New Zealand.**

The insurance industry in New Zealand is comprised of about 40 companies of which 90 per cent are foreign-owned, that is, owned mainly by companies from Australia, the United Kingdom and the United States. US insurance companies are not dominant in New Zealand but US companies own 50 per cent of the insurance organisations worldwide. Insurance companies typically offer insurance policies to individuals and businesses on a direct basis rather than dealing through brokers. However, brokers may also sell insurance policies by acting as agents for the various insurance companies. Brokers relieve insurance companies of sales effort and claims administration and receive a commission from insurance companies. Individuals and organisations may then claim insured losses from insurance companies through the brokers.

A background player in the primary insurance market is the re-insurer. The role of the re-insurer is to allow insurance companies to cover the risk of 'over-exposure' during unusual conditions such as natural disaster. Should the claims against the company's insurance policies then exceed available funds, re-insurers cover the difference between the insurance company's exposure to these claims and the available funds of the insurance company. For example the Earthquake Commission is currently the only organisation in New Zealand which offers insurance in the event of an earthquake. The Earthquake Commission is re-insured by the UK firm Lloyd's of London, the world's largest re-insurer.

Insurance companies manage the funds generated both from the sales of insurance policies and from retirement and savings plans of businesses or individuals. Fund management is of central importance to the profitability of the insurance companies. Fund management is primarily investment in real estate and stocks which are subject to the vagaries of the stock market and the economy. Effective fund management requires great skill and judgement, and the appropriate use of the latest computer technology.

Retirement savings have been dampened by the New Zealand government's policy to tax retirement savings plans. New Zealand taxes retirement savings or collects what is known as a superannuation surcharge. Australia allows retirement savings to be tax exempt. Stuart Fish, Convenor of the Superannuation Committee of the Life Office Association of New Zealand, notes that retired people are still unhappy with the superannuation surcharge. More than one Minister of Finance has promised to review the need for this surcharge. Elimination of the surcharge would make retirement saving more attractive to New Zealanders, providing increased opportunities for insurance companies.

There is a growing trend in fraudulent insurance claims. For example, a householder may claim for a loss which did not in fact occur, or may have occurred in circumstances different than that described to the insurance company or insurance broker. Insurance companies are having to employ additional staff or hire private investigators to investigate such claims, driving up the cost of insurance. Policies generated by telephone sales and telephone claims, such as Tower's Fintel, are experiencing higher than normal numbers of fraudulent claims.

From the public's viewpoint, there is also increasing concern about the availability and affordability of some types of insurance coverage. One doctor illustrated this concern, stating, 'A woman with breast cancer was at first told by her doctor she needed a mastectomy at a private hospital, but was turned away when he heard she did not have medical insurance.' (*The Dominion*, 25 July 1996, p. 3).

Performance and Innovation at Tower

Every month all the profit and growth figures of each company are presented in a predetermined format and first sent to the Tower Group holding company and then the information is reported to the board. There are two levels of reporting: one managerial and the other financial. The financial statements for the past four years, 1992 to 1995 inclusive, are presented as Appendix 3 and Appendix 4.

The investment performance of New Zealand operations and Australian operations are considered separately. While Tower encourages decentralised retail operations, investment operations are tightly controlled from head office. As group managing director, James Boonzaier ensures accountability of the managing directors (MDs) of each of the operating companies by approving, or otherwise, any changes in the conditions affecting themselves or their executive team, including especially salary increases or changes in responsibilities given to their general managers (GMs). For example, in the case of firing a GM, or restructuring a GM's responsibility, the managing director of an operating company must first talk to and gain approval of James Boonzaier. Beyond these general conditions, the MDs are free to look after their companies.

James Boonzaier explains what he looks for in Tower's executive managers:

> I look for a 'big picture ability', strategic ability; general managers do have to have the ability to see a larger picture. I certainly look for innovation in those types of people. Most of the people that are called general manager have to be generalists and go beyond the level of technicians, as a general rule. Certainly I look for people who are able to work in teams – if you can't work in teams in modern business, it becomes very difficult for a company.
>
> I also look for real intellect, for people who are smart and who have a sound customer orientation.
>
> We are a financial services group and the heart of it for us still is insurance. I look for prudence and integrity, almost as a given. Anybody who lacks integrity in this business wouldn't last more than a month – it is so fundamental to the whole ethos of this (Tower) Group; I think people know that, or they learn that very, very quickly.
>
> Fairness is fundamental. I have very strong feelings about justice and fairness. We have a strong equal opportunity policy in the business – now I'm not just thinking of men and women, or black and white; it's just simply giving everybody an equal opportunity. It's not about giving everybody the same. Quite the contrary, I think we're very much a meritocracy. I don't often throw my weight around, but in areas like that I have been known to.

Tower has now appointed a general manager to oversee technology development and innovation for the Group. The idea is that other group companies come in very early in the life of pilot projects which use new technology so that they benefit as well. An example is distribution through the Internet. Instead of three companies spending money in trying to find innovative ways to distribute products and services through the Internet, only one company piloted the new system. A learning environment was created so other companies learned most of the lessons before they moved into the new arena.

Tower sees the role of technology as both helping deliver 'the right kind' of financial services and keeping costs competitive. This belief in the importance of both people and service through technology means that technology is considered a key strategic resource.

People's Attitude at Tower

In 1994, the Tower Group of Companies celebrated their 125 years of history. A video captured people's sense of commitment to the 'new Tower' and to each other. Excerpts from statements made during this 1994 video production are given in Figure 11.2.

Loyalty and commitment are seen as a two-way process:

1 people are expected to develop themselves and their skills, so as to offer better service

2 the company is expected to provide opportunities and to reward self-development and skills.

Figure 11.2 Excepts from 1994 Video of Tower Corporation

1 'What we say we are, we are. We all complement each other. If one of our businesses has not got it [the service], some other will; we keep it in the family.' (Cathie Cook, Customer Officer)

2 'We would expect to provide as good a quality service as anywhere. Technology is required to analyse a huge amount of data and help us make decisions but there is always the overriding human consideration.' (Frank Jasper, Manager, Investment Accounting)

3 'It gives me great satisfaction to give customers peace of mind about their assets, their long-term care and their retirement. If we can help them, it is very satisfying.' (Carol Robinson, Client Services Manager)

4 'It is great to be able to explain our decision to our agent or broker and know that they go away knowing we have done the best we can for them.' (Devi Uka, Regional Underwriter)

5 'We have terrific, committed people, and as long as you have got that, it's exciting. I'm glad to be part of it.' (James Boonzaier, Group Managing Director)

James Boonzaier asks: 'Why should anyone have any commitment and loyalty to the organisation that has none towards them?'

Tower also believes in the many positive attributes of an old culture, especially if that culture leads to giving people ownership. The idea is that no one can say, 'I don't buy into the philosophy because I didn't participate in this development.'

James Boonzaier believes his philosophy of justice and integrity, together with the training and experience he received, has affected his management style. For example, he spent some years in the insurance industry after completing an undergraduate degree. Then he returned to university to complete a master of business administration (MBA) degree. This is the way James Boonzaier describes his return to university and his views on education:

> So at 29 I packed in my job, put on a pair of jeans and went back to school full time for 18 months and got an MBA. It really changed my world-view.
>
> I believe very firmly in education. Over the years I've had a very firm policy of requiring senior executives to go do a long programme at a university business graduate school as a requirement to progress in the organisation. Since I became general manager 15 years ago I would have put two dozen people through extended executive programmes.

However, Boonzaier is realistic about the limits to some people's readiness to learn the 'real' lessons. He concludes:

> I find about two thirds of people really benefit but one third of people learn 'wonderful' buzz words and don't change at all – distorted philosophies and 'clever' language.

The managing director of each of the nine companies in the Tower Group contributes to the overall strategic plan, as well as the strategy for their company.

James Boonzaier comments on the process and responsibility for changing strategy:

> But when the deal's done, the deal's done. It's to do with the integrity thing.
>
> I hate rule breakers but I love rule changers. If you don't like the darn rules, then let's sit down and change them. But when the rules are there, they must be kept because if you run a decentralised, diversified group like this you must trust the people out there to be playing by the same rules. That's why we get pretty ferocious when people break the rules. But we love it when people change them. In proper consultation of course.

The philosophy of 'putting people first' is reflected in the saying of 'being soft on people but hard on performance'. There is an aversion to laying people off until every avenue is pursued so as to give people the opportunity to deliver results. This approach was first reflected in Boonzaier's turnaround of Tower in 1990.

Overstaffing was apparent in 1990. But a conscious decision was made not to lay off staff and more than 80 per cent of staff reduction was handled by normal turnover. Other redundancies were mainly voluntary as some people were uncomfortable with the new philosophy or decentralisation or both. But most people were keen to try something new.

One of the most remarkable changes at Tower in 1990 involved a unique way to flatten the hierarchy by eliminating levels of managers reporting to each other. Instead of discharging 'surplus' managers, employees were divided among the existing managers with no new hiring of employees. Employees, however, could apply for vacancies within the Tower Group of companies. This created a unique 'internal labour market'.

Since managers could only employ existing employees, the situation encouraged managers to find more productive ways to engage and so retain their employees. One of the best tactics under this new structure was for both managers and employees to work together to find ways of generating new business for Tower, or to increase efficiencies, or both. Productivity and new business increased dramatically.

This philosophy of treating people well also applies in cases where people are not performing. The idea is to make sure that the reward system, the training, and the development are all consistent with what Tower is trying to achieve. The selection process is reviewed in the unlikely event that the person is not suited to the job.

Similarly the 1993 merger of Friends Provident and Adriatic Life to create a larger Tower Australia meant overstaffing in some areas. For example, there could not remain two chief executives (MDs) of the one company. But top Tower managers ensured the treatment of people was fair. And Tower Australia treated surplus staff as humanely as possible, with no difference in treatment of people old or young, new or longer service, men or women. Tower Australia has gone from strength to strength. In 1996 Tower won the life insurance company of the year award in Australia, a remarkable accomplishment for a company that has only operated in Australia for six years. Unsurprisingly, the people of Tower are very pleased about the award.

The Structure of Tower Group of Companies

Each of the operating companies within the Group has a highly autonomous board, typically an independent chairperson and a majority of directors from outside the Tower Group.

The Tower Group is structured as a holding company, as indicated in Appendix 5. The structure is comprised of four distinct groups:

1 Tower Mutual which owns all assets of the Group
2 Tower Corporation Holdings, the holding company for all subsidiary companies
3 seven retail companies –Tower Retirement Investment, Tower Trust (unit trusts), Trustees Executors (trustee services), National Insurance (fire and general insurance), National Insurance Life and Health (disability, medical and term insurance), Fintel (telemarketer of fire and general insurance), Tower Life Australia, and Austrust (trustee services)
4 two wholesale companies, Tower Portfolio Management New Zealand and Tower Portfolio Management Australia.

Tower Mutual has only two office bearers, James Boonzaier and the company secretary. Tower Corporation is headed by James Boonzaier in his capacity as group managing director.

The managers of the seven retail companies and the two wholesale companies all report to the group managing director. These managers have high discretion of autonomy, subject to the overall purpose and aims of the Group, including financial aims, overseen by James Boonzaier. The board of directors of each operating company is typically comprised of at least four persons, including James Boonzaier, the only permanent director. The board of the Holding Company is comprised of eight directors elected by the policy holders of the Group, and the group managing director.

The two wholesale companies, Tower Portfolio Management New Zealand and Tower Portfolio Management Australia, are what is known as 'fund mangers'. Fund managers first invest the funds of the retail companies of the Group and, second, they obtain wholesale funds from outside the Group. As an example of the latter, they invest for the Reserve Bank's pension fund, the National Provident Fund, and the Australian Savings Bank's 'Easy Plan'. There are about one billion dollars in wholesale funds that are invested by the two wholesale companies in the Tower Group.

The directors on a Company Board usually include the managing director of the operating company and other influential people including, wherever possible, high profile chairpersons such as Sir Colin Maiden who chairs Tower's National Insurance (Sir Colin Maiden also is chairman of Fisher and Paykel Limited and Independent Newspapers Limited) and Paul Baines, the former managing director of First Boston who chairs Tower Retirement Investment. James Boonzaier describes his ideas on the structure at Tower:

> Tower uses a holding company structure. The reason is that I believe that no company in the Tower group should have more than 400 employees. The average size of a company in the Tower group would be about 200 employees, so they are meant to be small companies, going from 30 people up to about 380 people in size.

> Focus is fundamental for us as a group. You've got to know your target market and you've got to know what kind of value you deliver, and I don't want group companies being broadly unfocussed. Small companies are better focussed; they are much more flexible; they have such a strong sense of identity; they are more accountable; and they are more fun!
>
> I think small companies are more motivational than big companies. On one hand, you need to get the economies of the Group as a whole. On the other hand, you need to have all the advantages of smaller companies. That's why what we're trying to do is, to a greater and greater extent, exploring the synergies in the larger group while not losing the advantages of the small autonomous businesses that give us a strong sense of identity.

An ownership option is to change from a mutual cooperative to a public company in order to increase the capital base of the company. Such a change is known as de-mutualising, that is, taking the mutual 'public', changing the articles of association, registering the organisation as a limited liability company, and listing it on the Stock Exchange with the intention of raising additional investment capital. National Mutual de-mutualised in October 1996, with Sovereign Assurance and Colonial Mutual preparing to follow. Tower Corporation is considering the idea of 'restructuring by de-mutualisation' and Tower management are carefully observing the progress of companies which do de-mutualise.

Summary of Recent Performance and Future Challenges

At the end of 1995 Tower acquired Austrust, a medium-sized trustee services company, from the South Australian Government. As usual, this acquisition was not opportunistic but carefully planned. James Boonzaier explains the process of acquisition and operation of the acquired businesses in the Tower Group:

> We carefully selected the companies that we wanted, a very proactive approach. I met the Chairmen of these companies well before the time to make sure that we did have an interest registered. I always felt that we had an edge because we had a good reputation and we had a business philosophy which typically went down well. I was able to look people in the eye and say, 'Look we're acquiring the business because we want the people; yes we want the assets, we want the image, we want all those things; but we also want the people'. For example, at Austrust not a single person has been laid off. The only changes that took place were at the board level. I let them resign; I didn't fire them.
>
> The general philosophy of allowing people a lot of autonomy within very firmly agreed guidelines is very motivational for people. It really works well, setting clear guidelines that are general and then letting people have choices: 'You know your market better than we do; as long as you stick to the deal, you do it'. We monitor very carefully; make no mistake. I sit on all the boards and I have my Head of Finance, my brilliant colleague, who runs through the board papers before each board meeting.

Tower uses return on investment (ROI) as the key measurement of financial performance, and refers to international standards of ROI for comparison. A 10 per cent nominal ROI is considered an acceptable return in today's low-inflation environment and over 20 per cent is considered very good performance. Tower has consistently generated returns of 15 per cent ROI. Tower's solid performance has been recognised by the financial industry's 'Fund Manager of the Year' awards for 1994 and 1995. Competition for these awards is fierce and competitors include AMP, Australia's largest trust, and Citibank, one of the world's largest and most successful financial institutions. The Tower Group is now about the tenth largest insurance group in Australasia. With the sale of New Zealand's Trust Bank to Australia, Tower is now the largest New Zealand-owned financial institution.

Strictly speaking, the Tower Group is not solely New Zealand-owned as 55 per cent of the voter-owners reside in New Zealand and 45 per cent of the voter-owners reside in Australia. Tower's financial statements are publicly available because of government legislation of mutual trusts. It is expected that the Annual Report on the1996 financial year will show significant growth in assets and improved financial performance over 1995.

Tower is well known in New Zealand, and in Australia the company is building its Australian profile. Management believe that Tower must become more well-known in Australia to realise its aim to become recognised as a diversified Australasian financial services business. Another challenge is to keep up with and even surpass competitors in using technology to appropriately deliver products and services more efficiently and more effectively.

Some competitors are pouring in hundreds of millions into technology while Tower's technology expenditure is 20 to 30 million dollars NZ a year. Somehow Tower must find ways to use the resources more effectively than competitors. Changes in technology may favour this to some extent. Tower may also need to look at strategic alliances with people from such giants as Electronic Data Systems (EDS) or IBM in order to leverage Tower's resources.

By the year 2000, Tower hopes to have 50 per cent of its business distributed directly, like that of Fintel's telemarketing of household insurance. For example Tower companies may try to directly sell Waikato University a range of financial and insurance products using the Registrar's office as a distribution centre. Here again Tower would be eliminating an intermediary between itself and the customer or customer group. Advantages are that customer loyalty would reside with Tower rather than with the intermediary, and an expensive, extra link in the chain is eliminated. Tower and the other insurance companies also hope to win the war with the banks.

In Tower's view, the banks have potential to market insurance and savings plans directly to customers. But so far the banks have not been very good at selling or developing these products. The power may be in distribution and there are many interesting distribution channels, such as Internet, which could be valuable in the future.

There are only four mutuals left in Australasia, including Tower. Growth of mutuals is from retained earnings as legislation prevents mutuals from raising money in capital markets. In the future, these mutuals may need sources of capital beyond those generated from retained earnings. This may involve applying to change the ownership structure from a mutual organisation to corporate ownership (de-mutualisation). The directors, James Boonzaier and the top managers of the Tower Group of Companies have considered these and the many other important issues affecting Tower and the insurance industry. They all agree that Tower looks secure. But three observations, each with a key question, dominate their concerns about Tower's long-term future. These questions are:

1 Service is seen as more important since service may be the only sustainable advantage that insurance companies can have. But is Tower large enough to compete with such industry giants as AMP in terms of cost and price?

2 Product innovation can be highly effective in the short term but it is expensive. Others soon copy a successful new product or service or marketing initiative. How can Tower keep up?

3 Tower may have been the best in the country for the past two years, if 'best' means superior investment performance in Australia and New Zealand. But how is Tower to survive, and thrive, in the competitive insurance and financial services industry of the future?

Appendix 1: Tower Group Mission and Objectives

Key Objectives and Outcomes

To achieve sustainable revenue growth

Target for Group Revenue: $1,397 million Result: $1,377 million

Group revenue grew by close to 5 percent during the year ended 30 September 1995. Growth in investment income was very strong, trebling in size to $428 million. Along with steady growth in regular premiums, this more than offset the fall in contributions from single premiums where high interest rates tended to favour bank deposits as a savings medium. Tower Portfolio Management New Zealand had a very successful year with substantial new funds coming under its management.

To improve operational productivity and profitability

Target for improvement in Group staff productivity: 10 percent

Result: 10 percent

Group Companies achieved good staff productivity gains in the year. Overall, the Group recorded a productivity improvement of 10 percent. Over the past five years, productivity in the Tower Group has risen by about 80 percent. The profit performances from all Group operating companies for the twelve months to the end of September 1995 were positive although results were generally below the previous year's profit levels largely for cyclical reasons.

To pursue strategic asset growth and expansion

Target for Group Total Assets: $5,000 million

Result: $5,028 million

Total Group assets increased by over $300 million for the year ended 30 September 1995 to exceed $5 billion for the first time. Growth was strong in Australia where over the last two years, Tower Life Australia has grown dramatically, and now accounts for about 30 percent of the Tower Group's business. In New Zealand, with $1.2 billion in retail funds under management, the Tower Group maintained its position as the largest retail funds manager. Tower has held this ranking for the past three years.

To achieve highly competitive investment performance while maintaining focus on prudence and security

Investment markets recovered in 1995 and Tower Portfolio Management teams in both New Zealand and Australia led the competition in most areas. Tower's balanced funds' after-tax returns ranged from 7 to 9 percent in New Zealand, and from 10 to 12 percent in Australia – well ahead of the market. Tower's investment performance in New Zealand and Australia was recognised with major successes in both countries' prestigious industry awards. In New Zealand, Tower was named Joint Fund Manager of the Year in the IPAC awards, and in Australia, Tower won nine awards in the Personal Investment Magazine Insurance Company of the Year survey. The philosophy of investment diversification in asset classes and across global markets continues to be very successful for Tower.

Source: 1995 Annual Report on Tower Financial Services Group.

Appendix 2: Time Line (1991–96)

A Period of Rapid Progress

The first half of the 1990s has seen Tower transformed from a modest New Zealand Government Insurance Company to a significant Australasian Financial Services Group. Today Tower Group covers the spectrum of Investment and Insurance services and comprises: National Insurance, Tower Retirement Investment, Tower Trust, Trustees Executors, Tower Life Australia, National Insurance Life & Health, Austrust and Tower Portfolio Management (New Zealand and Australia). All are operationally autonomous but strategically coordinated – like a fleet of ships. The changes have been, by most standards, quite startling:

- Assets under management grew from $2.2 billion to $7.3 billion (average growth 25% p.a.)
- Annual Revenue grew from $0.5 billion to $1.7 billion (average growth 25% p.a.)
- Total Productivity improved by 70% and staff productivity by 90% (average improvement 12.14% p.a.)
- Investment returns (one to five years) on both sides of the Tasman consistently in top quartile (Mercers, Intech). Generally speaking our policyholders/investors have had an excellent deal from Tower: NZ Balanced Funds have returned 11% p.a. and Australian Balanced Funds 13% p.a. after tax over the past 5 years.
- Main Fund solvency improved from 10% to 20% (15% improvement p.a.)
- Offshore (non-New Zealand) business grew from 5% to 45% of the total. We have become truly Australasian.
- Life Assurance dropped from an estimated 2/3 to 1/3 of our business – we have become a diversified Financial Services business covering the whole range of non-Bank Financial Services from Insurance, through Unit Trusts and Managed Funds to Trustee Services.
- During the period Tower Group divested four businesses: Harcourts (Real Estate), NAB, New Zealand (Banking), Corporate Press (Printing), Centron (Computers), acquired three businesses (Adriatic Life, Friends Provident and Austrust) and launched two new businesses: National Life & Health and Fintel (Telesales).
- The success of our business diversification strategy is best illustrated as follows:

  During the period New Zealand Bonds returned an average of 8.5% pre-tax, and Group Operations returned 12.9% after tax (equivalent to about 15% pre-tax). Operations have been our highest yielding and most stable Asset class.
- The Tower Financial Services Group has established itself as a Quality operator on both sides of the Tasman having won "New Zealand Fund Manager of the Year" twice and "Australian Life Assurance Company of the Year" as well as the BRW/Alcatel "Business Achievement Award".

- In terms of the "pecking order" of the Australasian Insurance Groups, Tower has arguably moved from the "fourth rank" to the "third rank" (and into the "top ten"):

  First Rank: AMP, National Mutual/AXA.

  Second Rank: MLC, Colonial.

  Third Rank: GIO, Sungroup, Prudential, NRMA, Mercantile Mutual Tower.

  Fourth Rank: QBE, FAI, Sun, Royal, Zurich, NZI, Norwich.
- **In Summary**, the Group has had, in many regards, quite a remarkable five years which has been matched by only a few of our competitors. Much of our progress is due to single-minded focus on strategic objectives and a handful of identified 'key areas'. It makes interesting reading to review the Group's 1991 Strategic Plan which indicates the extent to which we have achieved what we set out to do when we developed our first Strategic Plan.
- The challenges for the next five years are clearly articulated in the Group Strategic Plan:
  - Positioning and Image in Australasian terms
  - Strategic technology
  - Direct distribution
  - Financial restructuring
  - World class service
  - Developing high performance management.

We are quite well positioned to meet these challenges – if we maintain the energy and momentum of the past five years.

Appendix 3: Tower Financial Services Group
Statement of Total Revenue and Payments ($000)
Year Ended 30 September 1992–1995

	1995	1994	1993	1992
Total Group Revenue				
Premiums, Contributions and Subscription	719 333	925 371	562 680	485 060
Investment Income	427 830	133 255	347 294	107 682
Net Growth in Trustee Administered Funds	41 839	44 743	42 852	78 110
Other including Managed Investment Funds	268 748	200 489	45 496	177 530
Currency Movement on Foreign Based Policyholders' Funds	(80 662)	11 899	-	-
Total Revenue	**$1 377 088**	**1 315 757**	**998 322**	**848 382**
Total Payments				
Payments to Policyholders and Withdrawals	755 063	732 442	478 129	370 807
Management and Sales Expenses	216 164	208 030	145 560	153 919
Interest and Investment Expenses	12 092	14 647	-	-
Other Payments (incl Taxation)	49 964	43 246	66 982	13 839
Total Payment	**1 033 283**	**998 365**	**702 807**	**538 565**
Minority Interests	(2)	(116)	132	45
Net Revenue	343 803	317 276	295 383	309 772
Acquisition of Friends Provident Life Assurance Co Ltd Policyholders' Funds	-	1 012 860	-	-
Net Increase in Funds	**343 803**	**1 330 136**	**295 383**	**309 772**

Source: Annual Reports.

Appendix 4: Tower Financial Services Group

Statement of Total Funds Under Management ($000)
As at 30 September 1992 to 1995

	1995	1994	1993	1992
Total Group Funds				
Life Assurance and Superannuation Funds	3 091 280	3 007 845	2 005 453	1 895 351
Unit Trust & Group Investments Funds	656 147	676 774	518 787	221 737
Trustee Administered Funds	366 496	324 656	279 913	438 925
Managed Investment Funds	616 174	377 021	251 162	205 561
Minority Interest	15	13	859	770
Total Group Funds	**4 730 112**	**4 386 309**	**3 056 174**	**2 762 344**
Represented by: Assets & Investments				
Fixed Assets	2 518 401	2 378 168	1772 292	1 681 731
Shares	1 539 242	1 482 067	824 728	629 820
Property	372 387	319 107	200 572	286 825
Other	339 486	304 307	205 206	147 923
Total Investments	**4 769 516**	**4 483 649**	**3 002 798**	**2 746 299**
Current Assets				
Cash	33 398	24 234	11 570	3 816
Accounts Receivable	131 081	108 826	143 924	94 411
Other Current Assets	16 343	30 262	47 443	48 069
Total Current Assets	180 822	163 322	202 937	146 296
Fixed Assets	77 485	71 199	79 445	59 752
Total Assets Under Management	**5 027 823**	**4 718 170**	**3 285 180**	**2 952 347**
Less Liabilities				
Borrowings	45 674	65 495	13 666	4 296
Insurance Provisions	148 558	123 436	114 595	116 417
Accounts Payable	104 042	114 241	96 392	67 970
Other Liabilities (inc Taxation)	(563)	28 689	4 353	1 320
Net Assets Under Management	**4 730112**	**4 386 309**	**3 056 174**	**2 762 344**

Source: Annual Reports.

Appendix 5: Tower Financial Services Group Structure

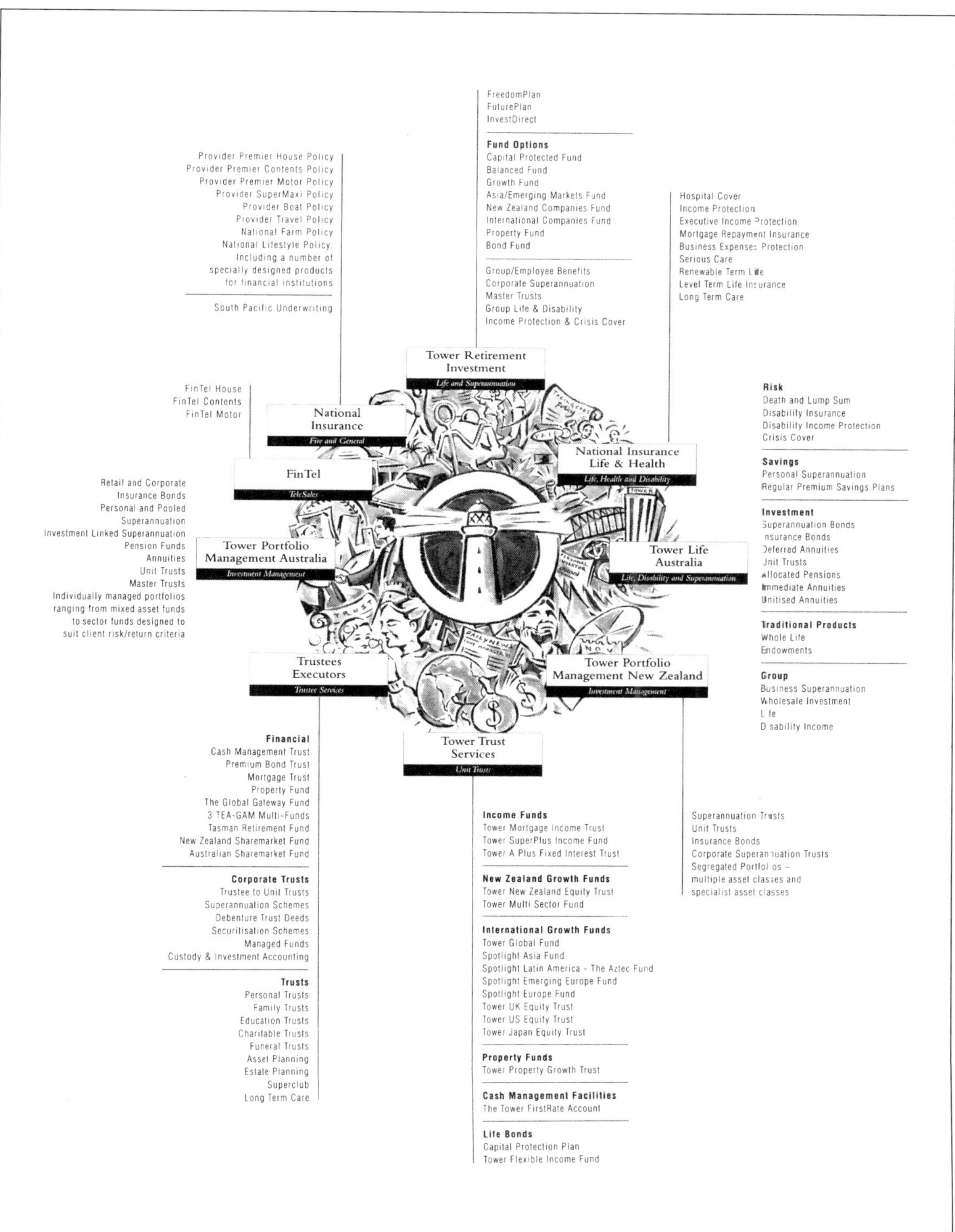

12 Wattie Frozen Foods

Well, yes, bottom-up empowerment did mean a lot of blood on the carpet to start with!

(Gerard La Rooy, General Manager, Business Improvement, 1994)

Introduction

This case is about improving overall company performance by making readily understandable business measures available on the production line each day. The provision of this information has been achieved by using a dynamic activity-based costing approach and the development of a work centre management system at production plants.

Wattie Frozen Foods Ltd (WFF) manufactures frozen and dehydrated foods through its four factories in Gisborne, Hastings, Feilding and Christchurch. Half the production is exported, mainly to Australia and the Asia/Pacific Rim countries, including Japan. In 1986 the company faced the prospect of a significant financial loss and elected to try a far-reaching strategic solution by attempting to change its traditional culture of 'top-down control' to one described as 'bottom-up empowerment'. Reorganisation involved dividing the processing plants into a comprehensive array of semi-autonomous work centres. Each work centre reflected the logical flow of a product through factory operations. Work centres were designed so they each had clear and complementary boundaries which did not overlap. Peripheral service functions became work centres in their own right.

The concept of work centre management at WFF embraces quality management, budgeting, cost control, physical and financial reporting, waste and loss management, training, performance improvement, capital expenditure justification, purchasing and asset management. The new culture required rigid adoption of the concept of internal customers, customers who must be satisfied

Acknowledgments This case study was developed for teaching by Bob Mills and is based on interviews with Gerard La Rooy, General Manager, Business Improvement, Heinz/Wattie and Gerald Townsend, Technical Development Manager, and invaluable contribution from Murray Norton. This case was originally commissioned by TRADENZ for an Innovation Leadership Programme for CEOs in the Food and Beverage Industry held at Hotel du Vin, 6/7 March 1995.The authors would like to thank Wattie Frozen Foods for their time and willingness to share their experiences and philosophies. The case is to be used as a basis for classroom discussion rather than to illustrate either effective or ineffective handling of an administrative or strategic situation.

and who could potentially refuse to accept substandard inputs from the preceding work centre or at least negotiate a lower transfer price. The focus that developed within each work centre was toward continuous process improvement instead of merely the achievement of an end result.

Physical measurements, readily understood by and accessible to all staff within each work centre, have been used as the linkage between factory floor and company financial systems. Useful information is made available at the 'workface' each day, helping both supervisors and workers to own and improve key performance indicators.

The implementation of work centre management has not been without distress to staff but the result, particularly in the difficult area of overhead management, has been worthwhile. Specific benefits include improved final product quality, more timely and accurate information allowing proactive control, and the reduction of waste and losses – all of which have improved staff morale.

Eight years after starting the stepwise strategy implementation each of the four production sites has been transformed. WFF see it as 'the way to go'.

The Company and its Situation

Wattie Frozen Foods, formed in 1986 to manufacture frozen and dehydrated foods, faced the prospect of a $10 million loss in its first year of operation. As a new Goodman Fielder Wattie Business Unit, it had significant resources available, but needed major changes in the way it ran its business to achieve a competitive edge and move to profitability.

The executive management team of Peter Lucas, Gerard La Rooy, Hamish Stevens and John Dunstan met, exchanged ideas and models for change and chose to promote the concept of developing a work centre management system.

They had identified three distinct needs of the company at the four processing sites:

1 A move from 'reporting to head office' to 'managing at site'
2 An improvement in the understanding and management of costs
3 An improvement in operations.

Addressing the first need, the team recognised that monthly costing reports, even if produced promptly, are useless for 'real-time' control and improvement of the operation. To be effective, site management needed to be proactive rather than reactive. However, to achieve this, relevant and preferably 'on-line' information for decision making was needed at the workface.

Overhead allocation was an example of an area causing difficulty. There had been a drift from the preferred arrangement, where direct costs are allocated to specific areas of operation, to the convenience of spreading costs across a number of accounting sectors. This drift had been caused in part by the increased use of computer systems across the company by management. Overheads of this type, which tended to be spread across cost centres, are difficult to manage tightly. Clearly defined responsibilities for costs and the power to manage them were seen as essential at WFF. In accounting terms there was a need for 'meaningful cost centres in the general ledger and associated authorities to operate them'. An improvement in direct cost management systems was seen as essential if cost control was to be managed from the workface.

Staff training in financial matters was required to meet the second identified need. The purpose of this exercise was to increase local understanding and promote the correct response to daily situations as they arose. Delayed financial analysis at Head Office in Auckland was too far removed for site action to be effective. As well, the analysis required translation from dollars or ratios to adjustments that could be affected on the processing equipment to resolve the problem.

An increased focus on using physical measurements, rather than on the dollar costs they represented, was selected as the appropriate way to describe situations to operations staff. Physical units, like tonnes per hour and litres per load, are readily understood by all the workforce and allow a quicker and more detailed understanding of process parameters that might need to be changed. A particular benefit of adopting this approach is in the understanding of costs associated with waste and loss. Financial consequences of product loss in a processing system can be readily understood at all levels in the company by using the work centre approach. Appendix 1 describes the difference of approaches by way of a practical example.

The third need, that of operational improvement and its consequential direct involvement from site staff and related workers, was viewed from three perspectives:

1 Timely, good quality and detailed information is essential for useful corrective responses during processing. Further, as a corollary, both product quality and the cost of achieving it can be managed more effectively within each stage of a process rather than at the end. Focus on the importance of each process step can emphasise the contribution each individual makes in reaching overall profitability. Making key performance indicators understandable and within the control of an individual team member provides the right tools at the right time and places them in the hands of those who are best situated to manage.
2 Information collected merely for passing on to 'the hierarchy' is unlikely to be 'owned' by staff. On the other hand, where information is provided primarily to assist the actual day-to-day operation at the workface, ownership and diligence in its collection and interpretation is much more likely. Further, the dumping of costs incurred or derived by a third party into a cost centre or the posting of inaccurate cost information into it will almost certainly result in a lack of responsibility for that element. Lack of ownership results in delays, inaccuracies, fiddling and fudging and, more importantly, lack of resulting action.
3 Given sound information and proper ownership, the basis is established for performance improvement, not just overall control. Information produced just for top level management at Head Office will not provide the basis for performance improvement. Detailed, factual and process-related information is needed.

As a consequence of these considerations, financial information flow systems at WFF were seen as vitally important to the daily quest for profitability and, it was believed, not isolated for the remote and delayed contemplation of upper management.

Organisational Structure

The needs of WFF and the consequent empowerment of staff and workers toward management of their particular process element made change of organisational structure and company culture inevitable. Work centre management was not considered compatible with the traditional hierarchical management structure.

Two concepts needed to be instilled into the thinking of staff to underpin work centre management. Firstly, the responsibilities that are associated with empowerment and secondly the development and maintenance of customer relationships had to be fostered.

Empowerment in the eyes of WFF required the devolution of all the following activities to the work centre:

- Quality Systems and Control
- Budgeting
- Control of all costs
- Physical/financial reporting
- Waste and loss management
- Training
- Performance improvement
- Justification for capital works
- Purchasing
- Asset management.

Most of the responsibilities associated with these functions have traditionally been the strict preserve of 'corporate beings', because of the cost of duplication across sites and the access to power that acquiring key information brings. However, the advent of new technology provides the opportunity for raw information to be entered into the system only once at source. The regular manipulation of data can also be done in a routine and automated fashion following expert rules expressed through common spreadsheet formulae and report forms.

All work centres have customers, be they internal or external. Internal customers at WFF are considered to have the same rights as external ones. They have a right to be satisfied. They can refuse to accept substandard or wrongly quantified inputs and can negotiate deals for extra costs incurred in correcting errors. In some cases, such as engineering services, external contractors can be brought in, although a weighting related to the cost of the company maintaining its own services is factored into bid assessment.

Clearly, work centre managers have key responsibilities and must be highly competent themselves or have assistants that can deal in areas where competency is lacking. These managers must understand the full workings of the business under their control. Work centres must be fully responsible for their use of inputs, resources and outputs; this means taking responsibility for labour, plant, services and stocks.

The perishability of partially processed stock is the prime reason for the need to make rapid decisions at WFF sites. However, traditional manufacturing industries have similar 'in-progress' work cost problems.

Designing the Work Centre

Gerard La Rooy advises that to design appropriate work centres to embrace these concepts, the whole operation should be divided into self-contained units small enough to ensure focused management and accountability. For WFF this translated to around 70 work centres at the four production sites. Each unit employed between 5 and 30 people. These work centres are defined as the smallest units of management and are the building blocks of the whole organisation. These centres should:

- Reflect the logical flow of the operation as much as possible
- Have clear and agreed boundaries
- Have no overlaps
- Cover the complete operation (no 'no-mans-land')
- Have only one manager
- Provide for measurement (as much as possible) of all labour, materials and resources consumed by the work centre
- Be mirrored in the accounting General Ledger (although several physical work centres could conceivably feed into a single cost centre).

All work centres at WFF can be charted to show work or product flow from suppliers to customers. In fact, a work centre chart is seen as being much more meaningful in describing the organisation's core business than traditional organisation charts (which are more concerned with internal company power structures and leave out any reference to the customer). Figure 12.1 shows an example of a work centre chart. Again, in the case of WFF there is a site manager whose role is to support work centres at individual sites and solve or mediate any difficulties that arise between different centres. Daily contact between work centre managers and staff is essential since both have instructions about the prompt resolutions of all issues affecting quality, quantities and services.

Figure 12.1 The Work Centre Chart: Main Processes, Suppliers and Customers

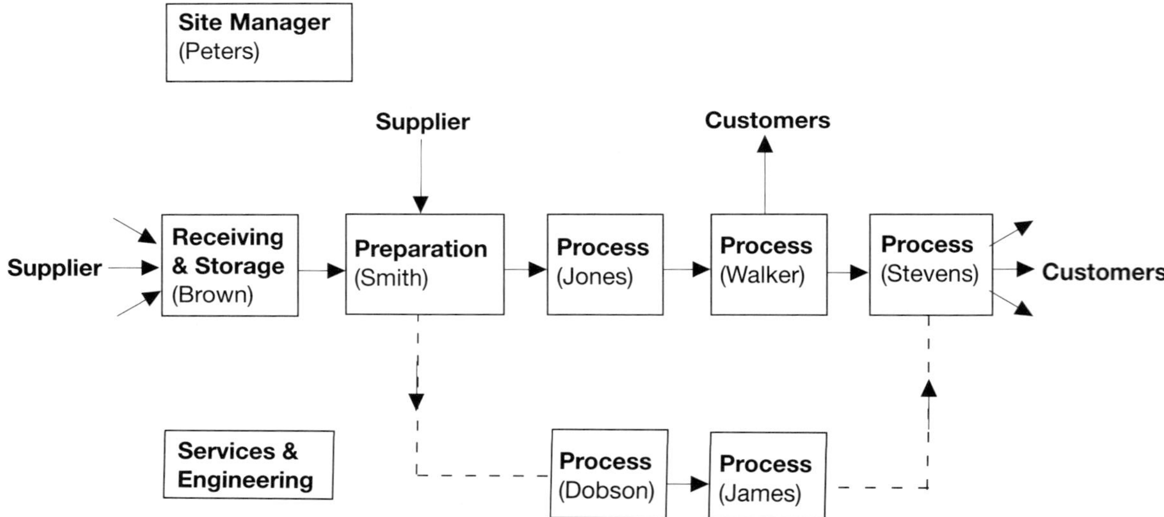

The new culture of work centre management requires widespread retraining. Indeed, WFF found that some key people frequently needed to learn to use business management tools that were new to them. Work centre managers, for example, need to understand the concepts and importance of:

- EBIT (Earnings before interest and tax)
- PFO (Profit from operations)
- ROFE (Return on funds employed)
- Profit and Cash
- Effect of assets on company performance
- Sunk costs
- Incremental analysis
- Statistical variability
- Capacity calculation
- Throughput monitoring.

Beyond mere knowledge of these measures is a requirement to recognise and apply appropriate tools to situations that arise on the job. Statistical charts required for quality control provide an example of such a tool which was formerly used only by specialists. Performance measures like plant utilisation and availability, productivity and wastage are also powerful management tools which need to be developed and incorporated into the everyday language of each work centre.

Gerard La Rooy is convinced that 'Pondering or agonising over results in terms of sales or costs may provide no insight into how the situation may be improved'. Rather, improvement can be best achieved by monitoring and understanding underlying processes. Appendix 1 shows, for example, how wastage is viewed by WFF. The culture must therefore support a focus on improvement rather than merely controlling or maintaining the status quo. Staff must be encouraged to be pro-active in seeking improvement opportunities. At WFF there are over 200 formal improvement projects reported on each year. Many smaller in-process enhancements are implemented as well. The company supports site field-days for improvement project outcomes to be displayed, explained and acknowledged. Each year the best two improvement project teams from each production site are selected to attend a national event and compete for a $3000 prize awarded to the winning site for staff recreation purposes. Winners are selected for cleverness, savings and quality of presentation.

The shift of emphasis from 'end result' to 'process improvement' means that there is a likelihood and expectation that improvements will be ongoing and therefore help maintain a competitive advantage into the future.

The Work Centre Management Information System

The work centre management information system as developed by WFF welds together the philosophies, practices and culture that have been described. In one respect it is a unique solution and has proved a decided advantage for WFF. The principles espoused could be applied to any similar processing industry. Its conceptual development and database design were carried out at WFF by a consulting team in conjunction with Business Systems Manager, Gerard La Rooy. The database and program construction was undertaken by Datacom Systems Ltd, and was developed in the software package ORACLE to run on WFF's own SEQUENT computer.

The information system provides:

- Formal control and accountability of all production and processing costs (including losses)
- Measures of the quality of output at each stage of production
- A reliable cost basis for assessing product contributions and transfer pricing across work centres
- Resource management information
- Information useful as a basis for performance improvement.

At WFF the management information system covers the total remote factory environment from harvesting to final production. The accounting base for the system has been designed to describe the business in terms that require virtually no general overhead loading. Ultimately even 'management' work centres can exist only if they provide a service that production centres need, this being no different to other service functions. The system provides ready information at the factory floor to enable daily control to be exercised with proper accountability. Management of the information system is of course decentralised with the main inputs, outputs and enquiries handled at work centre level. Costs are posted and can be controlled at the time of the event (or very shortly after) and assigned to processes or product at the source on the basis of actual consumption of resources for its transformation or 'value addition'. This feature sets work centre-based management systems apart from traditional Activity Based Costing (ABC), since it does not employ 'after the event' formulae to allocate costs.

All controllable costs are treated as variable costs wherever possible. Physical units like hours and tonnes are used rather than dollars for 'on the spot' control. A translation from the physical quantities used in the work centres into dollar values is made as required for direct posting to the General Ledger.

Direct access to appropriate, complete and relevant information together with the transparency of the system is believed to encourage improved production and performance levels at each work centre. Values for all the inputs, products or services are available to a work centre at the standard all-inclusive cost at that point. This is described as input consumption. Any losses are directly attributable to the work centre where and when they happen and are able to be loaded with their true costs. Likewise, the system values the output, or production, from a work centre . Incidentally, a work centre can consume its own output as in the case of, say, engineers working on their own machinery. Goods and services, as well as consumables, going out to another work centre are considered as 'production'.

The comprehensive new information system was implemented by first setting up the physical measurements for each work centre in turn. The old financial system was then operated and financial comparisons made until there was confidence that the physical data generated could be used to directly drive the General Ledger. Gerard La Rooy is convinced that taking this stepwise and parallel approach was a sound strategy, since there was not the trauma associated with making the entire system operate at the changeover date. The data are used as the basis for work centre reporting without the need for duplication or reformatting for different management levels to understand. As well, the information is used to automatically generate performance measures like quality, throughput, and plant availability for each work centre. Each employee or team has 'key performance indicators' for which they take responsibility, all of which are made available on the information system at the work centre. With the routine collection of performance data established, then more energy is able to be put into improving performance and implementing new ideas.

The Benefits

The work centre management system has been completely implemented at each of the four factory sites, with operations at Christchurch exhibiting particular benefits through the leadership of site manager Murray Norton. Enhancements to improve system operation have been identified and proposals to incorporate them are being planned. However, clear benefits showing significant cost reductions are already evident, especially in services work centres, for example, engineering and fork-lifts. In one branch alone, the number of fork-lift vehicles in operation was reduced from 18 to 16, saving $100,000 in the first six months. Savings were also made in the arrangements for purchasing fuel, a job once done by engineering and now done directly by the harvesting group. There have been many other similar instances where significant savings have been made.

The company acknowledges that the work centre philosophy and practice has been a major, if not the major, reason for the turnaround from a potential loss of $10 million in 1986 to a profit of some $18 million in 1994. These improved financial results have been achieved through staff having both a better understanding and better control of factors which lead to profitability. The understanding has been gained through shortening the route and time frame for feedback of information between events at site and their consequential effect on financial outcomes. Control has been improved by providing timely information at the workface for corrective action to be undertaken.

It is now perceived by all staff that there are no 'free' resources. There is also a better appreciation of the concept of internal customers and a real reluctance by work centres to either supply or accept substandard product. From the company accountants' point of view it has been observed that both the costing and inventory information have become more reliable. Mistakes are generally picked up at the time they occur rather than during balancing. This in turn has led to fewer 'surprises' at the end of the month!

Reliable daily financial reports are now available and monthly reports require much less time to produce. The way in which waste and loss costs accumulate is also now better understood, which leads to improved decision making. Staff morale has improved through their ability to own information and the freedom to make their own decisions in managing their work centre. In fact, work centre management has simultaneously changed the company profitability, culture, and the accounting system.

The Future

Wattie Frozen Foods have moved significantly from 'traditional' managing, accounting and reporting practices. It is expected that the concepts can be extended to include other corporate activities like:

- Work centre stock control
- Work centre fixed assets

- Work centre ROFE
- The sales work centre.

Since the introduction of work centres in 1986, various changes have occurred in company ownership, notably its acquisition by H.J. Heinz in 1992, but each owner has retained and encouraged the development of the work centre concept. In fact, Heinz plans to adopt the approach for its Australian operations.

The work centre management system is believed to be readily adaptable to other processing-based companies, if they are first willing to accept the dramatic changes it brings and then commit themselves to making it work.

Appendix 1: Consideration of Waste and Loss Calculations (Example)

Buy in 100 tonnes of crop @ $400/tonne to produce 80 tonnes of finished product. Assume direct and indirect costs of production are $80,000.

Traditional Approach

Recovery = $\frac{80t}{100t} \times 100\% = 80\%$

Loss = 20t @ $400/t = $8 000

Cost per tonne = $\frac{[(100t \times \$400/t) + \$80\,000]}{80t} = \$1\,500/t$

Showing this in a diagrammatic form

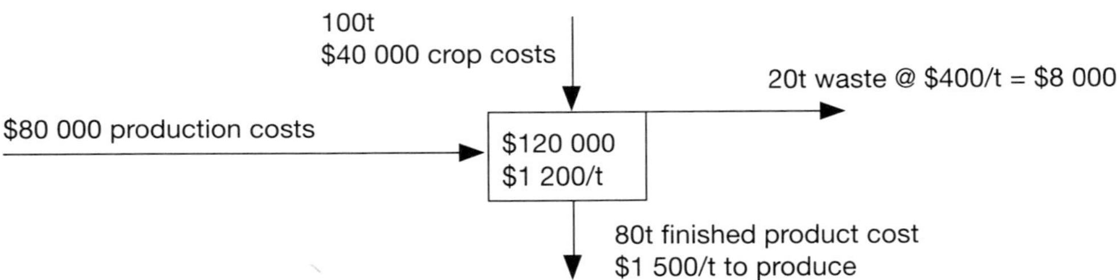

Added Value Approach

It should be considered that *all* the unit production cost contributed to the fraction that was eventually wasted or lost. In this case the cost of wastage would be 20t @ $1 200/t = $24 000.

Showing this in a diagrammatic form

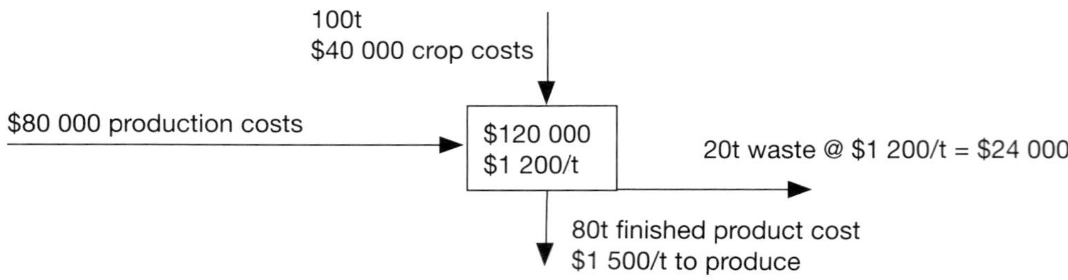

Wastage or loss calculated by the value added approach, however, assumes the retention of all product until the very end of processing and is not a particularly useful or helpful concept. A more realistic assumption is that loss occurs progressively through the process.

Cost Centre Approach

If we now consider a work centre approach, where four work centres sustain, say, equal production costs and tonnage losses, a more realistic assessment of the cost of the losses can be calculated. Further, the boundaries between the work centres can be characterised by physical quantities which can be translated into the cost of losses with each work centre.

Again in diagrammatic form

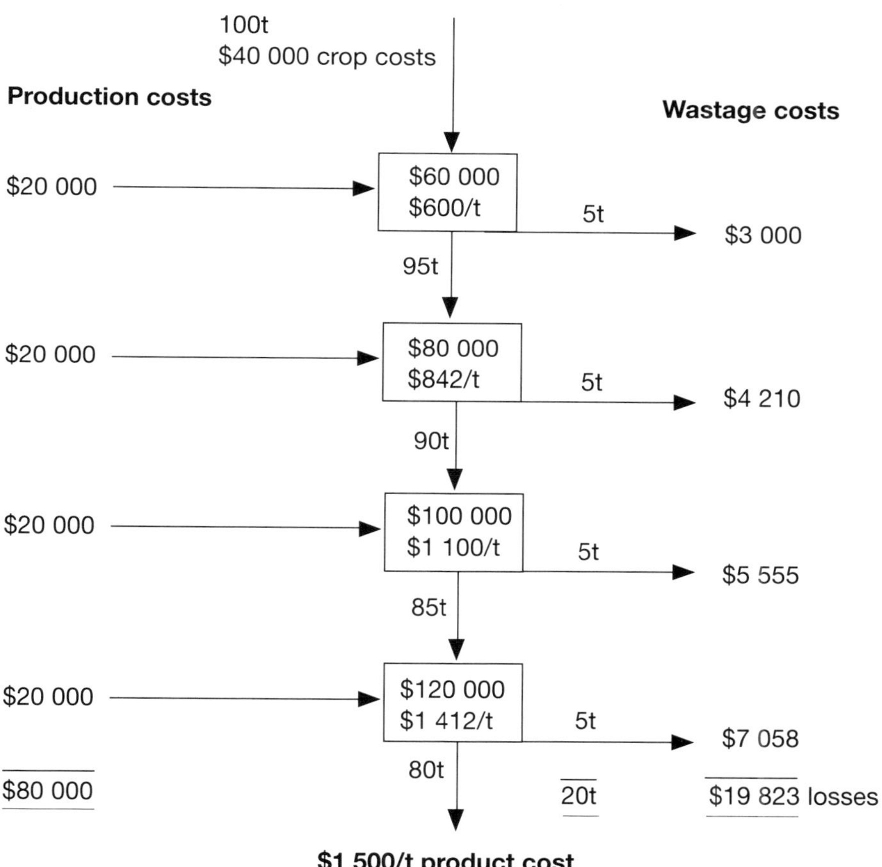